AMAZING
WORLD ATLAS

CONTENTS

How to Use This Book ✳ 4

Planet Earth in Space ✳ 6

Time Zones ✳ 8

Inside the Earth ✳ 10

Climate and Weather ✳ 12

The World's Oceans and Seas ✳ 14

16 ✳ The World's Population

18 ✳ Mapping the World

20 ✳ A Map for Every Occasion

22 ✳ A Physical Perspective

24 ✳ A Political Perspective

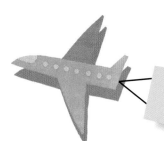

AROUND THE WORLD

NORTH AMERICA ✳ 26

Canada ✳ 30

Eastern USA ✳ 34

Western USA ✳ 38

Mexico, Central America and the Caribbean ✳ 42

SOUTH AMERICA ✳ 46

Northern South America ✳ 50

Southern South America ✳ 54

58 ✳ **EUROPE**

62 ✳ Northern Europe

66 ✳ Northwest Europe

70 ✳ Southwest Europe

74 ✳ Southeast Europe

78 ✳ Central Europe

82 ✳ Eastern Europe

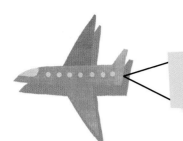

AROUND THE WORLD (CONTINUED)

ASIA ✳ **86**

Russia and its neighbours ✳ **90**

Central Asia ✳ **94**

East Asia ✳ **98**

Southern Asia ✳ **102**

Southeast Asia ✳ **106**

Southwest Asia ✳ **110**

114 ✳ **AFRICA**

118 ✳ Northern Africa

122 ✳ Eastern Africa

126 ✳ Central and West Africa

130 ✳ Southern Africa

134 ✳ **OCEANIA**

138 ✳ Australia and Papua New Guinea

142 ✳ New Zealand and the Pacific Islands

146 ✳ **ANTARCTICA**

QUIZ & INDEX

World quiz ✳ **150**

Index map ✳ **156**

158 ✳ Index

160 ✳ Acknowledgements

How to Use This Book

The *Amazing World Atlas* makes it easy to find the information you want.

These two pages will show you how it all works. Main entries begin with one of the seven continents: North America, South America, Europe, Asia, Africa, Oceania and Antarctica, in that order. Following each continental entry are pages devoted to regions and countries within that continent.

If you want to know about a specific region or nation, you can look it up in the index.

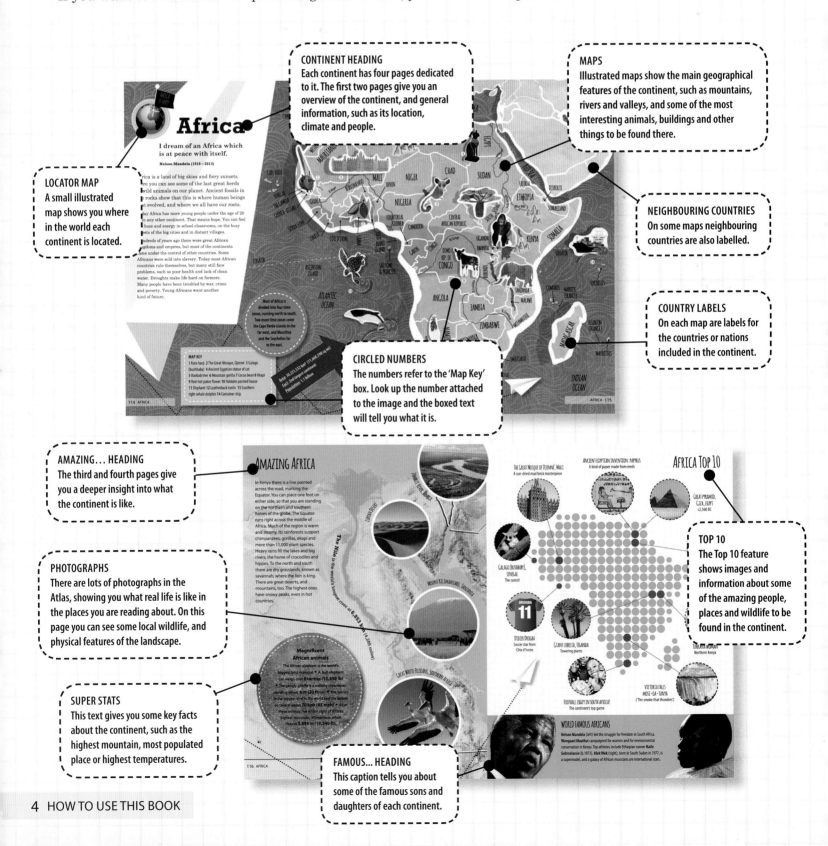

CONTINENT HEADING
Each continent has four pages dedicated to it. The first two pages give you an overview of the continent, and general information, such as its location, climate and people.

MAPS
Illustrated maps show the main geographical features of the continent, such as mountains, rivers and valleys, and some of the most interesting animals, buildings and other things to be found there.

LOCATOR MAP
A small illustrated map shows you where in the world each continent is located.

NEIGHBOURING COUNTRIES
On some maps neighbouring countries are also labelled.

COUNTRY LABELS
On each map are labels for the countries or nations included in the continent.

CIRCLED NUMBERS
The numbers refer to the 'Map Key' box. Look up the number attached to the image and the boxed text will tell you what it is.

AMAZING... HEADING
The third and fourth pages give you a deeper insight into what the continent is like.

PHOTOGRAPHS
There are lots of photographs in the Atlas, showing you what real life is like in the places you are reading about. On this page you can see some local wildlife, and physical features of the landscape.

SUPER STATS
This text gives you some key facts about the continent, such as the highest mountain, most populated place or highest temperatures.

TOP 10
The Top 10 feature shows images and information about some of the amazing people, places and wildlife to be found in the continent.

FAMOUS... HEADING
This caption tells you about some of the famous sons and daughters of each continent.

REGIONAL HEADING
Continental entries are followed by regional entries. These give more detail about the various countries and regions within the continent. Most regional entries cover four pages and, like the continental entries, the first two give you an overview of the country, nation or region, and the third and fourth provide more detail.

MAP
The map illustrates the region covered, and labels the countries or states included.

ENTRY HEADING
This heading tells you which part of the continent (countries and/or regions) the entry covers and, where necessary, lists the countries or states included.

CAPTIONS
Captions give information about real life, culture and history, valuable resources, statistics or landmarks found in the region.

ABBREVIATIONS
To save space, some words are abbreviated in this Atlas. They are listed below, with an explanation for each one.

°C = degrees Celsius
°F = degrees Fahrenheit
mm = millimetre
cm = centimetre
m = metre
km = kilometre
km^2 = square kilometre
kph = kilometres per hour
in = inch
ft = foot
yd = yard
mi = mile
sq mi = square mile
mph = miles per hour
g = gram
kg = kilogram
oz = ounce
lb = pound

INDEX
At the back of the book you will find an alphabetical index, where you can look to see if a particular place is covered in the atlas. The numbers following each index entry refer to page numbers.

There are also grid references that refer to the world map at the start of the index. These numbers and letters are in normal type.

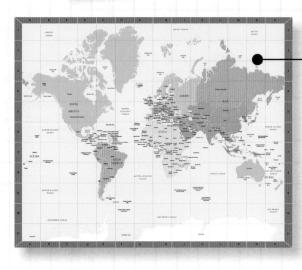

EXAMPLE:
Cambodia **86–89, 106–109** L6
Cameroon **114–117, 126–129** H7
Canada **26–33** C4

Don't miss our Amazing World Atlas game!

Become a super-explorer of continents, countries and cities around the world
✱
Test and grow your geography knowledge with interactive maps and games
✱
Discover fun facts about sights, wildlife, food and culture
✱
Challenge your friends and family

Download it today!
Search for Amazing World Atlas in the iOS App Store and on Google Play

For more information visit lonelyplanetkids.com

Planet Earth in Space

Our planet, Earth, is one of eight that orbit the Sun. It is the only one we know of that can support life, though the quest continues to find others.

The Sun is one of many stars in our galaxy, but it's the only one we can see during the day, due to its size and the heat it exudes. At its centre the Sun's temperature is about 15,000,000°C (27,000,000°F). And it measures over 1,000,000 km (620,000 mi) across its diameter – it's so big that a million Earths could fit inside it!

The surface of Earth is very young compared with that of some of the other planets. This is because it has changed a lot since it was first formed. Movement below the surface, such as earthquakes and erosion by water, reshapes it over time. More than two-thirds of Earth is covered in water. Ours is the only planet on which liquid water can exist, and water is essential for life.

The oceans also help keep the temperature stable, another factor that is important for life. They are aided in this by the carbon dioxide in our atmosphere, which traps warm air. This is known as the 'greenhouse effect'.

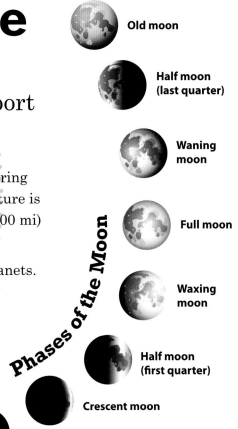

Phases of the Moon

Old moon

Half moon (last quarter)

Waning moon

Full moon

Waxing moon

Half moon (first quarter)

Crescent moon

New moon (invisible)

The light of the Moon is really light from the Sun, which reflects off the Moon's surface. As the **Moon orbits Earth**, we on Earth see this reflected light at varying angles. That's why the shape of the Moon appears to us to change. It takes about **29 days** for the Moon to orbit Earth, cycling through all the phases and arriving at the beginning again.

Our Unknown World
Up until the twentieth century we had no complete maps of the planet. Then we began to be able to take pictures of Earth from space. This allowed us to fill the gaps in our knowledge of the world. **Pictures from space** also help us predict the weather, and are especially useful in showing where hurricanes and other storms are going. Earth seen from space is a beautiful sight. It's mostly blue because of all the water on its surface, and it's often known as **'the blue planet'.**

Neptune
Neptune is the eighth planet from the Sun, and the fourth largest. It's a gas planet, with a rocky core. Its rings are dark, but we don't yet know what they're made of. Neptune has the fastest winds in the solar system, sometimes reaching up to 2000 km (1242 mi) per hour!

Uranus
Uranus is the seventh planet from the Sun, and the third largest. It is a gas planet with a solid metal core. Its blue colour is caused by methane gas clouds, which block out red light. Uranus' rings are dark and made of large objects, up to 10 metres (33 ft) across.

Solar System Data

	Mercury	Venus	Earth	Mars	Jupiter	Saturn	Uranus	Neptune
Highest Surface Temperature	430 ºC	480 ºC	58 ºC	-5 ºC	-148 ºC	-178 ºC	-216 ºC	-214 ºC
Lowest Surface Temperature	- 180 ºC	480 ºC	-90 ºC	-87 ºC	-148 ºC	-178 ºC	-216 ºC	-214 ºC
Diameter	4879 km	12104 km	12742 km	6779 km	139822 km	116,464 km	50,724 km	49244 km
Distance from Sun	58 million km	108 million km	150 million km	228 million km	778 million km	1.4 billion km	2.9 billion km	4.5 billion km
Length of Day	59 Earth days	243 Earth days	1 Earth day (24 hours)	1 Earth day	10 Earth hours	10.7 Earth hours	17 Earth hours	16 Earth hours
Length of Year (orbit around the sun)	88 Earth days	225 Earth days	365 Earth days	687 Earth days	4,333 Earth days	29 Earth years	84 Earth years	165 Earth years
Orbit Speed	170,503 kph	126,074 kph	107,218 kph	86,677 kph	47,002 kph	34,701 kph	24,477 kph	19,566 kph
Confirmed moons	0	0	1	2	50	53	27	13

Our Solar System

Saturn
Saturn is the sixth closest planet to the Sun, and the second largest. It is a gas planet, and has a solid core. Saturn is famous for its stunning rings. They are mostly ice, but may also contain bits of rock. The smallest particles are about a centimetre (half an inch) across.

Jupiter
Jupiter is the fifth closest planet to the Sun, and twice the size of all the other planets combined. It looks solid, but what you can see are actually clouds. Jupiter is a gas planet, probably with a solid core about the size of Earth. Its rings are difficult to see.

Mars
Mars is the fourth closest planet to the Sun, and the seventh largest. Mars has many interesting geographical features, including the largest mountain in the solar system, Olympus Mons, 24 km (15 mi) above ground level.

Earth
Earth is the third closest planet to the Sun, and the fifth largest. It's small and rocky, with lots of different geographical features, such as mountains, evergreen forests, rainforests, plains, deserts, valleys and, of course, oceans!

Venus
Venus is the second closest planet to the Sun, and the sixth largest. Like Earth, Venus is small and rocky, and probably once had water, but the high temperatures on the planet boiled it away. There are many active volcanoes on Venus.

Mercury
Mercury is the closest planet to the Sun, and the smallest. It is rocky, with lots of craters.

Sun

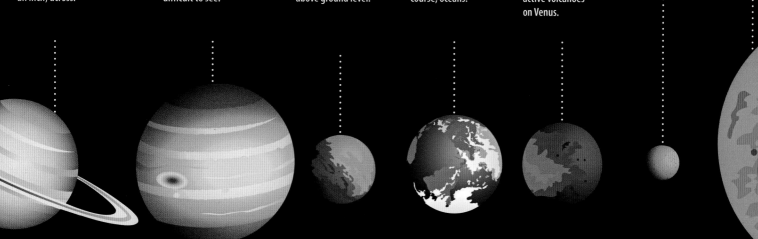

Time Zones

It might seem strange but different places around the world have different clock times. This is because, as well as orbiting the Sun, our planet spins around its own axis.

The axis runs North to South, from pole to pole. When the part of the Earth you are living on is facing the Sun, it's daytime. When it's facing away from the Sun, it's night time. Different parts of the world face the Sun at different times as the Earth spins. So if we want 'midday' to happen at more or less the middle of the day, we have to divide the world into different time zones.

For this reason, if you lived in Barcelona and got up at 8am and decided to call a friend in New York, they may not be all that happy as it would only be 2am there. Their 8am happens six hours later, when it's 2pm in Barcelona. Those six hours are the difference between the two time zones. Think that's complicated? Some countries have time zones of 15 or 30 minutes' difference from the next zone along, rather than a whole hour. And some also have 'daylight saving time', when they alter their clocks at certain times of the year to make the most of the light hours...

COORDINATED UNIVERSAL TIME (CUT)
Many timekeeping devices use this 24-hour time standard, set by highly precise atomic clocks. CUT (also referred to as UTC) is used interchangeably with GMT

| CUT -12 | CUT -11 | CUT -10 | CUT -9 | CUT -8 | CU |

Earth's seasons

The changing seasons on Earth are caused by its position relative to the Sun.

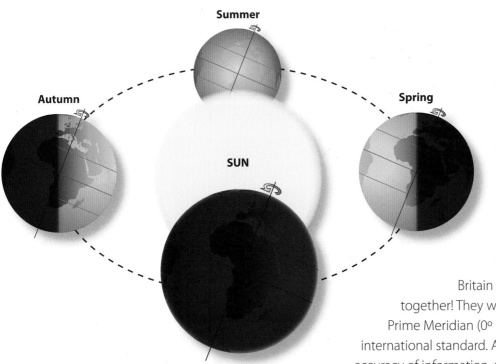

Summer

Autumn

Spring

SUN

Winter

OUTSIDE THE GREENWICH OBSERVATORY, IN SOUTHEAST LONDON, A METAL LINE DENOTES THE POSITION OF THE PRIME MERIDIAN.

Why Greenwich?

When the standard for time zones was set up, Britain had more ships than the rest of the world put together! They were all using the **Greenwich Meridian** as the Prime Meridian (0° longitude), so it made sense to adopt it as the international standard. And Greenwich Observatory was known for its accuracy of information, so people trusted it. Greenwich Mean Time, or GMT, became the time from which all international standard times are set.

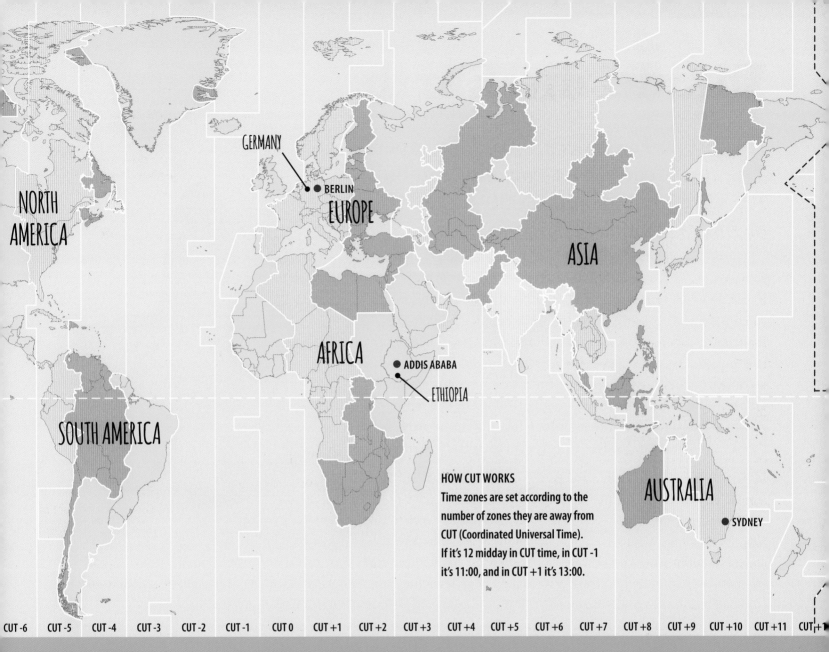

Labels on map: GERMANY · BERLIN · EUROPE · ASIA · NORTH AMERICA · AFRICA · ADDIS ABABA · ETHIOPIA · SOUTH AMERICA · AUSTRALIA · SYDNEY

HOW CUT WORKS
Time zones are set according to the number of zones they are away from CUT (Coordinated Universal Time). If it's 12 midday in CUT time, in CUT -1 it's 11:00, and in CUT +1 it's 13:00.

CUT -6 | CUT -5 | CUT -4 | CUT -3 | CUT -2 | CUT -1 | CUT 0 | CUT +1 | CUT +2 | CUT +3 | CUT +4 | CUT +5 | CUT +6 | CUT +7 | CUT +8 | CUT +9 | CUT +10 | CUT +11 | CUT +1

Time Zone Map

Each time zone is based on a central meridian. These are set at 15° intervals from the Prime Meridian, and cover the areas 7.5° to each side of the central meridian. New York City, for example, has the 75°W line of longitude as its central meridian, and its time zone includes all locations between 67.5°W and 82.5°W. Not all the time zones run in straight lines north to south. This is because many countries extend beyond their time zone, but want the same time zone throughout their territory.

Funky French Time
Until **1911**, many French maps still showed Paris as the Prime Meridian, at 0°. However, legal time was said to be Paris Mean Time minus **nine minutes, 21 seconds**. This was, in fact, **GMT!**

Quiz

Zone in!
If it's 10am in Berlin, Germany, what time is it in Addis Ababa, Ethiopia?

What does GMT stand for?

What is the number of hours' difference between CUT-3 and CUT +3?

If you lived in Vancouver, Canada and at 9am you telephoned someone in Sydney, Australia, what time would it be there?

How many 15° time zones are there?

ANSWERS: 12pm, Greenwich Mean Time, 6, 3am, 24

Happy New Year!
The first places to hit midnight on **31st December** are Christmas Island, Kiribati and Samoa, so they get to celebrate **New Year** before anyone else. Samoa used to be one of the last to see in the New Year, but it deleted a whole day, 30th December 2011, from its calendar and suddenly became the first place to see the sun set!

Inside the Earth

Inside the Earth there are four layers. The inner core is like a solid iron ball. It's white hot (about 5,000–7,000°C or 9,030–12,600°F).

That's up to 70 times as hot as boiling water! However, it is under so much pressure that it can't melt, and remains solid. The outer core is mostly iron and, although it's a bit cooler than the inner core (just 4,000–5,000°C or 7,239–9,030°F), it is liquid. This layer gives the Earth its magnetic field. As well as iron, both the outer and inner core probably contain sulphur and nickel, and small amounts of other elements. Above the outer core is the mantle, a layer of liquid rock. It flows very slowly and moves in currents as hotter rock from below rises and cools near the surface before sinking again. The crust is the part of Earth we know; the rocks, the soil, the ocean floor – and it's a very thin crust to contain all that heat!

The currents of moving rock within the mantle affect the crust. It has broken into pieces, called tectonic plates, which are constantly on the move. When they collide, they can push up mountains, and when they drift apart, huge trenches and valleys can appear. They also cause earthquakes and volcanoes. The plates that carry our continents have moved a lot since they first broke up. But you can still see some of the shapes that once fitted together.

Inner core
about 2400 km (1500 mi) in diameter

Outer core
about 2300 km (1430 mi) thick

Mantle
about 2900 km (1800 mi) thick

Atmosphere

Crust
just 8 to 40 km (5 to 25 mi) thick

NORTH AMERICAN PLATE

EURASIAN PLATE

ARABIAN PLATE

PACIFIC PLATE

PHILIPPINE PLATE

CARIBBEAN PLATE

PACIFIC PLATE

COCOS PLATE

AFRICAN PLATE

NAZCA PLATE

SOUTH AMERICAN PLATE

INDO-AUSTRALIAN PLATE

ANTARCTIC PLATE

Earth's riches

Fools and Their Gold

When gold is found somewhere, people flock to try and get some for themselves. Very few people find enough gold to live on, and many have sold everything they had to go searching for it. In commercial mining, a liquid metal called mercury is often used to separate the gold from the soil and other minerals around it. The mercury gets into the rivers and streams, and people and animals can be poisoned.

This we know, the Earth does not belong to us. We belong to the Earth.

Chief Seattle

How did Earth Form?

Like the other planets in the solar system, Earth probably formed about 4.6 billion years ago. The planets are made of molecules left over from the creation of the Sun. The molecules were floating about in a large cloud of dust and, eventually, some of them bumped into each other and stuck together. Gradually these small lumps of matter collided and expanded until they formed a planet. The Sun's gravity took hold of Earth and the other planets, and pulled them into its orbit, where they circle to this very day.

Precious Resources

Our planet is full of valuable resources, including precious metals, diamonds and fossil fuels such as oil and coal. It has moving air and water, both of which can provide electricity. The oceans are full of fish, and the land teems with animals and plants that provide us with food. Yet in the process of trying to get resources from the Earth a lot can be destroyed, including people's lives and livelihoods. People are only now beginning to realise how much of an impact we humans are having on our planet, and trying to find ways to protect it from too much damage.

Oil Spills

The oil we know about on the planet is going to run out in **less than a century**, so the oil companies are doing their best to get as much of it as they can. This includes using mining methods that harm local economies, and cause oil spills both in the ocean and on land, killing numerous plants and animals.

OIL-SOAKED JACKASS PENGUIN

Diamonds

We prize diamonds not only for their beauty, but also for their usefulness in cutting: they are the hardest known natural material in the world. Yet diamonds help finance wars, too. Diamonds, found in **war zones** and sold to provide money for wars, or terrorism, are called **'blood diamonds'**. These days, diamonds that can be proved to have come from good sources have a **special certificate**.

Climate and Weather

We all know how changeable weather can be – rain one minute, bright sunshine the next; two weeks of calm followed by sudden storms.

When we talk about the weather, we usually talk about short periods of time. Climate is like a long-term view of weather. We look at what the weather does in a particular area over a long period of time, work out the average temperatures, amount of rainfall and other figures, and these tell us what the climate is. Tropical rainforests, for example, have a hot, damp climate. Hot, dry deserts are – well – hot and dry! But they can also get very cold at night. So plants and animals have to be able to cope with the climate they live in.

Climates around the world differ for many reasons. At the equator, the central band running around the Earth, the Sun shines directly overhead. This makes the climate very hot. Away from the equator, the Sun's rays are more widely spread, making the climate cooler. Mountains are generally cooler than lower land nearby. The ocean protects the land close to it from extremes of temperature, because water releases heat more slowly than land. And climates can change over time, too. When we cut down part or all of a rainforest, the climate gets hotter. And it stays hotter for as long as it takes for the trees to grow back – if they do. This is a long-term climate change. Natural events can also change climate. El Niño, for example, is an area of unusually warm water in the Pacific Ocean that happens every two to seven years, and lasts for a few months to two years. It can cause severe drought (dry weather), floods and crop failure in countries close to the edge of the Pacific Ocean. Fortunately, though, this is a relatively short-term climate change.

Five main climates

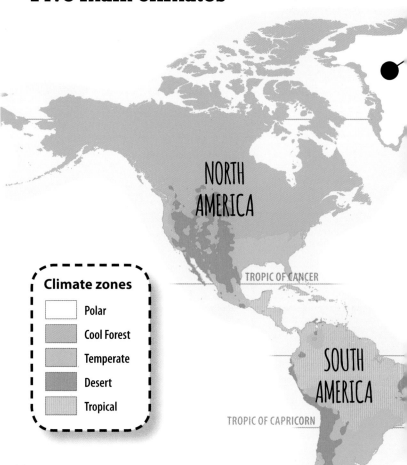

Climate zones
- Polar
- Cool Forest
- Temperate
- Desert
- Tropical

NORTH AMERICA

TROPIC OF CANCER

SOUTH AMERICA

TROPIC OF CAPRICORN

There are **five** main kinds of climate around the world, and they follow a rough kind of pattern. You can see this on the map above. At the extreme north and south of the globe are the freezing **polar climates**, named because these areas are close to the north and south poles. At the equator are the **hot, wet tropics**. The other climate areas are in between.

Why Does Weather Happen?

The differences in temperature around the planet mean air is constantly moving. Warm air in one place rises above cooler air, and the cooler air swirls in. In other places, cool air sinks and pushes warmer air out. Huge **'air masses'**, or bodies of air, carrying wet, dry, hot or cold air, are moved along by the wind. When two air masses meet, we get a **'front'**, and the weather changes.

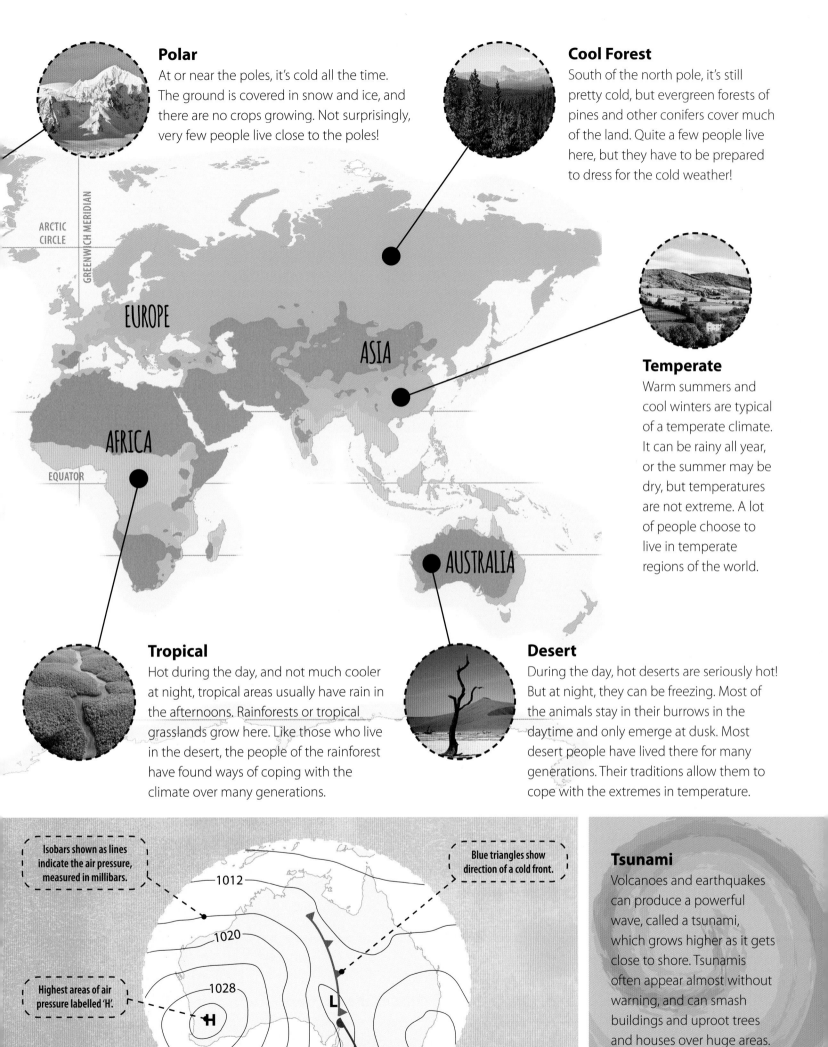

Polar

At or near the poles, it's cold all the time. The ground is covered in snow and ice, and there are no crops growing. Not surprisingly, very few people live close to the poles!

Cool Forest

South of the north pole, it's still pretty cold, but evergreen forests of pines and other conifers cover much of the land. Quite a few people live here, but they have to be prepared to dress for the cold weather!

ARCTIC CIRCLE

GREENWICH MERIDIAN

EUROPE

ASIA

AFRICA

EQUATOR

AUSTRALIA

Temperate

Warm summers and cool winters are typical of a temperate climate. It can be rainy all year, or the summer may be dry, but temperatures are not extreme. A lot of people choose to live in temperate regions of the world.

Tropical

Hot during the day, and not much cooler at night, tropical areas usually have rain in the afternoons. Rainforests or tropical grasslands grow here. Like those who live in the desert, the people of the rainforest have found ways of coping with the climate over many generations.

Desert

During the day, hot deserts are seriously hot! But at night, they can be freezing. Most of the animals stay in their burrows in the daytime and only emerge at dusk. Most desert people have lived there for many generations. Their traditions allow them to cope with the extremes in temperature.

Isobars shown as lines indicate the air pressure, measured in millibars.

Blue triangles show direction of a cold front.

1012

1020

1028

Highest areas of air pressure labelled 'H'.

H

L

H

Lowest areas of air pressure labelled 'L'.

1012

Red semicircles show direction of a warm front.

Tsunami

Volcanoes and earthquakes can produce a powerful wave, called a tsunami, which grows higher as it gets close to shore. Tsunamis often appear almost without warning, and can smash buildings and uproot trees and houses over huge areas.

The World's Oceans and Seas

We think of the Sun as the most important body affecting our weather. If it's a sunny day, it'll probably be warm, and if it's cloudy it'll be cooler.

In the main, that's true. However, the ocean soaks up and stores heat from the Sun. In fact, the top 3 m (10 ft) of the ocean hold the same amount of heat as the entire atmosphere does. The oceans also play a big part in whatever weather is coming our way, by flowing and drawing water and air in certain directions. The western coast of the United States, for example, is usually mild, because the winds there are warmed by the Pacific Ocean. And the oceans are also the source of most of the water in the rain cycle.

The rain cycle, also known as the water cycle, is the constant movement of water around our planet. Nearly all of the water on Earth is in the oceans and seas. When the Sun heats up water in the ocean, or rivers, or lakes, some of it turns into water vapour, or steam. Plants also release water vapour when they are warmed up. The vapour rises into the air until it gets cool again, and forms clouds of water droplets. When there are so many water droplets that the air can't hold them any more, we get rain (or snow, or hail). This falls back into the rivers, lakes and oceans or, if it falls on land, will run down a mountain, or soak into the ground and become ground water. Either way, it ends up back in the ocean and the whole process just keeps on going.

Fresh Water

Lakes and rivers are filled with fresh water, not salty water. Although fresh water only makes up a tiny amount of the water on the surface of Earth, it still plays a large part in the **water cycle**, producing water vapour that rises and forms clouds, and returning water that falls as rain or snow to the oceans.

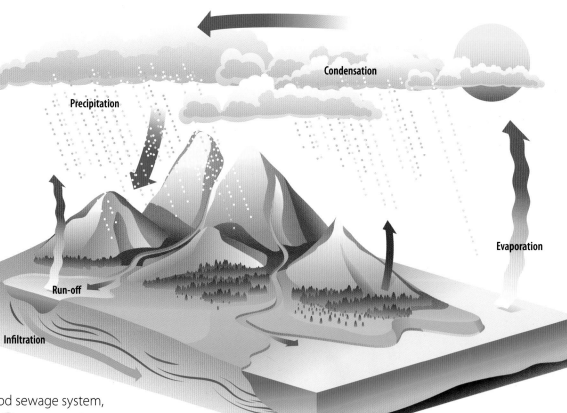

Pollution

In places where there is no good sewage system, human waste pollutes rivers and streams and can cause **disease** in people, plants and animals. In industrialised countries, pollution from factories can contain harmful chemicals that also cause damage. It is essential for good health that the fresh water on our planet remains fresh. Many countries have laws to prevent **water pollution**.

Under the Ground

Fresh water also flows underground, and is naturally filtered by the soil and stones it flows through. People dig **wells** to reach **groundwater**, and it is often so clean that it's safe to drink. Groundwater is topped up by rain and snow, and eventually flows back to the surface, in **natural springs**.

Pacific Ocean

The Pacific is the largest of all the oceans. It covers about a third of Earth's surface. The Portuguese explorer, Ferdinand Magellan, named it the 'Mar Pacifico', which means 'peaceful sea' in Portuguese.

Atlantic Ocean

The Atlantic is the second largest ocean. The world's longest mountain range is under the Atlantic. It's called the mid-Atlantic ridge, and it extends for more than 56,000 km (35,000 mi).

Arctic Ocean

The Arctic Ocean surrounds the North Pole. It is the smallest and shallowest ocean. For much of the year, the Arctic is covered in ice. When it melts, lots of fresh water enters the ocean. Because of this, on average, it's the least salty of all the oceans.

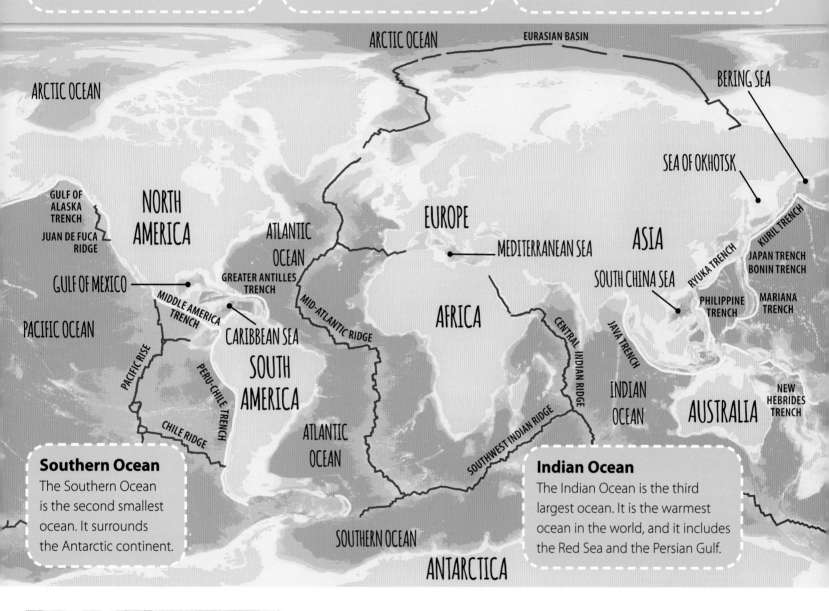

Southern Ocean

The Southern Ocean is the second smallest ocean. It surrounds the Antarctic continent.

Indian Ocean

The Indian Ocean is the third largest ocean. It is the warmest ocean in the world, and it includes the Red Sea and the Persian Gulf.

Why is the Sea Salty?

Rivers and streams on land carry fresh water. But they dissolve and pick up various **minerals** from the rocks and soil they pass through. Rivers carry the minerals with them until, eventually, they flow into the ocean. The **saltiness** of the oceans and seas comes from these minerals.

For most of history, man has had to fight nature to survive; in this century he is beginning to realise that, in order to survive, he must protect it.

Jacques-Yves Cousteau

The deepest part of the ocean is Challenger Deep in the Mariana Trench, at **10,924 m (35,899 ft)** below sea level.

The World's Population

In the 14th century, the total number of people in the world was less than 400 million.

Today there are more than seven billion (seven thousand million) of us! This might sound like a success story, but the more people there are, the more pressure there is on the environment, food supplies and other resources, such as energy. There are also more people living in poverty.

As you can see from the map on the right, people are not spread out evenly around the world. Some rich countries have a high population density, which you might expect, as they have good nutrition and health care, and enough work for most people.

Part of the problem is that our resources aren't spread out evenly, either. According to experts, we produce enough food to feed everyone, but it's not always in the right place. Some people have more than they need, and even waste food and water. More than 10 percent of the people in the world have too little food, and many have no access to clean water. Charities are doing their best to get food and water to those who need it, but it's a difficult job.

NORTH AMERICA

SOUTH AMERICA

Population Numbers by Continent	
Asia	4.3 billion
Africa	1.033 billion
Europe	733 million
North America	529 million
South America	386 million
Australia	36 million
Antarctica	1-5000

Cities are Great!

Most big cities and other large communities are close to water. Early people realised water from rivers and streams made it possible to grow crops, and feed and water animals (and themselves!). They used boats to explore, and met other people, with whom they could trade food and other supplies. For this they had to build more boats and ships – which created jobs. Many major cities grew up on the same spots people had first settled. Now, people still flock to them.

Cities are Awful!

Cities today are becoming more and more overcrowded. They are often expensive and polluted, and yet still people arrive from outside, looking for a better job and social life. Many find life in the city is harder than they expect. They may end up with no job, no home and no money. Even for those with good jobs, city life can be hard. Many adults move out when they have children. They believe they can have a better family life in a less stressful environment.

Cities by Population

1. Tokyo, Japan, 35.1 million
2. Chongqing, China, 28.8 million
3. Jakarta, Indonesia, 28 million
4. Seoul, South Korea, 25.2 million
5. Delhi, India, 22.2 million
6. Manila, Phillipines, 21.9
7. Mexico City, Mexico, 21.2 million
8. Shanghai, China, 20.8 million
9. Sao Paulo, Brazil, 19.8 million
10. Cairo, Egypt, 19.6 million

EUROPE

ASIA

AFRICA

AUSTRALIA

This map shows how early people from Africa may have spread around the world.

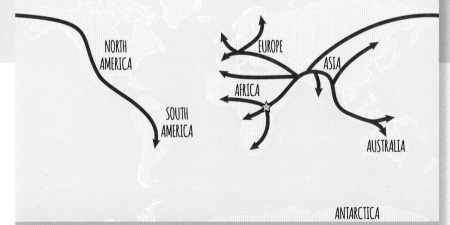

NORTH AMERICA

EUROPE

ASIA

AFRICA

SOUTH AMERICA

AUSTRALIA

ANTARCTICA

Where did we all come from?

The first hominids, or human-like mammals, developed from the ape family in Africa about five million years ago. Slowly (over millions of years) they began to walk upright, and their brains grew bigger. Living and travelling in groups, they gathered fruits and other foods, and hunted animals. Eventually, some of our direct ancestors moved beyond Africa and humans began to dominate life all over the world.

Why do People Live in Dangerous Places?

A surprising number of people live close to **volcanoes**, in **earthquake zones**, and areas prone to **flooding** and **forest fires**. However, close to the edges of the tectonic plates, for example, where most earthquakes and volcanoes happen, the soil is often very fertile. Precious minerals, such as gold and silver, are found there. In many cases, people moved there before we knew about **plate tectonics** and realised how dangerous it was, so there were huge cities already established. And tourists wanting to see the fantastic landscapes bring in money and jobs, too!

Mapping the World

"To put a city in a book, to put the world on one sheet of paper – maps are the most condensed humanised spaces of all...They make the landscape fit indoors, make us masters of sights we can't see and spaces we can't cover."

Robert Harbison

Maps are drawings of places around us. We use them to help us find somewhere we haven't been to before, and they've been around a very long time.

Early maps were very inaccurate compared with those we use today, but early cartographers (mapmakers) had no detailed knowledge of the world, and very often had to guess what was beyond what they knew. Gradually, better tools meant mapmakers could improve the quality of their maps. The invention of the magnetic compass, for example, allowed more accuracy. The arrival of the printing press meant that one good map could be copied many times, making maps more affordable.

For a map to be useful, it must be relatively easy to read. Cartographers use symbols, lines and colours to indicate different features, and usually list what they all mean in a 'legend', or key. Some elements of map-making are standard, and nearly all cartographers use them. Lines of longitude and latitude, for example, make finding a place on a map easy, so you will find these on nearly every map you see. However, to show a flat map of a spherical world is difficult, and there are many ways of doing it. That's why not all maps of the world are the same shape.

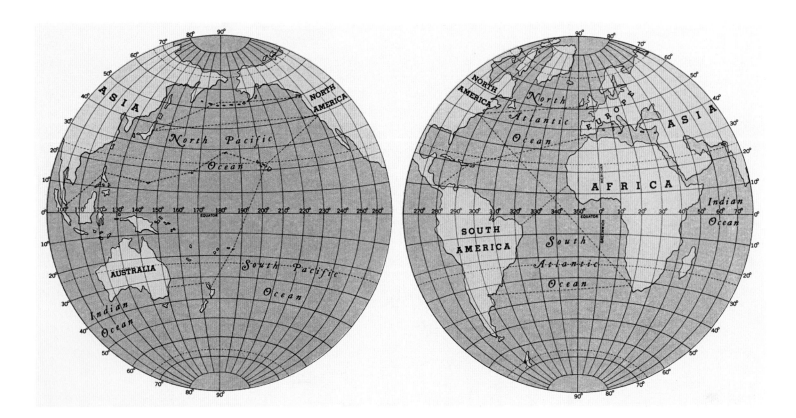

Mercator's projection

In 1659, Flemish cartographer Gerardus Mercator made a world map that presented the world as a flattened out cylinder (tube). It became the standard 'projection', or representation, of the world in two dimensions, especially for sailors, because it showed the meridians as straight lines. This made it easy to work out a course to the ship's next port of call. However, in Mercator's projection the scale (comparative size) increases towards the poles, distorting the shapes of some areas quite badly. Greenland, for example, looks larger than Africa, which is actually about 14 times bigger!

Robinson projection

In 1963, American cartographer Arthur H. Robinson made his world map projection an oval shape. This lessens the distortion at the poles, though it is still there. Robinson's projection is still a popular choice for maps and atlases today. However, no spherical object can be completely accurately represented in two dimensions. If you're interested in looking for different kinds of map projections, you may come across some quite weird and wonderful alternatives.

Ocean charts

Sailors have to know not only where a place is, but how they can get there by ship. Not easy when you can't see the ocean floor you're sailing over! So they have special maps, called nautical charts. Depending on the scale of the chart, it may show coastlines, water depths, currents and tides, and hazards (such as rocks and shipwrecks) to avoid.

A Map for Every Occasion

*"If I had a street named after me,
it would really put me on the map."*

Jarod Kintz

Today's maps are mostly based on satellite information, and are usually very accurate indeed. The satellites orbit Earth at a low height, and can record lots of detail.

But we still need cartographers to sort the information out and turn it into readable maps that are useful in everyday life. Modern cartographers use special mapping computer software to pick out the information they need to use and create a specific kind of map.

On these pages you will see a few of the many different maps people use in different situations. For example, to help us on short, local journeys, we use large-scale maps, which show a small area in great detail. For longer trips, we use small-scale maps, which show a large area in less detail. The maps you will see on later pages in this Atlas are small-scale.

Satellites

There are thousands of satellites orbiting Earth. Many of them have stopped working and are essentially just space junk. But a good many of those that still take pictures supply data used in making maps today.

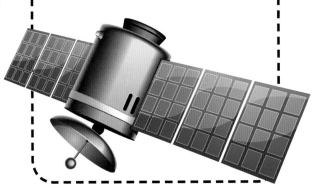

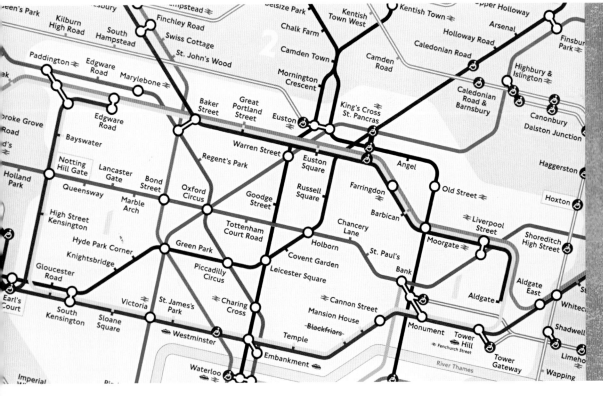

Topological Maps

A topological map is a very simple map. Maps like this usually ignore scale and detail in favour of simplicity and ease of use. Maps of underground railways are often topological, showing the system of lines and stations in a carefully laid out way, but disregarding their real life distance and exact position. Since passengers using an underground system really only want to get from one place to another, the basic information on the map is all they need.

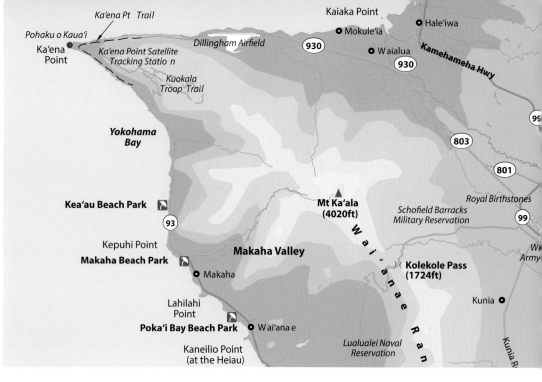

Topographical Features

A topographical map is primarily concerned with the description of surface features and shapes, such as hills, valleys and mountains. They can be shown in a number of different ways, but the most common are contour lines or shading, which show how high or low land is compared to that surrounding it.

Street view maps

These online maps provide a comprehensive view of a specific location. Just take a look at Google's street view maps as an example. Their 'Street View' option gives users the possibility of looking at a place almost as if they were actually there. You can zoom in, zoom out and see buildings and other features from street level.

These maps are made using cars with nine special cameras. Together, these take 360 degree images of the places they drive through. Narrow streets and other places too small for cars are mapped using tricycles, and even snowmobiles where necessary!

Flight Patterns

This map shows the flight patterns of some of the world's major airlines. It demonstrates how people travel around the globe, and some of the typical routes they take.

A Physical Perspective

"There isn't a parallel of latitude but thinks it would have been the equator if it had had its rights."

Mark Twain

Physical maps of the world show Earth's surface features. These usually include large ones, such as mountains, valleys, rivers and lakes, and sometimes smaller ones, such as hills, roads and railway lines.

What to include really depends on the size of the map, and what it will be used for. Because they are quite small, the maps in this atlas only show major features. But a map meant for serious study, or to locate particular features, would be very much more detailed – and probably very much larger!

The map on the right is a physical map of part of Switzerland. On it you can see major rivers, lakes, mountains, towns and cities, and even some of the shapes of the land. You can also see country borders. These are not always included in physical maps, but they often are, as it can be useful to know in which country certain features are found.

Legend

Rhine	River
Lago Maggiore	Lake
Oberalp Pass	Pass/Bridge
Mt Titlis (3239m)	Mountain

Grid references

If you want to find a specific place, say a town or city, on a map in an atlas, you will probably look it up in the index. This will give you the region or country the town is in, the page number, and a letter and number. The letter and number form the grid reference. Find them on the edges of the map (usually the letters are at the top and the numbers down the side of the page) and trace the column down and the row inwards until you find the box where they meet. Now you only have to look within that box!

Coordinates

On some maps, and especially on a globe, you might need to use coordinates to find what you are looking for. These are numbers that tell you the latitude (how far north or south somewhere is from the equator) and the longitude (how far east or west of the Greenwich Meridian). For example, the latitude and longitude of Port Elizabeth, South Africa is: 33° 55'S / 25° 34'E. This means it's 33 degrees and 55 minutes south of the equator, and 25 degrees and 34 seconds east of the Greenwich Meridian (each degree is divided into 60 minutes). So, to find it on a map, or globe, we look at the lines of latitude and longitude, find where these two coordinates meet, and we've found Port Elizabeth!

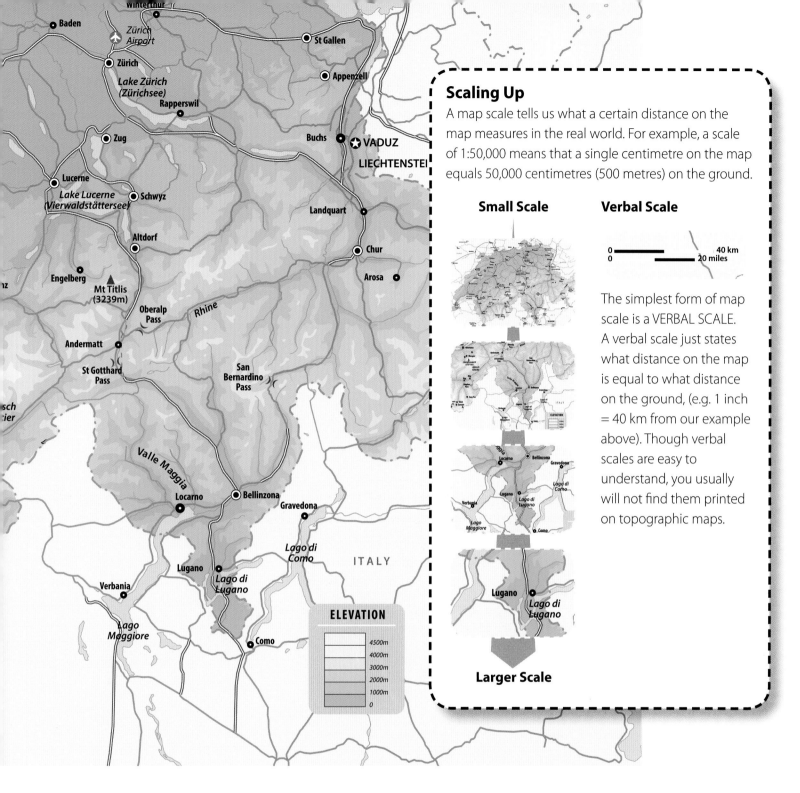

Scaling Up

A map scale tells us what a certain distance on the map measures in the real world. For example, a scale of 1:50,000 means that a single centimetre on the map equals 50,000 centimetres (500 metres) on the ground.

Small Scale

Verbal Scale

| 0 | 40 km |
| 0 | 20 miles |

The simplest form of map scale is a VERBAL SCALE. A verbal scale just states what distance on the map is equal to what distance on the ground, (e.g. 1 inch = 40 km from our example above). Though verbal scales are easy to understand, you usually will not find them printed on topographic maps.

Larger Scale

ELEVATION

	4500m
	4000m
	3000m
	2000m
	1000m
	0

How to read a hiker's map

Most of us don't need to know how to find our way around the world. Airplanes, railways and other kinds of transport usually take us long distances. But if we want to walk around a village, or explore the countryside, we need a map with good detail and landmarks that we can use to be sure we're going the right way! Large-scale maps, such as this hiker's map, show enough detail to allow you to be sure you're going in the right direction.

A Political Perspective

'You have brains in your head. You have feet in your shoes. You can steer yourself any direction you choose.'

Dr. Seuss

Political maps in a detailed atlas, like the one below, include specific kinds of information.

They are intended to show the nations or countries of the world, and the land that each controls. National and state borders are clearly marked, and not only capital cities, but also other cities and large towns are marked with a symbol and labelled. Often, nations are coloured differently from those next to them, to make it clear where each one begins and ends. There are special kinds of lines for borders that are in dispute – for example, where two countries are arguing or fighting over an area of land. Really large physical features, such as mountain ranges and major rivers, are sometimes shown, but not always.

Things change a lot in the political world! After World War II, for example, Germany was split into two – East Germany and West Germany. Maps had to be redrawn to show this. Then, in 1990, they were reunited, and the maps were redrawn again. Sometimes, places change their names to reflect new political leadership. The old name as well as the new one may be shown for a while, to help people who don't know about the change. Issues like this mean that political maps usually become out of date much more quickly than physical maps.

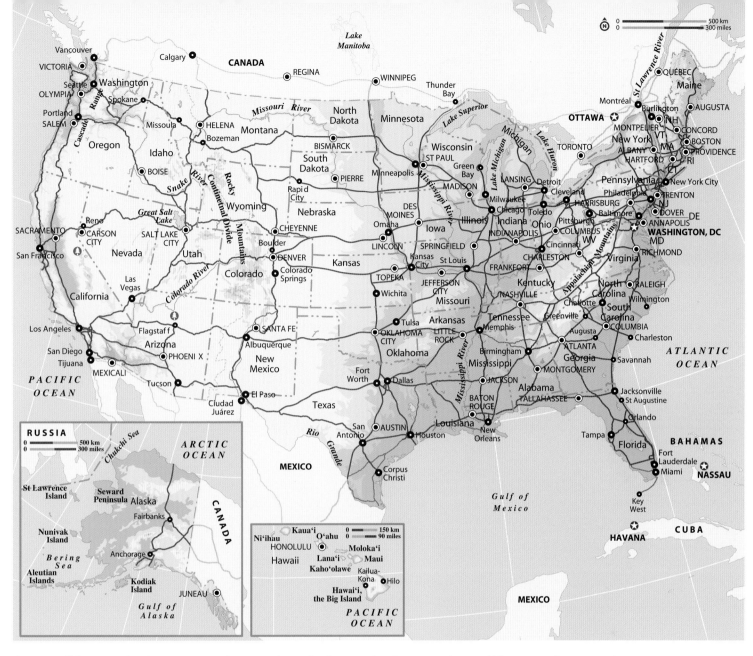

As you will have noticed, most countries or nations don't come in nice, neat shapes. Where a nation controls somewhere far away from its homeland, such as Alaska in the United States, cartographers often use a separate inset box to highlight that it doesn't physically belong in the part of the world shown on the map.

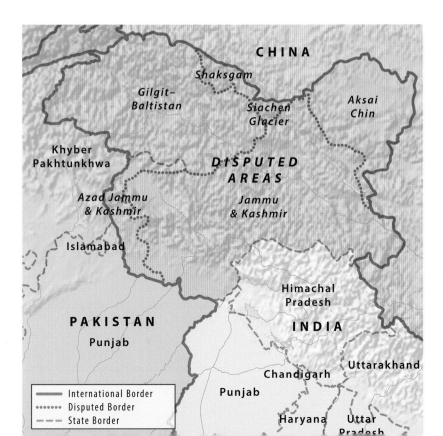

	International Border
.....	Disputed Border
- - -	State Border

Border fighting

Sometimes more than one country lays claim to a region or territory. Southern Asia's Kashmir, for example, has been at the centre of a dispute between India and Pakistan for more than 60 years! There is no international recognition of either claim to the area, so Kashmir is shown as a disputed territory on maps like this. Disputed territories have dotted borders on the maps in this book.

North America

America is so vast that almost everything said about it is likely to be true, and the opposite is probably equally true.

James T. Farrell

ALASKA

YUKON TERRITORY

BRITISH COLUMBIA

GULF OF ALASKA

WASHINGTON

OREGON

NORTH PACIFIC OCEAN

MAP KEY
1 Vaquita **2** Golden Gate Bridge **3** Giant Redwood **4** Canadian Goose **5** Moose **6** Puffin **7** Mount Rushmore **8** The Capitol building **9** Statue of Liberty **10** Midwestern farm **11** Mississippi steamboat **12** Alligator **13** Mexico City Metropolitan Cathedral **14** Mayan temple, Tikal **15** Ackee

Area: 24.5 million km² (9.5 million sq mi)
Fact: third largest (after Asia and Africa)
Population: 529 million

North America has 22 named time zones, but many of them are the same. In fact there are really only 5 different time zones on the continent.

HAWAII

North America is packed full of natural wonders. From Niagara Falls to Death Valley, and the Grand Canyon to Mount McKinley, it has some of the most amazing landscapes in the world.

It is the third largest continent and has all of the major climate types. This gives it a truly diverse range of plants and animals, including one of the smallest owls and the largest bears. The continent is also home to a multitude of people from all over the world, and contains some of the largest cities.

The first North American people were from Asia. They developed a number of different cultures and languages. Most hunted animals and gathered fruit, nuts and vegetables for food. In the south, some learnt how to cultivate crops, such as corn and tomatoes. The Maya people, in Central America, developed a system of writing and an advanced calendar. When European people arrived in the 16th century, not only did they bring a rich cultural heritage, but also diseases, such as smallpox and flu, that wiped out huge numbers of the Native Americans.

ARCTIC OCEAN

GREENLAND

BAFFIN BAY

6

NORTHWEST TERRITORIES

NUNAVUT

HUDSON BAY

QUEBEC

NEWFOUNDLAND & LABRADOR

5 ALBERTA

SASKATCHEWAN

MANITOBA

ONTARIO

PRINCE EDWARD ISLAND

4

MONTANA

N. DAKOTA

MINNESOTA

WISCONSIN

R. Mississippi

8

NEW YORK

MAINE

NEW BRUNSWICK

NOVA SCOTIA

WYOMING

IDAHO

7 IOWA

R. Missouri

ILLINOIS

INDIANA

OHIO

PENNSYLVANIA

NEW HAMPSHIRE
MASSACHUSETTS
CONNECTICUT
NEW JERSEY
DELAWARE

NEVADA

UTAH

COLORADO

NEBRASKA

KANSAS

MISSOURI

KENTUCKY

W. VIRGINIA

VIRGINIA

9

3

CALIFORNIA

2

ARIZONA

NEW MEXICO

10

OKLAHOMA

R. Ohio

TENNESSEE

NORTH CAROLINA

SOUTH CAROLINA

GEORGIA

BERMUDA

TEXAS

11

FLORIDA

NORTH ATLANTIC OCEAN

MEXICO

LOUISIANA

GULF OF MEXICO

12

BAHAMAS

13

CUBA

DOMINICAN REPUBLIC

14

BELIZE

15

CARIBBEAN

PUERTO RICO

GUATEMALA

HONDURAS

EL SALVADOR

NICARAGUA

CARIBBEAN SEA

1

COSTA RICA

PANAMA

SOUTH AMERICA

NORTH AMERICA – BIG AND BEAUTIFUL!

Sometimes it seems North America does everything in a big way! It's known for big buildings, huge lakes, enormous waterfalls and other physical features. North American people even think big; just look at the number of new ideas that have come from here. From walking on the moon to inventing the nuclear bomb, creating jazz, country and mariachi music and enormous theme parks. Not to mention Hollywood's booming film industry, which makes countless North Americans and others from around the world into huge, box-office-busting, money-making stars!

North America grows about half of the world's maize (corn)

BOURBON STREET IN THE FRENCH QUARTER, NEW ORLEANS

MORAINE LAKE IN THE CANADIAN ROCKY MOUNTAINS

THE GRAND CANYON, ARIZONA

GOLDEN GATE BRIDGE, SAN FRANCISCO

Why America?

America was named after the 15th century Italian explorer, Amerigo Vespucci. He was the first person to think that South America was not part of the East Indies, but a different land altogether, previously unknown to Europeans. The name 'America' was later extended to North America.

NORTH AMERICA TOP 10

BERING SEA
Separates the North American continent from the Asian continent

MOUNT McKINLEY (DENALI)
The highest mountain in North America at 6,193 m (20,320 ft)

GREAT BEAR LAKE
The largest lake in Canada

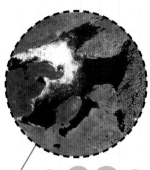

NIAGARA FALLS
Has the highest flow rate of any waterfall on Earth

EMPIRE STATE BUILDING
Built in 1931, it has appeared in over 250 movies

MOUNT RUSHMORE
Monument to 4 American Presidents

THE ELF OWL
Lives in the Sonoran Desert region of Arizona and migrates to Mexico in the winter

MEXICO CITY
One of the most populated cities on Earth, with 9 million inhabitants

CAPE CANAVERAL
Home to the Kennedy Space Center, space rocket launch site

PIRATE
Pirates in the Caribbean were also known as buccaneers

ALL-AMERICAN HEROES

You've probably heard of a lot of North Americans; for example, **Neil Armstrong** (left), the first man to walk on the moon. **Sitting Bull** was a Sioux medicine man and holy man, and defeated **General Custer** at the battle of Little Bighorn. Famous North American writers include **Mark Twain** (right) and **Maya Angelou**. Musicians such as **Dizzy Gillespie** and **Avril Lavigne** have made a splash, as have actors **Will Smith** and **Jennifer Lawrence**.

CANADA

ALBERTA - BRITISH COLUMBIA - MANITOBA - NEW BRUNSWICK
NEWFOUNDLAND & LABRADOR - NOVA SCOTIA - ONTARIO
PRINCE EDWARD ISLAND - QUEBEC - SASKATCHEWAN

Canada is a vast, rugged land. From north to south it spans more than half of the Northern Hemisphere. From east to west it stretches almost 7,560 km (4,700 mi). Winters can be very cold, with temperatures dropping below −40°C (−40°F) in some parts of the country. However, the huge forest that covers much of Canada's land is home to millions of different birds and other wildlife. Canada is famous for its large mammals, which include bears, caribou (wild reindeer), grey wolves, moose, mountain lions, musk oxen, walrus, and whales.

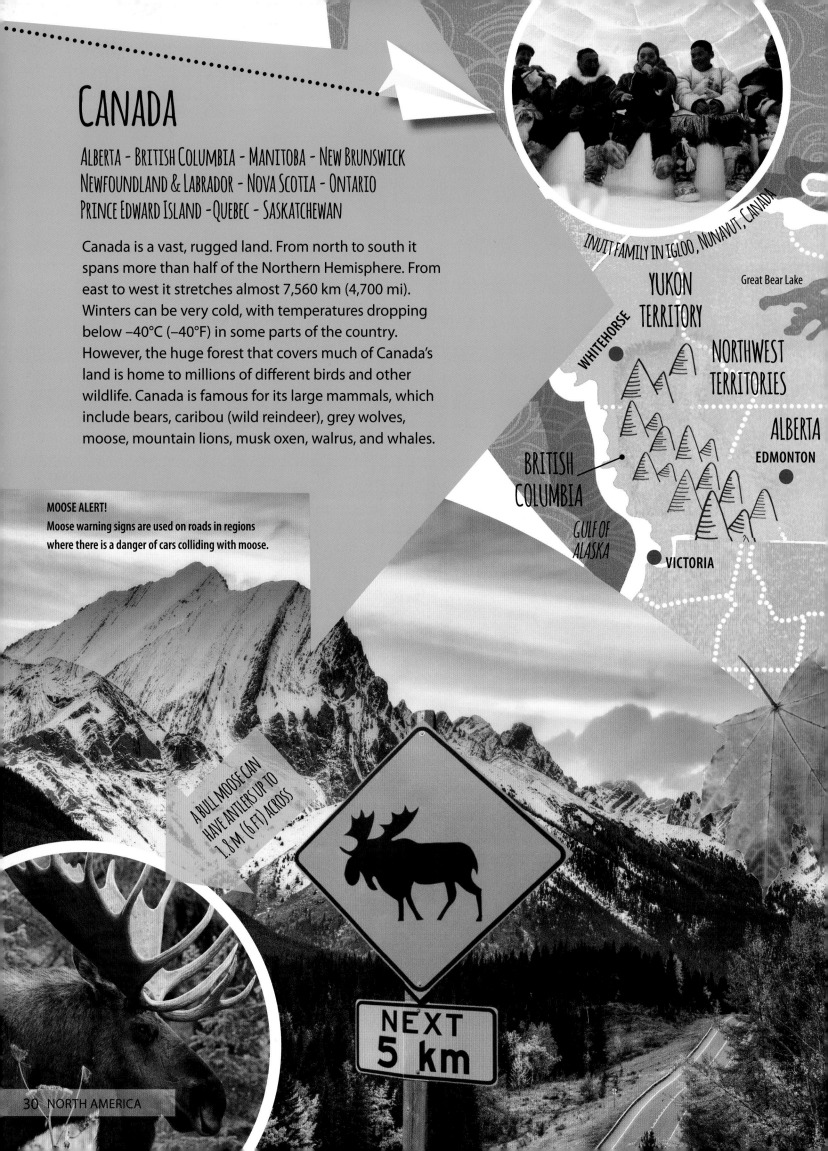

INUIT FAMILY IN IGLOO, NUNAVUT, CANADA

MOOSE ALERT!
Moose warning signs are used on roads in regions where there is a danger of cars colliding with moose.

A BULL MOOSE CAN HAVE ANTLERS UP TO 1.8 M (6 FT) ACROSS

NEXT 5 km

YUKON TERRITORY

WHITEHORSE

Great Bear Lake

NORTHWEST TERRITORIES

BRITISH COLUMBIA

ALBERTA

EDMONTON

GULF OF ALASKA

VICTORIA

ARCTIC OCEAN

GREENLAND

BAFFIN BAY

NUNAVUT

YELLOWKNIFE

Great Slave Lake

HUDSON BAY

NORTH ATLANTIC OCEAN

SASKATCHEWAN

MANITOBA

Lake Winnipeg

NEWFOUNDLAND & LABRADOR

REGINA

Lake Manitoba

ONTARIO

QUEBEC

WINNIPEG

PRINCE EDWARD ISLAND

QUEBEC CITY

ST. JOHN'S

Lake Superior

MONTREAL

NEW BRUNSWICK

OTTAWA

Lake Huron

TORONTO

FREDERICTON

HALIFAX

Lake Ontario

NOVA SCOTIA

Lake Erie

THE FAST AND THE FURRY

The fastest land animal in Canada is the pronghorn, which looks a little like an antelope. It can reach almost **55 mph (90 km/h)** over short distances.
The Atlantic puffin is the smallest puffin in the world, about the size of a pigeon. It has to flap its wings about **300 to 400 times** a minute to fly!
The arctic fox has the warmest pelt (fur) of all arctic animals and is the smallest of all canids (dogs, wolves, and foxes) in the Arctic.

AT HOME IN THE ROCKIES

The Canadian Rocky Mountains are part of a series of mountain ranges running from Alaska to the tip of South America. They are home to hundreds of elks, bighorn sheep, and moose, as well as many other animals.

BIGHORN SHEEP

? WHO OR WHAT AM I?

I hatch in a nest on the ground, in the mountains of Alaska and Canada. I'm white in the winter, but my back gets brown in the summer. My name begins with a silent letter.

ANSWER: A ptarmigan

WHO LIVES HERE?

The original inhabitants of Canada were the **Native Americans**, or First Nations people. **Europeans** settled the country in the 17th century, and their descendants also live here, along with more recent immigrants. Most **Canadians** speak English, but French is also an official language.

The name **Canada** comes from the word 'kanata' which means 'settlement' or 'village' in the language of the indigenous St Lawrence Iroquoians.

MAD ABOUT MAPLE

Since 1965, the maple leaf has been the centrepiece of the National Flag of Canada. Maple tree sap is used to make delicious maple syrup and it takes 30 to 50 gallons of sap to make just 1 gallon of syrup. In autumn, maple leaves change colour to vibrant oranges, reds and russets and the national parks publish colour reports so tourists can find the best places to spot this glorious sight.

8893 km (5526 mi) of border is shared between the **USA and Canada.** It's the largest shared border in the world

For 94 years, the **Jasper Raven Totem Pole** stood in Jasper National Park. But when it was found to be rotten it was sent back to the Haida Nation that had carved it. In 2011, the Two Brothers Totem Pole was sent to replace the original.

Canadians use a number of slang terms for their **money.** The one dollar coin, for example, has a picture of a common loon (a kind of bird), so it's often called a **'loonie'.** The two-dollar coin is called a **'toonie'**, a combination of the words 'two' and 'loonie'!

Canada has between **2 and 3 million lakes** – that's more than all the other countries in the world put together!

20% of all water on Earth is contained in Canada's lakes.

JOB:
Forestry

ART:
Inuit carvings in walrus ivory, muskox horn, caribou antler and soapstone, totem poles

WHAT TO SAY:
'Take off!' (You're kidding, no way)

WHAT NOT TO SAY:
Are you American?

FOOD:
Poutine - french fries, topped with a light brown gravy-like sauce and cheese curds

LEISURE ACTIVITY:
Trips to watch polar bears

SWEET TREAT:
Maple syrup

The game of **lacrosse** so many Canadians play today is based on traditional games played by a number of different **First Nations** communities. This makes it one of the oldest team sports in America! Traditionally, some games could last for days, and up to 1000 people from local villages took part.

Number plates for cars, motorbikes and snowmobiles in the Northwest Territories are the shape of a **polar bear.**

NORTHWEST TERRITORIES
T6I69
CANADA N.W.T. 85 1983

Canada is rich in minerals, including zinc, nickel, lead and gold. Since the 1500s it has exported fish and furs around the world.

Canadians eat more macaroni and cheese than any other people in the world!

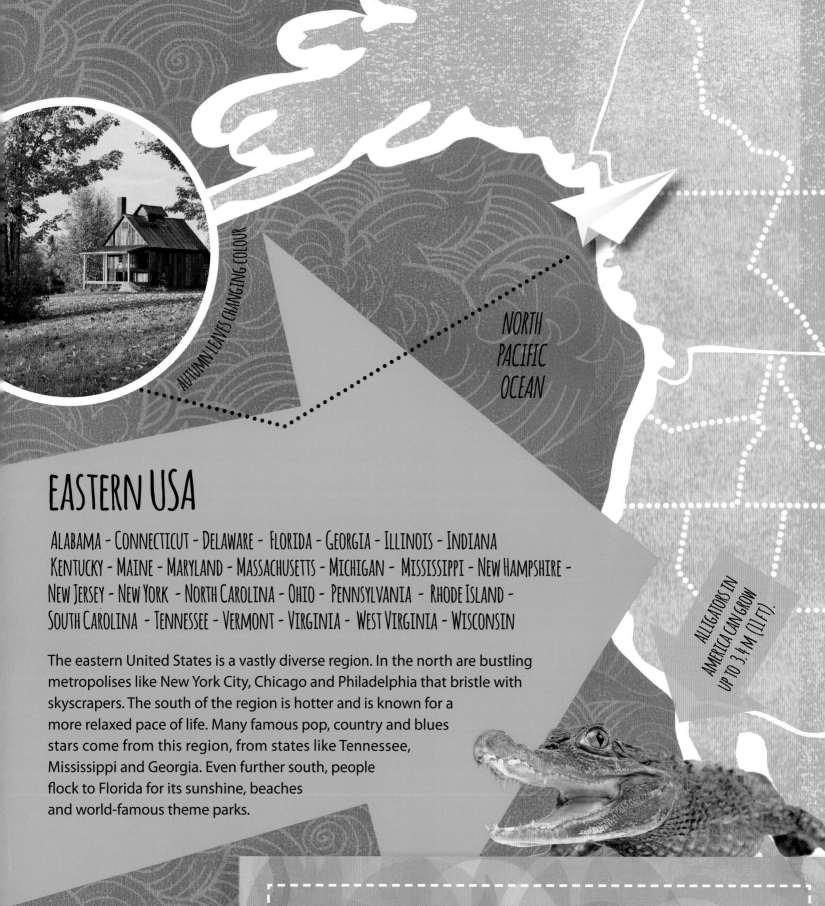

AUTUMN LEAVES CHANGING COLOUR

NORTH
PACIFIC
OCEAN

EASTERN USA

ALABAMA – CONNECTICUT – DELAWARE – FLORIDA – GEORGIA – ILLINOIS – INDIANA
KENTUCKY – MAINE – MARYLAND – MASSACHUSETTS – MICHIGAN – MISSISSIPPI – NEW HAMPSHIRE –
NEW JERSEY – NEW YORK – NORTH CAROLINA – OHIO – PENNSYLVANIA – RHODE ISLAND –
SOUTH CAROLINA – TENNESSEE – VERMONT – VIRGINIA – WEST VIRGINIA – WISCONSIN

The eastern United States is a vastly diverse region. In the north are bustling
metropolises like New York City, Chicago and Philadelphia that bristle with
skyscrapers. The south of the region is hotter and is known for a
more relaxed pace of life. Many famous pop, country and blues
stars come from this region, from states like Tennessee,
Mississippi and Georgia. Even further south, people
flock to Florida for its sunshine, beaches
and world-famous theme parks.

ALLIGATORS IN AMERICA CAN GROW UP TO 3.4 M (11FT).

THE FIRST, THE FURTHEST, AND THE TOOTHIEST . . .

America's first undersea national park, John Pennekamp Coral Reef State Park, was
created in 1960. It has an underwater statue of Jesus Christ, a submerged Spanish ship,
and lots of incredible, protected coral! ● The furthest south you can go in the continental
U.S.A is the end of Key West, Florida. It's marked by a giant concrete buoy and features in
many tourist photos ● Only one kind of crocodile and one kind of alligator live in the
USA, and both of them are found in the mangrove swamps of the Florida Everglades.

STATE OF THE NATION

The United States is a relatively young country. Its first people, the Native Americans, didn't see themselves as part of a larger nation. When European settlers arrived, they began to take over the land, fighting the Native Americans for control. In 1783, 13 colonies on the East Coast, previously under British rule, won their independence and the United States was born.

Lake Superior

Lake Huron

MASSACHUSETTS

NEW HAMPSHIRE
VERMONT

MAINE

WISCONSIN

Lake Michigan — MICHIGAN

Lake Erie

NEW YORK

BOSTON RHODE ISLAND

CHICAGO

PENNSYLVANIA

CONNECTICUT
NEW YORK CITY NEW JERSEY

ILLINOIS

INDIANA

OHIO

DELAWARE
MARYLAND

Mississippi R.

Ohio R.

KENTUCKY

W. VIRGINIA

VIRGINIA

WASHINGTON, D.C.

35
million Americans share **DNA** with at least one of the 102 pilgrims who arrived aboard the **Mayflower** in 1620.

TENNESSEE

N. CAROLINA

NORTH
ATLANTIC
OCEAN

MISSISSIPPI

SOUTH
CAROLINA

GEORGIA

ALABAMA

FLORIDA

TAMPA

MIAMI

THE STATUE OF LIBERTY

The seven rays on the crown of the **Statue of Liberty** represent the seven continents. Each measures up to **2.7 m (9 ft)** in length and weighs as much as **70 kg (150 lb).**

U.S. POSTAGE 11¢
IN GOD WE TRUST
LIBERTY

WHO LIVES HERE?

The United States' population is made up of people from all over the world. As well as **Native American** families and the descendants of the European settlers, there are **African Americans**, many of whom are descended from freed slaves. And people flock to the United States today, seeing it as a land of opportunity, and wanting their chance at the 'American Dream'.

The world's **first ever skyscraper** was built in Chicago, Illinois, in 1884

The most populous **city** in the United States is **New York City,** followed by Los Angeles and Chicago.

In 1620, **settlers from the UK** arrived in what is now Massachusetts. Their first winter was very difficult, with little food to eat. But some **Native Americans** taught them how to farm local crops, and in their second year they had a good harvest. They invited the Native Americans who had helped them to join them for a meal. That meal is still celebrated today, as **Thanksgiving Day.**

GRUB'S UP

American food has been influenced by cuisines from all over the world. However, there are some dishes that Americans really can call their own – and they're delicious! Corn dogs were invented in Texas, and Ruth Graves Wakefield of Massachusetts came up with the chocolate-chip cookie.

THE EASTERN USA REAL DEAL!

WHAT TO SAY:
Have a nice day!

WHAT NOT TO SAY:
Football is stupid!

FAMOUS FOR:
Key lime pie

SPORTS:
Football, surfing, inline skating

DRINKS:
Ginger ale, iced tea

FOOD:
Hot dogs, clam chowder, fried green tomatoes

300

George Washington Carver, who lived in Alabama, discovered more than **300** uses for **peanuts.** Carver wanted to help poor farmers by finding alternative crops to cotton, such as peanuts and sweet potatoes, which would also help feed the farmers' families.

6% of people in the **USA** believe nobody has ever landed on the **Moon.**

In 2014 the US became the biggest producer of oil in the world, overtaking Saudi Arabia and Russia. Much of the oil comes from offshore drilling in the Gulf of Mexico.

The American **one-dollar bill** contains several hidden images, including a spider in the upper-right-hand corner.

BIG AND BOLD

The tallest trees on Earth are giant redwoods, reaching up to **115.5 m (379 ft)** in height (without the roots) and up to **7.9 m (26 feet)** in diameter ● Alaska is the best place to see the aurora borealis (northern lights). This amazing natural light display is caused by electrically charged particles from the Sun. When they hit the gases of our atmosphere, they begin to glow. Some Alaskans have an aurora alert – when they see it displaying, they start off a chain of phone calls to let other people know!

HAWAII

WESTERN USA

ALASKA – ARIZONA – ARKANSAS – CALIFORNIA – COLORADO – HAWAII – IDAHO – IOWA – KANSAS – LOUISIANA – MINNESOTA – MISSOURI – MONTANA – NEBRASKA – NEVADA – NEW MEXICO – NORTH DAKOTA – SOUTH DAKOTA – OKLAHOMA – OREGON – TEXAS – UTAH – WASHINGTON – WYOMING

DUSTY DESERTS
Most of Arizona is made up of deserts.

In the western states are many of the incredible landscapes that the United States is famous for. Much of the middle of the country is covered in prairies – grasslands that are perfect for farming. Further west are the towering snowy peaks of the Rocky Mountains, as well as one of the hottest places on earth – a sweltering desert called Death Valley, in the state of California. West of the deserts and mountains lie the high-tech cities of the West Coast – where new phones and computers are invented and movies are made.

TEXAS LONGHORN

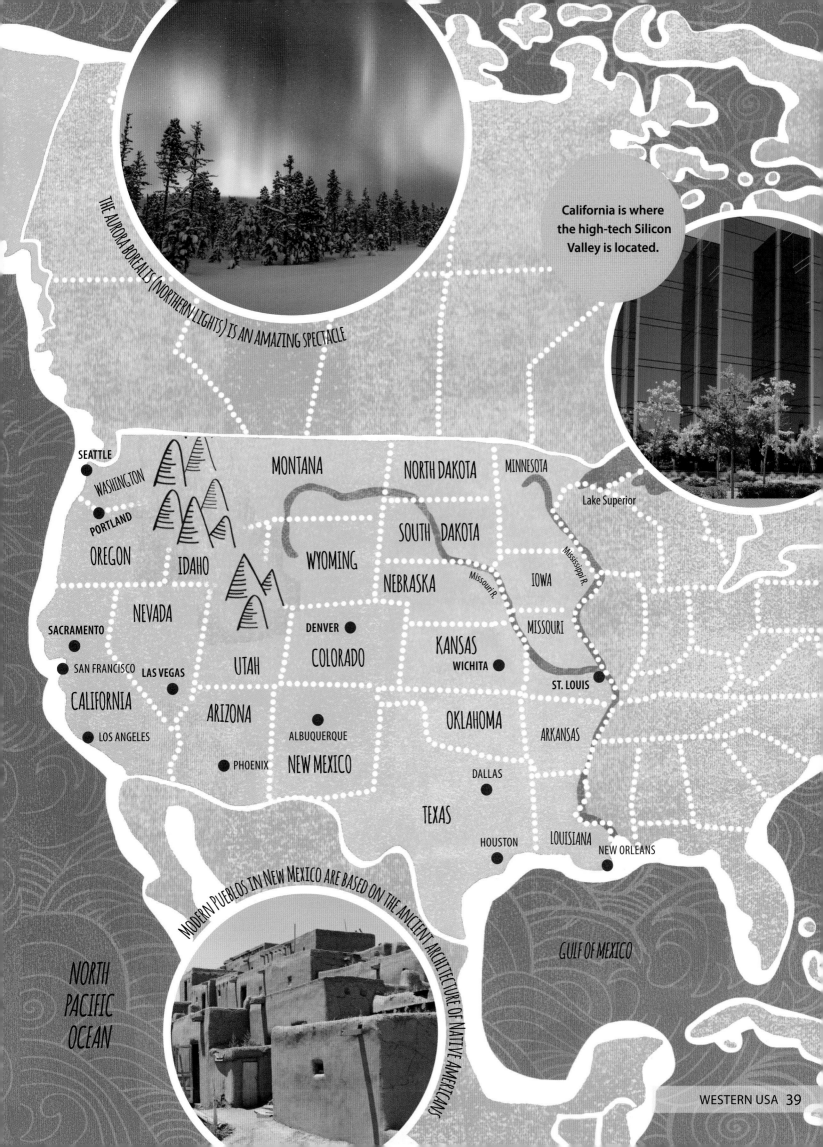

THE AURORA BOREALIS (NORTHERN LIGHTS) IS AN AMAZING SPECTACLE

California is where the high-tech Silicon Valley is located.

SEATTLE

WASHINGTON

PORTLAND

OREGON

IDAHO

MONTANA

NORTH DAKOTA

MINNESOTA

Lake Superior

SOUTH DAKOTA

WYOMING

NEBRASKA

Missouri R.

IOWA

Mississippi R.

NEVADA

SACRAMENTO

SAN FRANCISCO

LAS VEGAS

UTAH

DENVER

COLORADO

KANSAS

WICHITA

MISSOURI

ST. LOUIS

CALIFORNIA

LOS ANGELES

ARIZONA

PHOENIX

ALBUQUERQUE

NEW MEXICO

OKLAHOMA

DALLAS

ARKANSAS

TEXAS

HOUSTON

LOUISIANA

NEW ORLEANS

MODERN PUEBLOS IN NEW MEXICO ARE BASED ON THE ANCIENT ARCHITECTURE OF NATIVE AMERICANS

GULF OF MEXICO

NORTH PACIFIC OCEAN

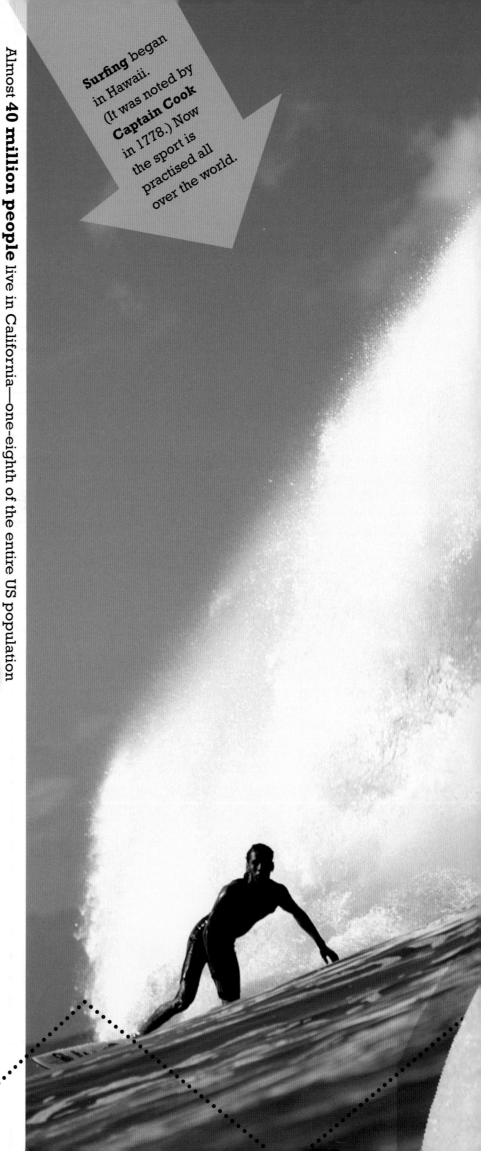

Surfing began in Hawaii. (It was noted by **Captain Cook** in 1778.) Now the sport is practised all over the world.

WHO LIVES HERE?

In the Southwest of the United States it is common to find inhabitants with Mexican ancestry. There's also a strong mix of Hispanic people from Central and South America, as well as descendants of European settlers and African Americans.

Hawaii is the most recent of the 50 states in the USA (it joined in **1959**).

SURF'S UP!

ALOHA, HAWAII

Many people dream of living in a place like Hawaii. It's certainly beautiful, warm, and sunny, and it is the centre of the surfing world, with some of the tallest and cleanest waves around. Oahu's North Shore has many surfing destinations that play host to thousands of amateurs, pros, and wannabe pros from around the world each year.

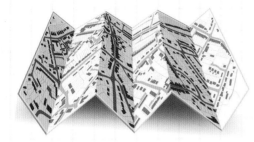

WHAT TO SAY:
"Howdy!"

FAMOUS FOR:
Cowboys

INFAMOUS FOR:
Hollywood

POPULAR FOOD:
Peanut butter and jelly sandwiches

HOBBY:
Storm chasing

PLANT:
Saguaro cactus

The **USA** bought Alaska from **Russia** in 1867 for **$7.2 million.** It's the largest state in the country.

In **California** you can go from **86 m** (282 ft) below sea level in Death Valley to **4,418 m** (14,494 ft) above at the top of Mt. Whitney in less than a day.

US Highway 550 in Colorado became known as Million Dollar Highway because its roadbed was paved with low-grade gold ore.

At over **5,000** years old, a **bristlecone pine** in California's White Mountains is the **oldest** known **living tree** in the world.

500,000

or so measurable seismic tremors happen in California each year.

Silicon Valley in California is home to many of the world's most famous companies including Apple, who make phones and tablets, and Pixar, who make animated movies.

The tallest mountain in Hawaii is **Mauna Kea**. It's **4,205 m** (13,796 ft) above sea level.

However, when measured from the sea floor, it is more than **10,000 m** (32,000 ft) high, making it taller than Mount Everest (Earth's highest mountain above sea level, at **8,848m** (29,028 ft).

98% of the world's crayfish are caught in the state of Louisiana.

Mexico, Central America and the Caribbean

Belize - Caribbean Islands - Costa Rica - El Salvador - Guatemala - Honduras - Mexico - Nicaragua - Panama

Mexico is a land of extremes, with high mountains and deep canyons in the centre of the country, sweeping deserts in the north, and dense rainforests in the south and east. Southeast of Mexico is Central America, a narrow strip of land that connects North America to South America. Overall, the land is fertile and rugged, and dominated by a series of volcanic mountain ranges.

Central America is bordered by Colombia, the Caribbean Sea and the Pacific Ocean. Directly to the east are the islands of the Caribbean. The rainforests and coastal wetlands of eastern Mexico are home to thousands of tropical plant species and exotic animals, such as jaguars and quetzal birds. Few nations on Earth support as many plant and animal species as Mexico does. Rainforests are also common in Central America, especially Panama and Costa Rica.

GREAT VIEW!
The church of Nuestra Señora de los Remedios in Mexico was built on top of the ruins of the ancient pyramid Tlachihualtepetl. It looks out towards the active volcano Popocatépetl.

MEXICO

NORTH PACIFIC OCEAN

FRENCH PIRATE FRANÇOIS L'OLONNAIS OPERATED IN THE CARIBBEAN IN THE 1660S

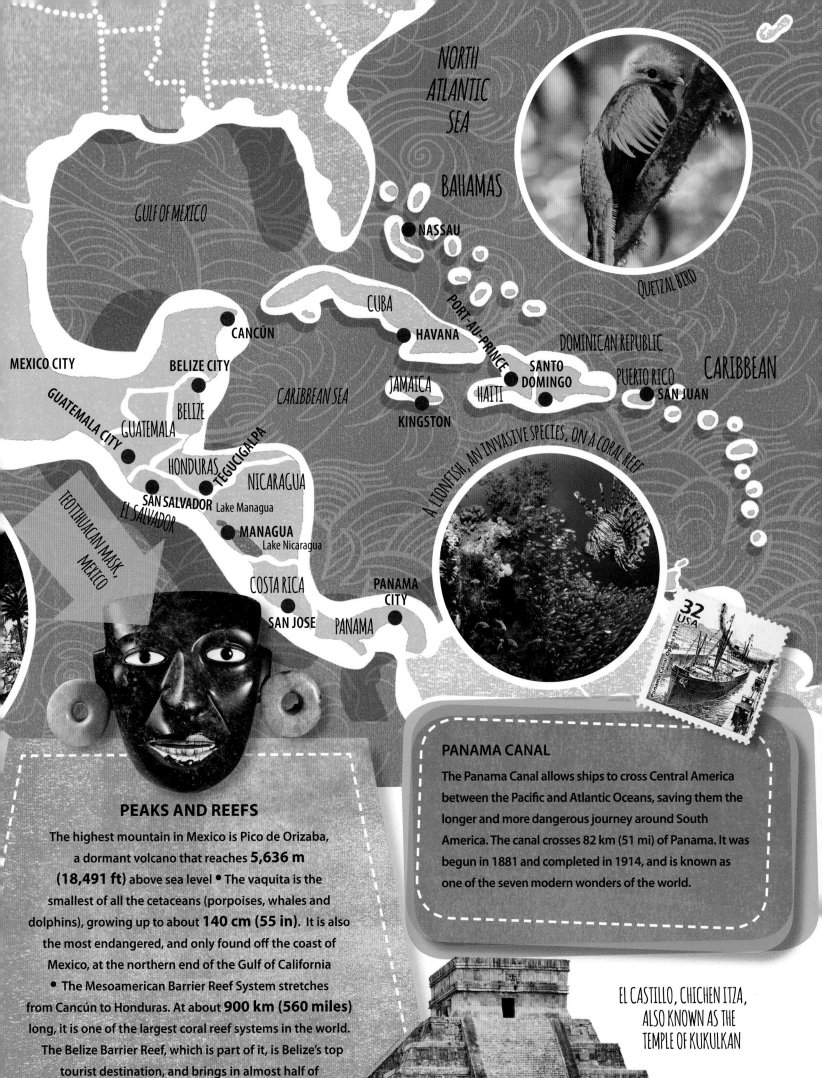

NORTH ATLANTIC SEA

GULF OF MEXICO

BAHAMAS

NASSAU

QUETZAL BIRD

CUBA

HAVANA

PORT-AU-PRINCE

DOMINICAN REPUBLIC

CANCÚN

MEXICO CITY

BELIZE CITY

SANTO DOMINGO

PUERTO RICO

CARIBBEAN

GUATEMALA CITY

BELIZE

CARIBBEAN SEA

JAMAICA

HAITI

SAN JUAN

GUATEMALA

KINGSTON

HONDURAS

TEGUCIGALPA

NICARAGUA

A LIONFISH, AN INVASIVE SPECIES, ON A CORAL REEF

TEOTIHUACAN MASK, MEXICO

SAN SALVADOR

Lake Managua

EL SALVADOR

MANAGUA

Lake Nicaragua

COSTA RICA

PANAMA CITY

SAN JOSE

PANAMA

32 USA

PEAKS AND REEFS

The highest mountain in Mexico is Pico de Orizaba, a dormant volcano that reaches **5,636 m (18,491 ft)** above sea level • The vaquita is the smallest of all the cetaceans (porpoises, whales and dolphins), growing up to about **140 cm (55 in)**. It is also the most endangered, and only found off the coast of Mexico, at the northern end of the Gulf of California • The Mesoamerican Barrier Reef System stretches from Cancún to Honduras. At about **900 km (560 miles)** long, it is one of the largest coral reef systems in the world. The Belize Barrier Reef, which is part of it, is Belize's top tourist destination, and brings in almost half of its **260,000** or more annual visitors.

PANAMA CANAL

The Panama Canal allows ships to cross Central America between the Pacific and Atlantic Oceans, saving them the longer and more dangerous journey around South America. The canal crosses 82 km (51 mi) of Panama. It was begun in 1881 and completed in 1914, and is known as one of the seven modern wonders of the world.

EL CASTILLO, CHICHEN ITZA, ALSO KNOWN AS THE TEMPLE OF KUKULKAN

La Catrina is an icon of Mexican pop art. She is often seen on display during **Día de los Muertos (Day of the Dead)** celebrations in Mexico.

The islands of the **Caribbean** trade in fish, aluminium, iron, nickel, petroleum and timber

WHO LIVES HERE?

Native Americans were the region's first real occupants. From the 16th century onwards the majority of the area was colonised by **Spain**. Most of today's Central Americans and Caribbean people are of mixed heritage, and the population includes **African, Asian, European and native American people.**

The Spanish invaded **Yucatan** in the 16th century. It's said they gave it its name because whenever they asked a question the indigenous Mayas replied **'uh yu ka t'ann'**, which meant **'Hear how they talk'!**

MAD ABOUT FOOTBALL

Mexicans adore football – it's their most popular sport, and they're pretty good at it, with the national team reaching the World Cup quarter finals twice. At the national stadium, Estadio Azteca in Mexico City, you can regularly see the 'Mexican Wave'. This is when supporters stand up one after another and raise their arms above their head, creating a ripple effect in the crowd. The wave got its name after becoming really popular during the 1986 World Cup, held in Mexico.

97% of **Barbadians** can read and write. The island nation's educational system is not only very good, but also free to all children.

117 million people live in **Mexico**. It is the 11th most populated country in the world.

MUSIC:
Mexican Mariachi bands

FOOD:
Mole is a Mexican savoury sauce

PLACE:
Trafalgar Falls, Dominica

FESTIVAL:
Día de Los Muertos (Day of the Dead)

SAYING (JAMAICAN) :
Wan han wash de oda (One hand washes the other)

GAME:
Lotería is a popular game, similar to bingo, but with singing and picture cards

SPORT:
Football is the top sport in Mexico, but other favourites include baseball and jai alai, a handball game that began in Spain

FRUIT:
Ackee is a yellow fruit that must be eaten ripe – it's poisonous otherwise!

Mexicans take sports seriously. In ancient times, losers of a ritual ball game were **put to death**. In some dangerous sports, such as bullfighting and **rodeo** (which was invented in Mexico), competitors still put their lives on the line.

42 million people live in Central America.

Mexico produces oil, silver, copper and agricultural products. Central America mines copper, gold, silver and zinc.

There are many **volcanoes** in Central America (it's on the **Ring of Fire**), including 28 active ones.

Saint Lucia changed hands between the French and British **14 times** in the 17th and 18th centuries.

South America

"The forest is not a resource for us, it is life itself. It is the only place for us to live."

Evaristo Nugkuag Ikanan, Peruvian campaigner (born 1950), activist for the Aguaruna people of the Peruvian rainforest

South America is a land of legends. Hundreds of years ago, explorers from Europe heard rumours of lost kingdoms and cities, of fabulous treasure, and of peoples living deep in the forests. The truth was more wonderful than the tales. South America had ancient civilisations, great empires – such as that of the Incas – skilled goldsmiths, builders and craftspeople, and chocolate!

Spanish and Portuguese invaders arrived in the 1500s. They had guns, ships and horses, and were greedy for land and gold. They ruled for almost 300 years.

But today's independent South American nations are home to a rich mixture of peoples, beliefs and cultures. Their roots are indigenous, European, African and Asian. Yet amidst the farms, the factories, the slums and the skyscrapers, the ancient spirit of South America survives, in a love of ritual and spectacle, of music and colour, of people working together. The mountains and ancient forests are still there too, but in many places they are under threat from loggers and miners. For the future of South America and the rest of the world, they too must survive.

NORTH AMERICA

GALÁPAGOS ISLANDS (ECUADOR)

EQUATOR

12

EASTER ISLAND (CHILE)

SOUTH PACIFIC OCEAN

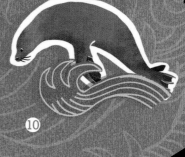
10

Area: 17,840,000 km² (6,890,000 sq mi)
Fact: 4th largest continent
Population: 389,860,000

MAP KEY
1 Ocelot 2 Red cayenne peppers 3 Green turtle
4 Machu Picchu 5 Scarlet macaw 6 Sawn logs 7 Totora reed canoe, Lake Titicaca 8 Coffee beans 9 Christ the Redeemer, Rio de Janeiro 10 South American sea lion
11 Iguaçu Falls 12 Easter Island Statue

MALPELO ISLAND
(COLOMBIA)

R. Orinoco

VENEZUELA

GUYANA

SURINAME

FRENCH GUIANA

COLOMBIA

1

ECUADOR

PERU

Amazon Basin

R. Amazon

EQUATOR

2

3

BRAZIL

5

6

Brazilian
Highlands

Andes

4

Lake Titicaca

BOLIVIA

8

9

Atacama
desert

7

PARAGUAY

Gran Chaco

CHILE

Mar Chiquita

11

URUGUAY

Andes

ARGENTINA

Pampas

SOUTH
ATLANTIC
OCEAN

Patagonia

FALKLAND ISLANDS
(UK)

SOUTH GEORGIA
(UK)

TIERRA
DEL FUEGO

CAPE HORN

Incredible South America

The Amazon River rises in Peru, in the Andes mountains. It flows eastwards across Brazil to the Atlantic Ocean. Small motor boats beat against the current, passing remote fishing and trading villages. The Amazon Basin forms the green heart of South America, and is covered by the world's largest rainforest. To the north, the Guiana highlands drop to tropical plains beside the Caribbean Sea and the Atlantic. Westwards, the dizzying peaks of the Andes form a long, rocky backbone, parallel to the Pacific coast. Along the Atlantic coast are huge cities. As the landmass narrows in the south, there are coffee plantations, hot and dusty scrub, cattle ranches and grasslands. In the far south, bleak valleys stretch towards frozen Antarctica.

The **Andes mountain** chain is the world's longest, at approx **7,000 km** (**4,300 miles**)

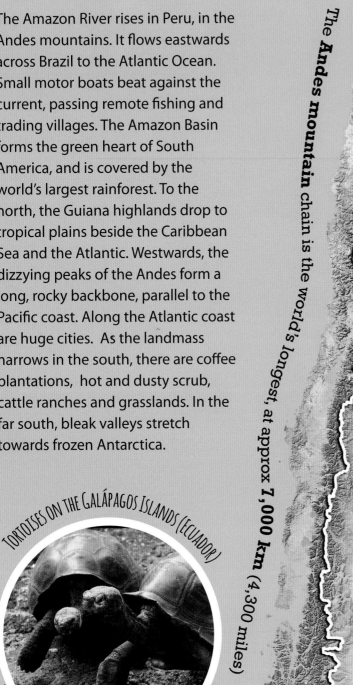

LAKE TITICACA, BOLIVIA

TIERRA DEL FUEGO

ERUPTING VOLCANO, CHILE

TORTOISES ON THE GALÁPAGOS ISLANDS (ECUADOR)

AMAZON RAINFOREST

Awesome Amazon

The Amazon rainforest covers approximately **5.5 million km²** (**2.1 million sq mi**) • It takes in 9 countries • It receives a massive **2,743 mm (108 in)** of rainfall a year • The trees produce about **one-fifth** of all our planet's life-giving oxygen • The forest supports a greater **variety** of species than anywhere else on Earth • **10%** of the world's known species and **20%** of the world's bird species live here • There are **500** mammal species, an estimated **2.5 million** different **insects**, and **40,000** different **plants**.

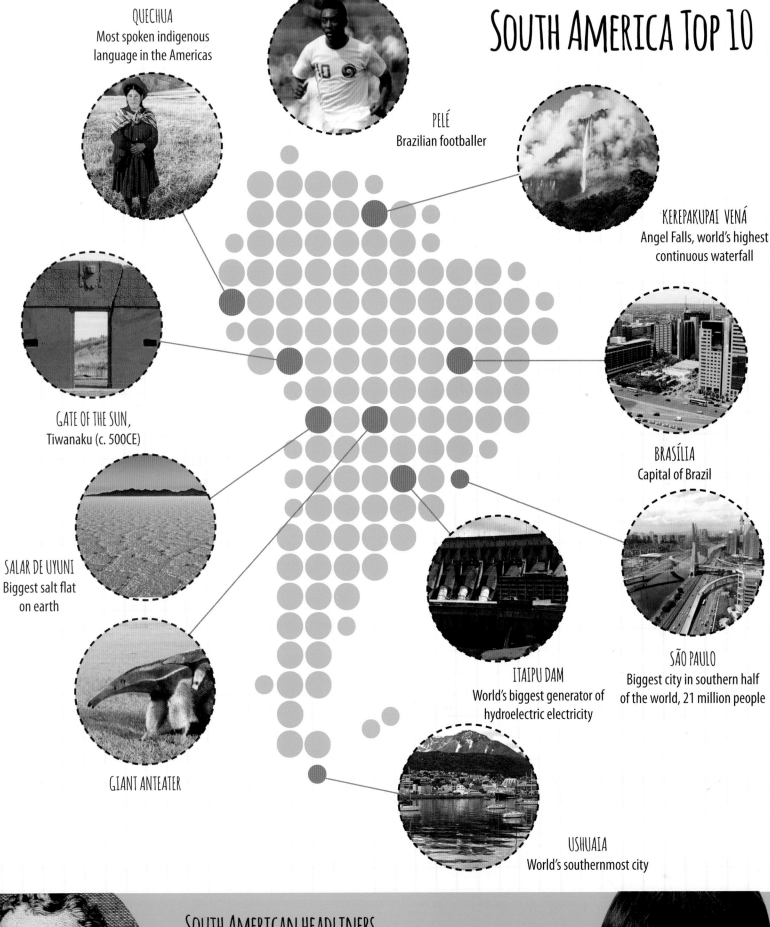

QUECHUA
Most spoken indigenous language in the Americas

PELÉ
Brazilian footballer

KEREPAKUPAI VENÁ
Angel Falls, world's highest continuous waterfall

GATE OF THE SUN,
Tiwanaku (c. 500CE)

BRASÍLIA
Capital of Brazil

SALAR DE UYUNI
Biggest salt flat on earth

SÃO PAULO
Biggest city in southern half of the world, 21 million people

GIANT ANTEATER

ITAIPU DAM
World's biggest generator of hydroelectric electricity

USHUAIA
World's southernmost city

SOUTH AMERICAN HEADLINERS

In the 1800s the armies of **Simón Bolívar** (left) helped large areas of South America break away from rule by the Spanish empire. Brazilian **Chico Mendes** (1944-88) campaigned to protect the Amazon rainforest. **Rigobeta Menchú** (born 1959) won the 1992 Nobel Peace Prize and Prince of Asturias Award in 1998 for her human rights work in Guatemala. South America's soccer superstars have included **Pelé** (born 1940), **Diego Maradona** (born 1960) and **Lionel Messi** (born 1987) (right).

Northern South America

BOLIVIA - BRAZIL - COLOMBIA - ECUADOR - FRENCH GUIANA
GUYANA - PERU - SURINAME - VENEZUELA

Big cities rise from the Atlantic and Caribbean coasts. Gleaming, smart skyscrapers tower over beaches and busy avenues. But clinging to the hillsides are *favelas* or shanty towns, which are home to many poor people. In the northeast are the forests and rivers of the Guiana Highlands, and the sugarcane and rice fields of the coast. In the northwest, the flooding Orinoco River spills out across the Llanos grasslands, where millions of cattle are herded by cowboys. Venezuela also has some of the world's biggest reserves of oil. In the west, the land rises through the mist to the high peaks of the Andes, where the air is cool and dry. The Pacific coast and the mountains too have seen civilisations rise and fall for thousands of years. Here are today's high altitude cities such as Bogotá, Quito and La Paz, and beside the Pacific, Lima and Callao.

RICH AND POOR, RIGHT NEXT DOOR
The huge statue of Christ the Redeemer looks out across Rio de Janeiro. Spread out below are the makeshift houses of the poor, the luxury apartments of the rich, the city's green hills and the blue of the ocean.

MACHU PICCHU, CITY OF THE INCAS

GALÁPAGOS ISLANDS
(ECUADOR)

PACIFIC OCEAN

CATTLE ROUND UP IN THE MATTO GROSSO, BRAZIL

MACAWS IN THE
AMAZON RAINFOREST

CARACAS

Lake Maracaibo

VENEZUELA

R. Orinoco

GEORGETOWN

PARAMARIBO

CAYENNE

Angel Falls

GUYANA

BOGOTÁ

COLOMBIA

Guiana
Highlands

SURINAME

FRENCH GUIANA
(FRANCE)

QUITO

ECUADOR

Amazon Basin

EQUATOR

PERU

R. Amazon

Andes

BRAZIL

Lake
Titicaca

LIMA

SALVADOR

Brazilian
Highlands

BOLIVIA

LA PAZ

BRASÍLIA

RIO DE JANEIRO

SÃO PAULO

SNUG! A BABY FROM OLLINTAYTAMBO, PERU

RECORD BREAKERS

Kerepakupai Vená, or Angel Falls, in Venezuela is the world's highest uninterrupted waterful, tumbling **979 m (3,212 ft)** • Lake Titicaca is another record breaker. It is **3,812 m (12,507 ft)** high in the Andes mountains, on the border between Bolivia and Peru. It is the highest lake on Earth to be navigated by big boats. (But the locals use canoes, made from a kind of rush called totora) • The Galápagos Islands are home to the world's largest tortoises, with some exceeding **1.5 m (5 ft)** in length and reaching 250 kg (550 lbs).

A DESERT MYSTERY

In Peru's Nazca desert, there are 1,500-year-old lines scraped onto the surface. Some form patterns or pictures of monkeys, hummingbirds and fish. They are gigantic and only make sense when seen from the air. Despite many theories, no one is really sure how they got there.

WHO LIVES HERE?

Who doesn't? It's quite a mix! In Brazil most people speak Portuguese. In Guyana they speak English. In Suriname it is Dutch and in French Guiana, French. In the rest of the region, Spanish is the top language. But hundreds of other languages are spoken too, because many people are descended from other **European, African, Asian or indigenous 'Indian'** peoples such as the **Yanomami** of Brazil, the **Tukano** of Colombia or the **Quechua** of the Andes.

Brazil is the largest country in all of South America: **8,515,767 km²** (3,287,597 sq mi)

Rio de Janeiro stages the world's most **spectacular carnival**, with glittering costumes and parades – and 2 million people out on the streets dancing the samba.

THE KIDS FROM THE BARRIO

In Colombia, a city neighbourhood is called a *barrio*. About 10.8 million people live in the area around Bogotá. Many are poor people from the countryside. They've come to look for work, but haven't got enough money to buy a house or rent a flat. They live in shacks made of odds and ends. The hillsides are covered in these homes.

Did you know that **mummies** didn't just come from Ancient Egypt? They have also been found high in the **Andes**. Bodies were left in stone towers called *chullpas*, and preserved by the dry and cold air. Some were human sacrifices.

The hunters of the **Colombian rainforest** use poison darts to bring down wild animals. They collect the poison from a **gold coloured frog** that contains just 1 mg (0.000035 oz) of a deadly toxin. This is enough to kill thousands of mice or 20 humans!

In **Peru and Ecuador**, make sure you wear **yellow** underpants on New Year's Eve. If you don't have any, buy them at any street stall.

Yellow means good luck in the year to come. Wear **red** ones if you want to fall in love!

Thanks to oil, **Venezuela** is the wealthiest country in South America.

'HELLO' IN THE QUECHUA LANGUAGE:
Napaykullayki

MAKING MUSIC:
Pan-pipes of the Andes

UNUSUAL FOOD:
Roasted 'big-bottom' leafcutter ants (Colombia)

MOST PRECIOUS BIRD POO:
The guanay cormorant from Peru produces valuable guano for fertiliser

SLOWEST MAMMAL ON EARTH:
The three-toed sloth

TRAFFIC MADNESS:
São Paolo has had traffic jams of 295 km (183 miles)

MOST FIFA WORLD CUP WINS:
Brazil has won football's World Cup five times

THE TOOTHIEST LAND MAMMAL:
The giant armadillo has between 80 and 100 teeth

MOST LOGGED IN:
Brazil is the world's second biggest user of Facebook and Twitter (after the USA)

Wake up and smell the coffee! Brazil produces the most coffee in the world – 2.6 million tonnes a year.

The railway from Lima to Huancayo in Peru reaches **4,829 m (15,843 ft)** above sea level – on track for the top of the world!

Southern South America

Argentina - Chile - Falkland Islands/Islas Malvinas
Paraguay - South Georgia - Uruguay

It's a tough ride on horseback across the Gran Chaco – a hot, dry plain that stretches into Paraguay. Most Paraguayans live in the eastern part of the country, which is easier to farm. In Uruguay cattle graze the hills and valleys, while farmers grow fruit and vegetables in the countryside near the Atlantic coast. Most Uruguayans live in Montevideo, a city on the north bank of the River Plate. On the south bank of the Plate is Buenos Aires, capital of Argentina. This country stretches west to fertile valleys and vineyards beneath the high Andes. The wide grassland region of the Pampas is cattle country and was once famous for its cowboys, known as Gauchos. The climate cools southwards to Patagonia and its dry, windswept valleys. Between the Andes and the Pacific Ocean, Chile is the longest and thinnest country in this atlas. It has deserts, copper mines, vineyards and forests, ragged coastlines and active volcanoes. Chile and Argentina both occupy Tierra del Fuego, at the chilly southern tip of the continent.

GREAT CHUNKS OF ICE!
Patagonia's Perito Moreno glacier is an awesome sight.
It is 30 km (19 mi) long and 170 m (558 ft) thick.

VALLEY OF THE MOON, ATACAMA DESERT, CHILE

CHILEAN VINEYARD

ANDEAN LLAMA, CHILE

TANGO DANCERS, ARGENTINA

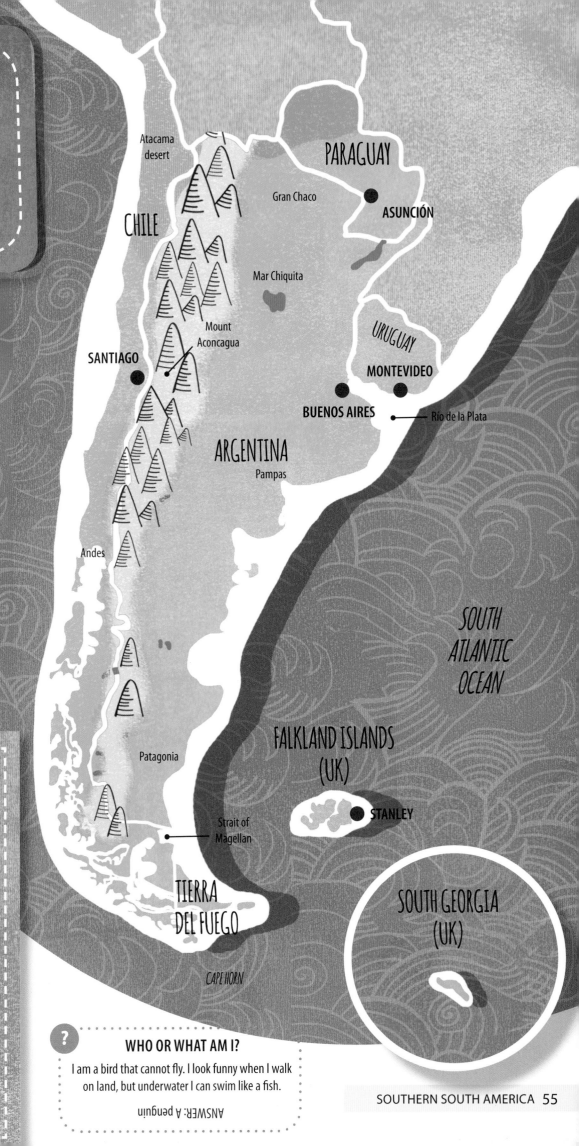

DRY AS A BONE
The driest and oldest hot desert on the planet is Chile's Atacama. In some parts it hasn't rained for hundreds of years! Some say it looks like the surface of the planet Mars.

BUENOS AIRES

PACIFIC OCEAN

LANDS OF ICE AND FIRE
The River Plate (Rio de la Plata) is **220 km (140 mi)** across its mouth, making it the widest river in the world • Mount Aconcagua in the Argentine Andes is a double record breaker. It is the highest peak in the southern half of the world, and also the highest in the western part of the world. Its height? A dizzying **6,961 m (22,387 ft)** above sea level • The rim of the Pacific Ocean is notorious for its earthquakes and volcanoes. Chile has **137** active volcanoes.

Atacama desert

CHILE

PARAGUAY

Gran Chaco

ASUNCIÓN

Mar Chiquita

Mount Aconcagua

SANTIAGO

URUGUAY

MONTEVIDEO

BUENOS AIRES

Río de la Plata

ARGENTINA

Pampas

Andes

SOUTH ATLANTIC OCEAN

Patagonia

FALKLAND ISLANDS (UK)

STANLEY

Strait of Magellan

SOUTH GEORGIA (UK)

TIERRA DEL FUEGO

CAPE HORN

?

WHO OR WHAT AM I?
I am a bird that cannot fly. I look funny when I walk on land, but underwater I can swim like a fish.

ANSWER: A penguin

WHO LIVES HERE?

The Indian peoples of the region include the **Guaraní**, the **Mataco** and the **Mapuche.** The years of rule by Spain, from the 1500s, mean that **Spanish** is still the main language today. All kinds of other immigrants came to settle here over the ages – **Italians, Germans, Jews, Russians, Welsh, Poles, Syrians, Lebanese, Japanese and Koreans.**

Argentina is the largest country in southern South America: **2,766,890km²** (1,068,300 sq mi)

The **Andean condor** has a gigantic wingspan of up to **3.2 m (10.5 ft)**.

The **Drake Passage** between Cape Horn and Livingston Island in Antarctica is just **809 km (503 miles)** across.

A STORY OF HOPE

In 2010, 33 Chilean miners were trapped deep underground after a rock fall. One of the men, Ariel Ticona, missed the birth of his daughter while he was stuck underground. He sent a message to his wife on the surface saying the new baby should be called Esperanza, which means 'hope'. Incredibly, all 33 men were rescued after 69 days.

In 2009 the **Uruguayan** government gave every school kid in the country a free laptop.

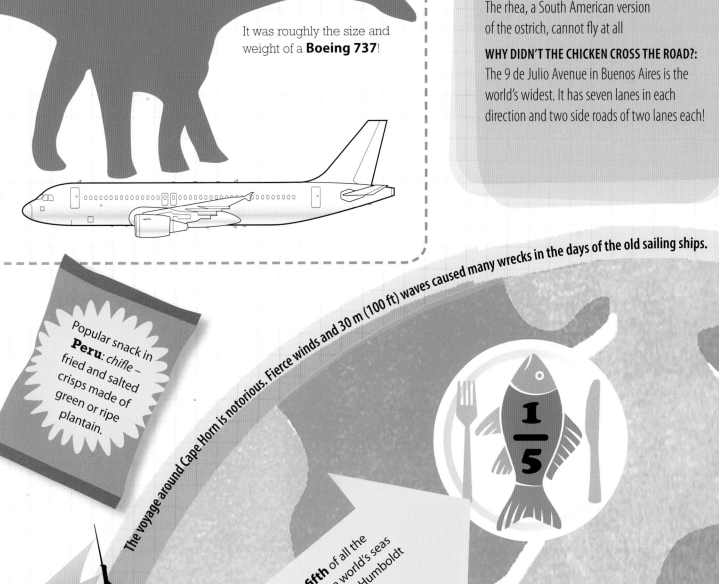

Probably the biggest dinosaur known to have existed was discovered in **Patagonia in 2014**. This titan was **40 m (131 ft) long** and **20 m (66 ft) tall**. It weighed **77 tonnes**.

It was roughly the size and weight of a **Boeing 737**!

'HELLO' IN THE GUARANÍ LANGUAGE:
Mbaé'chepa

NATIONAL SIZZLER OF ARGENTINA:
Asado (beef barbecued in an outdoor pit)

BIGGEST CITY POPULATION:
Greater Buenos Aires -12.8 million

HARDEST TREE TO CLIMB:
Chile's national tree, the Chilean Pine (also known as the monkey puzzle tree)

MOST DRAMATIC DANCE MOVES:
The tango, invented in Buenos Aires

NON-FLYING BIRD:
The rhea, a South American version of the ostrich, cannot fly at all

WHY DIDN'T THE CHICKEN CROSS THE ROAD?:
The 9 de Julio Avenue in Buenos Aires is the world's widest. It has seven lanes in each direction and two side roads of two lanes each!

Popular snack in **Peru**: chifle – fried and salted crisps made of green or ripe plantain.

The voyage around Cape Horn is notorious. Fierce winds and 30 m (100 ft) waves caused many wrecks in the days of the old sailing ships.

Nearly **one-fifth** of all the fish caught in the world's seas come from the cold Humboldt current, which sweeps northwards along the coast of **Chile and Peru.**

Europe

Learn from yesterday, live for today, hope for tomorrow.

Albert Einstein

There are snowy northern forests, green fields and woods full of wild flowers, moors and heaths. There are awesome mountain ranges such as the Alps, and lowlands crossed by rolling rivers. There are olive groves, vineyards and sunny beaches. Europe is not one of the bigger continents, but here you can meet all sorts of different peoples, hear many languages and see a fantastic variety of landscapes.

In the north, Europe borders the icy Arctic Ocean. The Atlantic Ocean brings rain to western shores. Europe's sunny south meets the warm blue waters of the Mediterranean and the Black Sea. The continent stretches eastwards to the Caucasus and the Ural mountains. Beyond lies Asia. In fact Europe and Asia together make up one mega-landmass, called Eurasia.

As well as Europe's big modern cities you can still see prehistoric stone circles, beautiful cathedrals and castles from the Middle Ages, and factories and railways from the industrial age of the 1800s. At that time European empires ruled large parts of the world, spreading languages such as Spanish, French and English around the globe.

Five nations cross the divide between Europe and Asia – Russia, Turkey, Azerbaijan, Georgia and Kazakhstan. They appear in the Asia section of this book.

ICELAND

FAROE ISLANDS (DENMARK)

NORTH SEA

ATLANTIC OCEAN

REPUBLIC OF IRELAND

UNITED KINGDOM

NETHERLANDS

BELGIUM

LUXEMBOURG

R.Seine

R.Loire

SWITZERLAND

FRANCE

PORTUGAL

ANDORRA

MONACO

SPAIN

R Guadalquivir

MEDITERRANEAN SEA

NORWAY
SWEDEN
FINLAND
BALTIC SEA
ESTONIA
LATVIA
LITHUANIA
BELARUS
RUSSIA
DENMARK
POLAND
GERMANY
R.Rhine
R.Danube
R.Oder
CZECH REPUBLIC
UKRAINE
R.Dniester
R.Dnieper
MOLDOVA
SLOVAKIA
LIECHTENSTEIN
AUSTRIA
HUNGARY
ROMANIA
SLOVENIA
CROATIA
BLACK SEA
BOSNIA
& HERZEGOVINA
SERBIA
BULGARIA
SAN MARINO
KOSOVO
MACEDONIA
MONTENEGRO
TURKEY
ALBANIA
ITALY
VATICAN CITY
GREECE
Sardinia
Sicily
MALTA
Crete
CYPRUS

Today 28 nations are linked as members of an international organisation called the European Union (EU).

Area: 10,180,000 km² (3,930,000 sq mi)
Fact: 6th largest continent
Population: 741.2 million

MAP KEY
1 Portuguese fishing boat
2 Oranges 3 Mont Saint Michel,
France 4 Bagpipes 5 Stave church
6 Brandenburg Gate, Berlin
7 European Bison 8 Painted eggs
9 Pelican 10 Greek windmill
11 Dolphin 12 Gondola, Venice
13 Duomo, Florence 14 Sagrada
Familia, Barcelona

Exploring Europe

Fly into cities such as London, Paris, Rome or Berlin and you will see modern business districts built of steel and glass next to ancient buildings dating back hundreds or even thousands of years. You will see traditional ceremonies and festivals alongside the latest in fashion, art and pop music. You can shop in shiny stores or busy street markets. There is often a lively coming together of cultures and peoples from around the world. There are suburbs too, poorer areas and regions, industrial zones and seaports, and landscapes shaped by thousands of years of farming.

The **Scandinavian** peninsula is about **1,850 km (1,150 miles)** long

BUDAPEST ON THE RIVER DANUBE

GRIVOLA AND GRAND NOMENON MOUNTAINS, AOSTA VALLEY, ITALY

WHITE STORK

Lands and seas

Western Europe is kept warm by an ocean current called the North Atlantic Drift, which keeps the climate mild • Eastern Europe is further from the sea, and has greater extremes of hot and cold • Mediterranean means 'in the middle of the land'. This sea covers an area of about **2.5 million km²** **(965,000 sq mi).**

Inventive Europe

Europe is famous for some amazing inventions. These include
• the thermometer **(c1593)**
• the newspaper **(1605)** • the telescope **(1608)** • the steam locomotive **(1803)**
• photography **(1822)** • the saxophone **(1846)** • the motor car **(1885)**
• the television **(1926)**
• ballpoint pens **(1938)**
• the world wide web **(1989).**

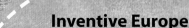
STEAM LOCOMOTIVE

EUROPEAN TOP 10

THE SHARD, LONDON
(312.7 m, 1,112 ft tall)

ATLANTIC PUFFIN
Seabird found in the
North Atlantic Ocean

EURASIAN ELK
World's biggest deer

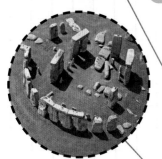

STONEHENGE
Prehistoric monument
(c3000-2000 BC)

HUNGARIAN GOULASH
Spicy stew of meat,
noodles and vegetables

EIFFEL TOWER, PARIS
City landmark (1887)

ALHAMBRA PALACE, GRANADA
Moorish palace (889)

MONT BLANC
(4,810 m, 15,781 ft tall)

VATICAN CITY
Centre of the Catholic Church
and the world's smallest state

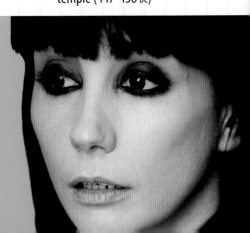

THE PARTHENON, ATHENS
Ancient Greek
temple (447-438 BC)

EUROPEAN HALL OF FAME

Harry Potter, the boy wizard of the stories by JK Rowling, was
played on screen by English actor **Daniel Radcliffe** (left, b.1989).
Serbian **Novak Djokovic** (b.1987) is a top-ranking world tennis
champion. **Tamara Rojo** (right, b.1974) is a Spanish ballet dancer
and artistic director of the English National Ballet. **Jean Paul
Gaultier** (b.1952) is a French fashion designer.

Northern Europe

Denmark - Estonia - Finland - Iceland
Latvia - Lithuania - Norway - Sweden

You know you're way up near the Arctic Circle when the sky flashes green and pink with the Northern Lights, when it stays light all night at midsummer and is dark during the days of midwinter. Welcome to Europe's far north.

Norway, Sweden and Denmark are sometimes known as Scandinavia. This region include forests of spruce and birch, lakes, mountains and deep sea inlets called fjords. Winters are snowy, but summers can be warm and sunny. The living is easier in the farms and the cities of the south. Iceland is known for its volcanoes and hot springs, which provide heat and power for housing and greenhouses.

Across the Baltic Sea is Finland, another land of lakes and forests, with its capital at Helsinki. Estonia, Latvia and Lithuania have historical links with Germany and Poland, and were part of the Soviet Union (Russia) until 1991.

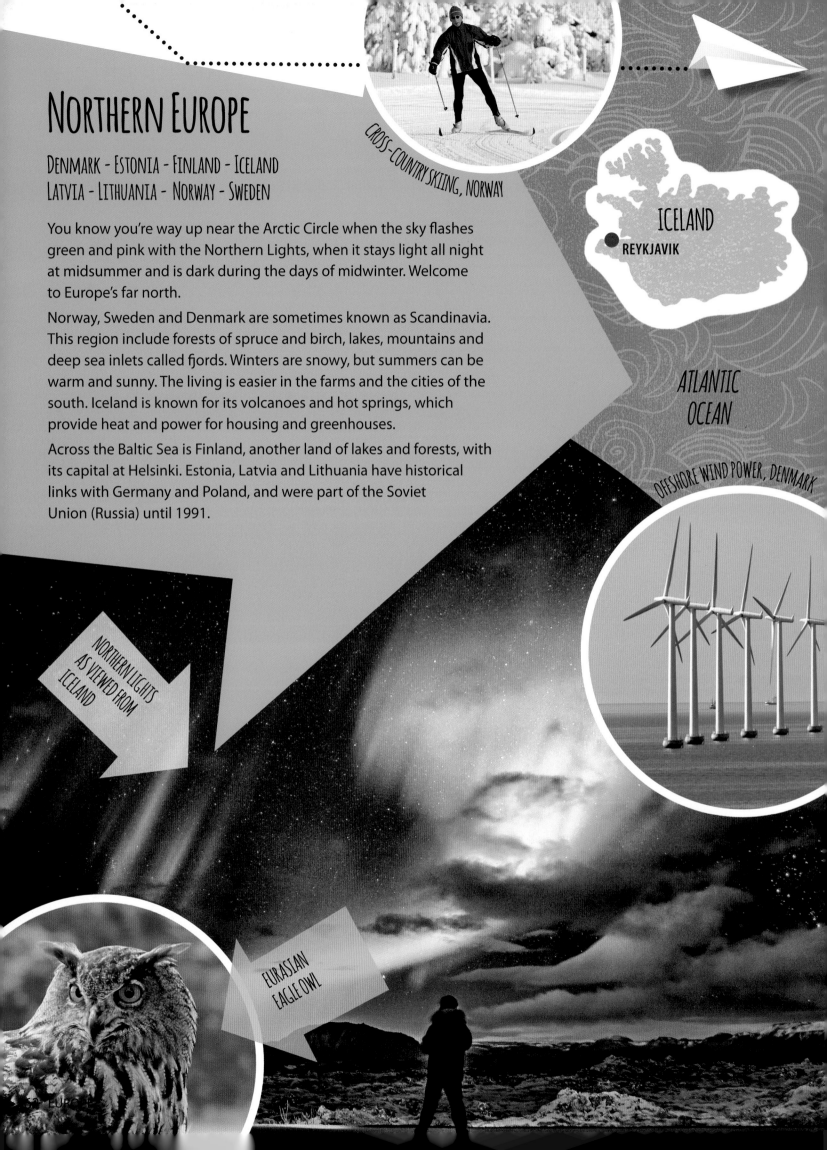

CROSS-COUNTRY SKIING, NORWAY

ICELAND
REYKJAVIK

ATLANTIC OCEAN

OFFSHORE WIND POWER, DENMARK

NORTHERN LIGHTS AS VIEWED FROM ICELAND

EURASIAN EAGLE OWL

NORWEGIAN
SEA

MARAUDING VIKINGS

About 1,200 years ago
Scandinavia was home to the
Vikings, who were brilliant
seafarers and traders. They were
fearsome warriors too, with
scary names like Eirik Bloodaxe!

FAROE ISLANDS
(DENMARK)

Lapland

FINLAND

NORTH
SEA

NORWAY

SWEDEN

BALTIC SEA

TAMPERE

HELSINKI

TALLINN

ESTONIA

OSLO

STOCKHOLM

RIGA

GOTHENBURG

LATVIA

AARHUS

LITHUANIA

DENMARK

COPENHAGEN

MALMÖ

VILNIUS

KALININGRAD
(RUSSIA)

STAVE CHURCH, NORWAY

Northern
moneymakers

Fish from the North Sea
• Timber and paper from the forests
• Oil and gas from the North Sea
• Danish wind turbines • Danish bacon
and butter • Iceland's greenhouse
produce • Cars and lorries
• Electronics

?

WHO OR WHAT AM I?

I sail in a longship, I live in a longhouse,
I have a long beard, a long sword and a long,
deadly axe – so watch out you wimps!

ANSWER: A hairy old Viking

WHO LIVES HERE?

The Danes, Swedes, Norwegians and Icelanders are all **Germanic** peoples and speak closely related languages. The **Sami, Finns and Estonians** are also related. The Letts (Latvians) and the Lithuanians are **Baltic** peoples.

Reykjavik in **Iceland** is the world's northernmost national capital.

LOVE LEGO

Lego was first made in Denmark back in 1949. Since then about 560 billion bricks, parts and figures have been manufactured. And where better to see them than at the Legoland theme park in Billund, Denmark, right next door to the original Lego factory?

Sweden is the biggest of the Nordic countries by area: **450,295 km²** (173,860 sq mi)

Many northern European countries have **festivals of light** during the dark days of midwinter. Swedish girls often wear a crown of glowing candles for **St Lucy's Day** (13 December).

The famous Øresund road plus rail bridge joins up with the Drogden tunnel to link the Danish capital, Copenhagen, with Malmö in Sweden.

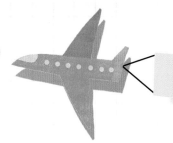

All steamed up! There are over **2 million** saunas in **Finland.**

An ancient rock carving from **Alta, Norway,** suggests people were skiing here about **4,000 to 5,000 years ago.**

HELLO IN FINNISH:
Hei

SHORTEST PLACE NAME:
A fishing village called Å, in Norway's Lofoten Islands

BALTIC JEWELLERY:
Amber is a fossil tree resin which glows yellow, brown or orange

MAKING MUSIC:
The 1970s Swedish pop group Abba sold 380 million albums worldwide

BESTSELLER:
Books about Pippi Longstocking, a character created by Swedish author Astrid Lindgren, were translated into 64 languages

MIDNIGHT SUN:
At Noordkapp in Norway the sun never sets from 14 May to 15 July

VOLCANOES:
Iceland has over 20 active volcanoes

Copenhagen's most famous tourist attraction is a statue of the **little mermaid**, from the 1837 tale by Hans Christian Andersen.

Iceland's parliament or Althing is one of the world's oldest. It was founded in the year **930.**

IKEA is a Swedish company which has 349 furniture stores in 43 countries. It is said to use about 1 percent of the world's wood supply!

Did you know the **Vikings** discovered **North America** nearly **500 years** before Christopher Columbus?

The Danes snack on over **100 million** hot sausages in bread each year.

NORTHWEST EUROPE

AUSTRIA - BELGIUM - FRANCE - GERMANY - LIECHTENSTEIN - LUXEMBOURG
MONACO - NETHERLANDS - REPUBLIC OF IRELAND - SWITZERLAND - UNITED KINGDOM

Atlantic breakers roll in to meet high cliffs on the west coast of Ireland, a land of green grass and low hills. Northern Ireland, together with England, Scotland and Wales on the larger island of Great Britain, is part of the United Kingdom. Here you travel through rolling farmland, moors and highlands, small villages, historic market towns and large, busy cities such as London.

England is linked to France by a rail tunnel beneath the Channel. A high-speed TGV train whisks you to Paris, or southwards through vineyards and river valleys to the warm and sunny Mediterranean coast and the little city-state of Monaco. High mountains occupy the southeast of France, part of the Alpine ranges. Switzerland, tiny Liechtenstein and Austria are beautiful countries with rich histories and cultures.

Germany stretches from the Alps to the North and Baltic Seas, crossed by great rivers such as the Rhine and the Elbe. Here are forests and heaths, mountains and plains, with many large industrial cities as well as historic castles and traditional houses.

THE KING'S CASTLE
King Ludwig II of Bavaria had a bit of a thing about castles. In 1869 he set about building the ultimate fairytale castle. It was called Schloss Neuschwanstein and today is one of Germany's top tourist attractions.

TGV/HIGH-SPEED TRAIN, FRANCE

RED DEER, SCOTLAND

BRANDENBURG GATE, BERLIN, GERMANY

Scotland

NORTH SEA

EDINBURGH

Northern Ireland

BELFAST

REPUBLIC OF IRELAND

DUBLIN

UNITED KINGDOM

Wales

England

CARDIFF

LONDON

ATLANTIC OCEAN

ENGLISH CHANNEL

HAMBURG

R.Elbe

NETHERLANDS

AMSTERDAM

BERLIN

GERMANY

BELGIUM

R.Rhine

BRUSSELS

FRANKFURT

PARIS

R.Seine

LUXEMBOURG CITY

R.Danube

R.Loire

LUXEMBOURG

LIECHTENSTEIN

VIENNA

Alps

SWITZERLAND

Alps

AUSTRIA

FRANCE

R Rhône

Alps

ZURICH

VADUZ

BORDEAUX

Pyrenees

MARSEILLE

MONACO

WOMAN IN BRETON COSTUME, FRANCE

Corsica (France)

AJACCIO

SUPER STATS

Monaco is the smallest country in the region, with an area of just over **2 km² (0.8 sq mi)**

• The Alps run across 8 countries and include about 100 peaks over **4,000 m (13,123 ft)**

• London is the biggest city in northwest Europe, with a population of over **8.3 million**

• Austria's rivers and lakes mean that it can produce over half of its electricity by hydropower.

SECRETS OF THE UNIVERSE

Deep beneath the French-Swiss border there is a huge underground tunnel called the Large Hadron Collider. This is where scientists send particles whizzing round at high speed until they smash into each other. It sounds like a fantastic game, but actually this is the world's biggest ever physics experiment.

Sunny or rainy, dry or muddy? Whatever the weather, English crowds love open air music festivals such as **Glastonbury.** Britain has been a centre of pop music and youth fashion ever since the 1960s.

WHO LIVES HERE?

The countries of northwest Europe grew up over hundreds of years from a patchwork of smaller states. A visitor might think of the nationalities as simply **French, German, Dutch or Swiss,** but within the borders there are in fact many peoples – **Scots, Welsh, Bretons, Walloons, Flemings, Frisians, Swabians, Bavarians**... Even little Switzerland has four official languages (French, Swiss-German, Italian and Romansh). Europe's historical overseas empires mean that many people are also descended from **African, Asian** and **Caribbean** roots.

Mainland **France** is the largest country in northwest Europe: **551,500 km²** (212,935 sq mi)

A big wall used to run through the centre of Berlin, with armed guards and barbed wire. From 1961 it divided the eastern part of the city from the west. The **Berlin Wall** was a harsh symbol of the **Cold War,** when Germany was divided into two separate countries. In 1989 the wall was knocked down and today Berlin is capital of a united Germany.

HOW LOW CAN YOU GO?

Belgium, the Netherlands and Luxembourg are sometimes collectively referred to as the Low Countries because they are situated in the low-lying delta of the Rhine.

THE NORTHWEST EUROPE REAL DEAL!

'HELLO' IN THE IRISH LANGUAGE:
Dia dhuit

FASHION CAPITAL OF THE WORLD:
Paris, France

HOME OF THE WALTZ :
Vienna stages over 200 grand balls each year, many in the Hofburg Imperial Palace

PUZZLING PASTIME:
Rolling cheese down a grassy hill, Gloucestershire, England

WITCHIEST PLACE :
The Harz mountains, Germany, home to many myths and fairytales

MOST FAMOUS CAR RACE:
The Monaco Grand Prix, Formula One race through the streets of Monte Carlo

LONGEST PLACE NAME:
Llanfairpwllgwyngyllgogerychwyrn-drobwllllantysiliogogogoch in Wales

MOST DELICIOUS SWEETS:
Belgian chocolates

Britain's National Health Service employs over **1.7 million** people.

The Dutch grow about **3 billion** tulip bulbs each year and export them around the world.

Luxembourg may be little, but its people are the second biggest wealth creators in the world (after the Qataris).

About **27%** of the **Netherlands** is below sea level.

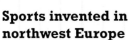

Sports invented in northwest Europe

- **Golf** (Scotland)
- **Curling** (Scotland)
- **Cricket** (England)
- **Rugby** (England)
- **Modern football/ soccer**(England)
- **Snooker** (England)
- **Hurling** (Ireland)
- **Gaelic football** (Ireland)
- **Real tennis** (France)
- **Pétanque** (France)

Germany produced **5.4 million** cars in 2013.

Southwest Europe

Andorra - Balearic Islands - Gibraltar - Portugal - Spain

A big slab of land juts out from Europe into the Atlantic Ocean, below the stormy Bay of Biscay. This is the Iberian peninsula, divided between Spain and Portugal. It is separated from France by the high mountains of the Pyrenees, where tourists visit the mini-state of Andorra. Spain is rimmed by other mountains around the central, flat Meseta region.

Spain's northwest coast is green from Atlantic rains, but much of the country is dry and dusty. Spain can be sweltering hot in the summer. There are villages of small white houses, oranges and lemons, fields of sunflowers and olive trees. You can see castles and ornate Roman Catholic cathedrals, and in the south the Islamic palaces and fountains of the Moors, who ruled here in the Middle Ages. Madrid is the biggest city.

At Spain's southern tip, the great rock of Gibraltar is UK territory, just 14 km (9 miles) from the coast of Africa. In Portugal there are river valleys and forests of cork-oak, fishing villages and beaches by the Atlantic surf, and the historic port of Lisbon.

A VISION OF THE FUTURE
Is it a ship or a castle? No, it's a fantastic modern art gallery built of stone, glass and gleaming titanium. The Guggenheim Museum, Bilbao, lies in the Basque Country, Spain.

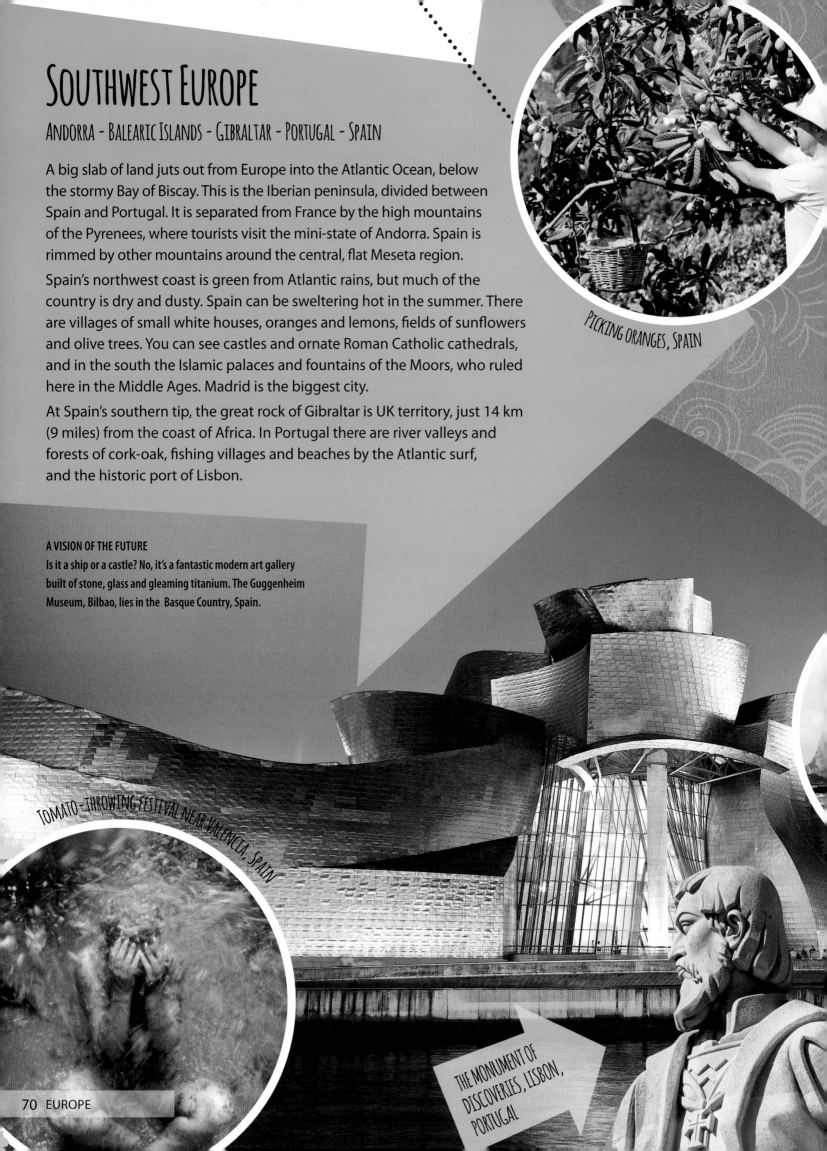

PICKING ORANGES, SPAIN

TOMATO-THROWING FESTIVAL NEAR VALENCIA, SPAIN

THE MONUMENT OF DISCOVERIES, LISBON, PORTUGAL

BAY OF
BISCAY

ATLANTIC
OCEAN

BASILICA OF THE SAGRADA FAMILIA, BARCELONA

Cantabrian Mts

PORTO

R Duro

PORTUGAL

SPAIN

BILBAO

ANDORRA

BARCELONA

R Tagus

MADRID

LISBON

BALEARIC ISLANDS

VALENCIA

PALMA

R Guadalquivir

THE ROCK OF GIBRALTAR

Sierra Nevada

SEVILLE

MEDITERRANEAN SEA

GIBRALTAR
(UK)

CAVE ART
At Altamira in northern Spain you can
see amazing cave paintings of animals
and hunters. They were made between
about 13,000 and 17,000 years ago, but
look as if they were painted yesterday.

SUPER STATS
The Tagus is the longest river in the
Iberian peninsula, flowing **1,083 km
(645 miles)** through Spain and Portugal
• The tallest mountain in Spanish territory is the
volcanic Pico del Teide in the Canary Islands off
Africa's west coast at **3,718 m (12,198 ft)**
• The Bay of Biscay is famous for its fierce winter
storms • The population of greater Madrid is
about **6.5 million**, making it the biggest
urban area in southwest Europe.

WHO LIVES HERE?

The Spanish and Portuguese languages have spread around the world. The Iberian peninsula has a patchwork of peoples and cultures. Some have their own languages or dialects. The **Catalans** live in the northeast, around Barcelona, as well as in Andorra and France. The Basque capital is at Vitoria-Gasteiz. The **Basques** speak a language which is not related to any others in Europe.

There's no **tooth fairy** in Spain – instead, they have a 'tooth mouse' called Ratoncito Pérez!

IT'S FIESTA TIME!

Spain is famous for its countless festivals and pageants, for processions, parades, horseback cavalcades, dancing and costume. These celebrations may be rooted in history, in Roman Catholic religious rituals or in ancient regional customs, and they are often spectacular.

Spain is the largest country in southwest Europe: **505,370 km²** (212,935 sq mi)

Flamenco is a style of singing, guitar playing and dancing popular in **southern Spain**. The dancers strut, shout, stamp and clap. OLÉ!

Portuguese fishermen catch more sardines than any other kind of fish. Sardines freshly grilled? **'sim por favor!** – yes please!'

Patterned tiles in dazzling colours decorate the **Alhambra,** a fabulous Moorish palace in **Granada, Spain.**

When the summer sun burns down at noon, the **Spanish** traditionally shut up shop and find a shady place for a **SIESTA**, or nap. Work starts up again when it gets cooler.

Spain produces over **41 percent** of the world's **olive oil.**

Portugal is famous for its wines, fruit and fish, but it is also a centre for the IT, biotechnology and aerospace industries.

Portugal and Spain produce over **90 percent** of the world's **corks.**

A riot of red – at **Buñol**, in the Valencia region of Spain, people gather each August to spend an hour throwing **150,000 squashed tomatoes** at each other.

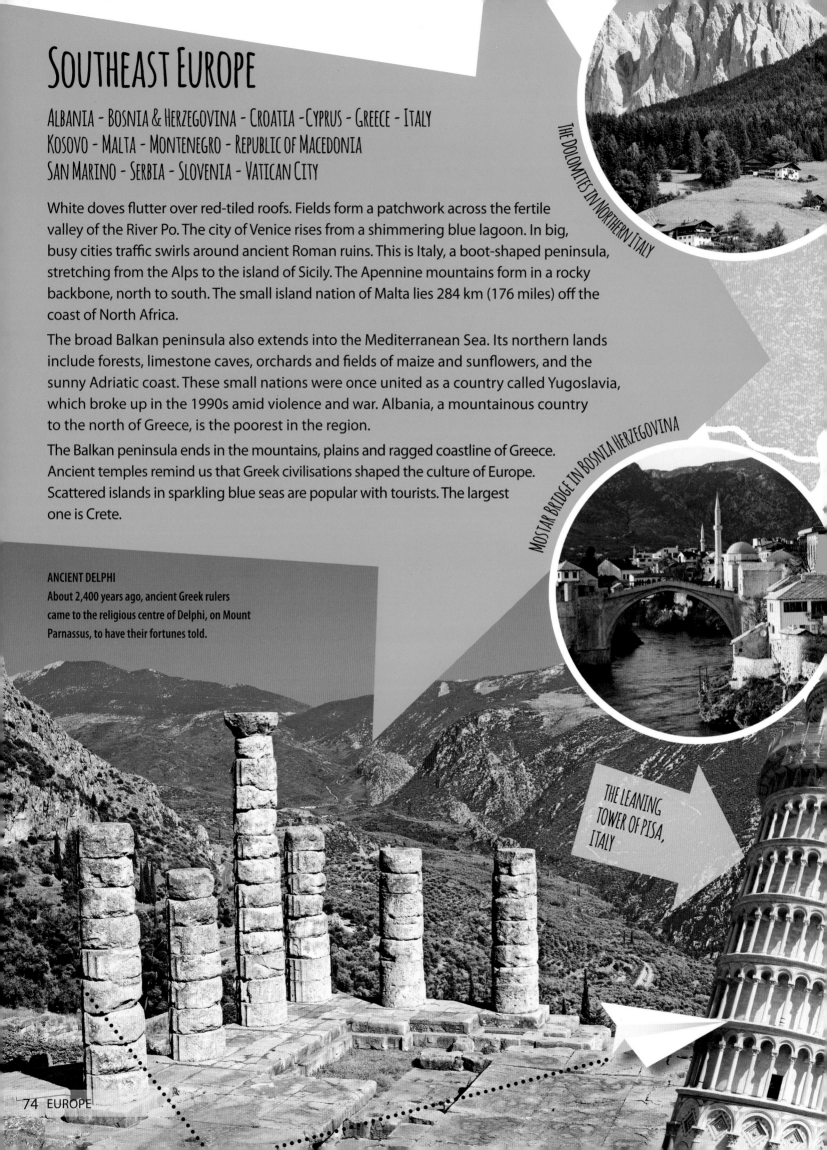

Southeast Europe

Albania - Bosnia & Herzegovina - Croatia - Cyprus - Greece - Italy
Kosovo - Malta - Montenegro - Republic of Macedonia
San Marino - Serbia - Slovenia - Vatican City

White doves flutter over red-tiled roofs. Fields form a patchwork across the fertile valley of the River Po. The city of Venice rises from a shimmering blue lagoon. In big, busy cities traffic swirls around ancient Roman ruins. This is Italy, a boot-shaped peninsula, stretching from the Alps to the island of Sicily. The Apennine mountains form in a rocky backbone, north to south. The small island nation of Malta lies 284 km (176 miles) off the coast of North Africa.

The broad Balkan peninsula also extends into the Mediterranean Sea. Its northern lands include forests, limestone caves, orchards and fields of maize and sunflowers, and the sunny Adriatic coast. These small nations were once united as a country called Yugoslavia, which broke up in the 1990s amid violence and war. Albania, a mountainous country to the north of Greece, is the poorest in the region.

The Balkan peninsula ends in the mountains, plains and ragged coastline of Greece. Ancient temples remind us that Greek civilisations shaped the culture of Europe. Scattered islands in sparkling blue seas are popular with tourists. The largest one is Crete.

ANCIENT DELPHI
About 2,400 years ago, ancient Greek rulers came to the religious centre of Delphi, on Mount Parnassus, to have their fortunes told.

THE DOLOMITES IN NORTHERN ITALY

MOSTAR BRIDGE IN BOSNIA HERZEGOVINA

THE LEANING TOWER OF PISA, ITALY

Dolomite Mts

SLOVENIA

LJUBLJANA

ITALY

R Po

ZAGREB

CROATIA

BOSNIA & HERZEGOVINA

SARAJEVO

SERBIA

R Danube

BELGRADE

MILAN

CITY OF SAN MARINO

SAN MARINO

Apennine Mts

MONTENEGRO

PODGORICA

KOSOVO

PRISTINA

SKOPJE

MACEDONIA

ROME

VATICAN CITY

NAPLES

TIRANA

ALBANIA

THESSALONIKI

Sardinia

GREECE

PALERMO

Sicily

ATHENS

MEDITERRANEAN SEA

ETRUSCAN SCULPTURE, 5TH CENTURY BC, ITALY

VALLETTA

MALTA

Crete

SUPER STATS

The awesome Roman empire was at its biggest in **117**BC, when it covered about **5 million km²** (**1,930,511 sq mi**)

• Vatican City State, the world headquarters of the Roman Catholic Church, is the smallest nation on Earth. It covers just **44 ha** (**110 acres**) within the city of Rome

• Mount Olympus in Greece is **2,918 m** (**9,573 ft**) high. The ancient Greeks believed it was the home of the gods.

NICOSIA

Cyprus

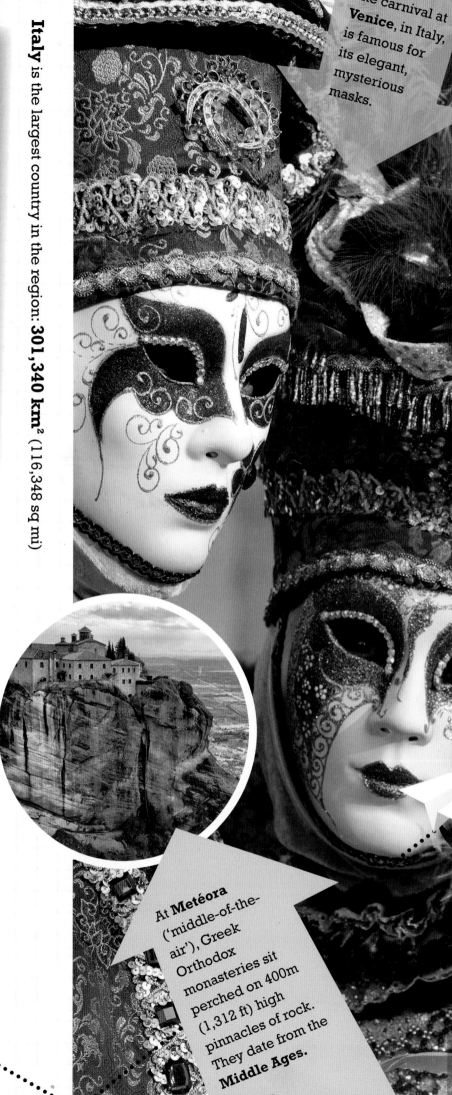

WHO LIVES HERE?

The Italian language has its origins in the **Latin** spoken in ancient Rome. The Maltese language is related to Arabic. Both Malta and Italy are **Roman Catholic** countries. Many peoples of the smaller Balkan states speak Slavic languages. They are mostly Christians, but some are Muslims, such as the **Bosniaks**. Many Albanians are Muslim too. **Roma communities** are found across the region. The Greeks have their own language and alphabet and many follow Greek Orthodox Christianity.

Italy is the largest country in the region: **301,340 km²** (116,348 sq mi)

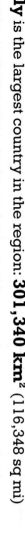

The carnival at **Venice**, in Italy, is famous for its elegant, mysterious masks.

ALBANIAN SCHOOLS

Albania is a country where many people are poor farmers, growing vegetables or olives. It is trying to improve its schools. A United Nations team has helped with rebuilding, repair, and with providing much-needed libraries and laboratories.

At **Metéora** ('middle-of-the-air'), Greek Orthodox monasteries sit perched on 400m (1,312 ft) high pinnacles of rock. They date from the **Middle Ages.**

From mountain top to seashore, Italy is home to over **57,000 animal species**, one-third of the European total. They include wolves, brown bears, wild boar and one of the tiniest mammals in the world, the Etruscan pygmy shrew – which weighs just **1.8 g (0.06 oz).**

Rome's **Colosseum** once saw deadly gladiator fights and mock sea battles. It opened in **AD 80** and could hold up to **80,000** spectators.

'HELLO' IN ITALIAN:
Ciao

BIGGEST LAKE IN SOUTHERN EUROPE:
Skadar (Albania-Montenegro, 370-530 km² (140-200 sq mi) in surface area)

WORLD'S OLDEST SURVIVING REPUBLIC:
San Marino (founded AD 301)

BIG BANG:
Mount Etna, Sicily, is Europe's highest active volcano

'THANK YOU' IN GREEK:
ευχαριστώ [say 'efcharistó']

MALTA'S ANCIENT MYSTERY:
Stone temples (c3600-3200 BC)

OLYMPIC GAMES:
Were held in Southern Greece as early as 776 BC

TOP SNACK IN ATHENS:
Koulouri (sesame bread ring)

FERRIES TO THE ISLANDS :
Piraeus in Greece is Europe's busiest passenger port with 20 million passengers a year

Greece exports tasty foods such as creamy yoghurts, cheeses, olives and olive oil, honey and melons.

Kosovo has the youngest population in Europe, with over half of the people **under 25.**

Many names in the history of fast cars are **Italian** – Ferrari, Lamborghini, Alfa Romeo, Maserati...

Central Europe

Bulgaria - Czech Republic - Hungary - Poland - Romania - Slovakia

Gdansk is a Polish port on the Baltic Sea. Poland lies across the huge plain which stretches eastwards into Russia, crossed by long rivers such as the Oder and the Vistula. Here are farms growing potatoes or beet, forests, lakes and industrial towns. In the centre is the busy capital city, Warsaw. Summers can be warm and winters very cold. Southern borders rise to the Sudeten and Tatra mountains.

The Czech Republic and Slovakia take in highlands, mountains, forests and farms, as well as industrial and mining regions. Many visitors come to admire the beautiful old city of Prague. Another grand capital is Budapest, on the banks of the Danube river. Hungary is a land of grassy plains, farms and orchards, forests and mountains.

Romania lies to the north of the Danube, and from the plains around Bucharest rises to form a great horseshoe of mountain ranges, known as the Carpathians and the Transylvanian Alps. Bulgaria takes up the northeastern part of the Balkan peninsula bordering Greece, Turkey and the Black Sea.

SMART PRAGUE
The Czech city of Prague has been a centre of learning, the arts and politics for over a thousand years.

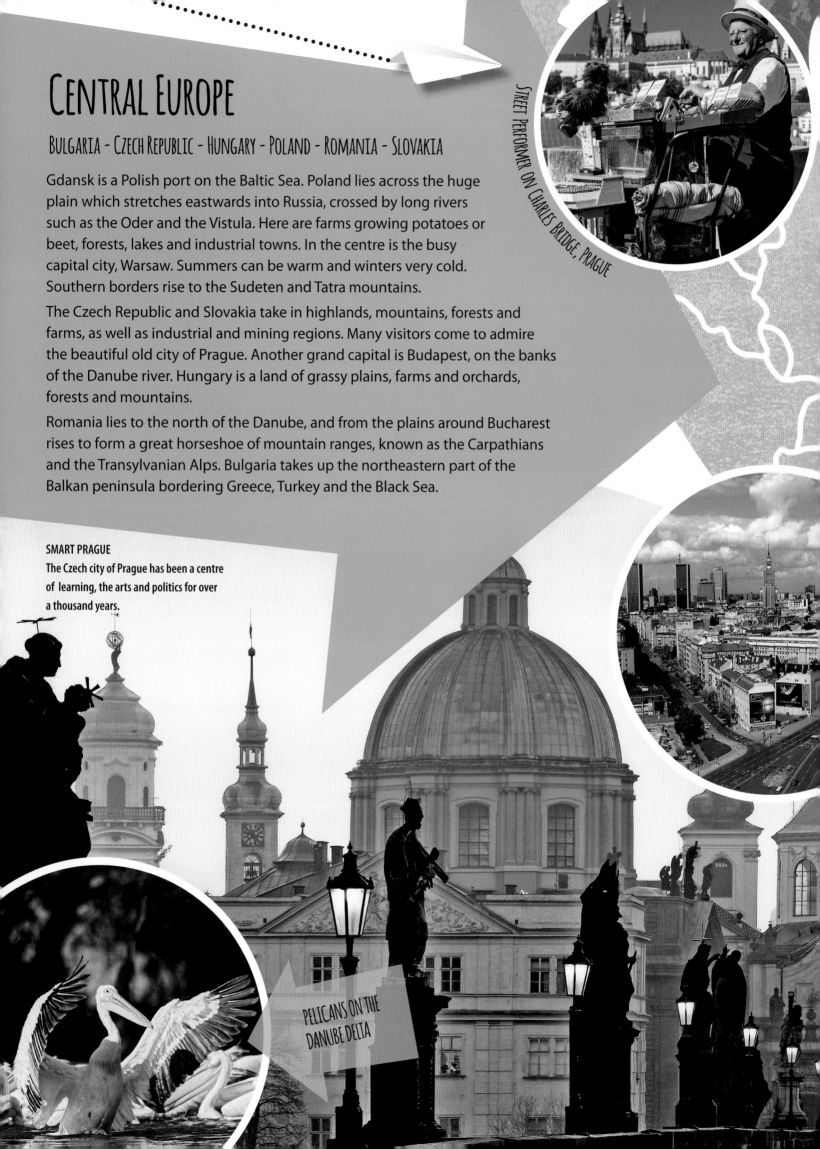

Street Performer on Charles Bridge, Prague

Pelicans on the Danube Delta

GDANSK

R Vistala

POLAND

R Oder

WARSAW

LODZ

KRAKOW

Tatra Mts.

PRAGUE

CZECH REPUBLIC

SLOVAKIA

BRATISLAVA

BUDAPEST

Carpathian
Mountains

HUNGARY

R Danube

ROMANIA

BUCHAREST

BLACK SEA

SOFIA

BULGARIA

DOWNTOWN WARSAW

WOODEN MONASTERIES, BÂRSANA, ROMANIA

SPARKLING GLASS

You need some puff to blow glass in the old-fashioned way. Fine glass has been made in the historical Czech region of Bohemia since the Middle Ages. The region is still famous for its crystal glassware.

SUPER STATS

Balaton in Hungary is the biggest lake in Central Europe (**592 km², 229 sq mi**) • Poland has **23** national parks, **1,269** nature reserves, and **100** bird sanctuaries • The People's Palace in Bucharest, Romania is the largest civilian building in the world, covering **340,000 m² (3,700,000 sq ft)**. It has **1,100** rooms, **12** floors, **4** underground levels with another **4** under construction • The oldest golden treasure (**6,000 years old**) in the world was found in Bulgaria.

?

WHO OR WHAT AM I?

I can be blue or brown, silver or green, and I travel a long, long journey from Germany, through Central Europe to the Black Sea.

ANSWER: The River Danube

79

WHO LIVES HERE?

The region includes Catholic, Protestant and Orthodox Christians, also Muslims and Jews. The **Poles, Czechs, Slovaks** and **Bulgarians** are all **Slavic** peoples with their own languages. The **Hungarians**, also known as Magyars, are a separate ethnic group. So are the **Romanians**, whose language comes from the Latin of the old Roman empire. Many other peoples live in the region, including the **Roma** – who are not the same people as the Romanians.

Let's dance the **polka**! This lively folk dance from **Central Europe** conquered the world's ballrooms in the 1800s and is still popular today.

STEW-PENDOUS!

In Hungary they call their national dish *Gulyásleves* ('herdsman's soup'), but it is also popular across Central Europe and known in English as Goulash. This is a spicy beef stew seasoned with paprika, herbs and garlic, and may include vegetables such as diced potatoes. It's a winter warmer!

Poland is the largest country in Central Europe: **312,685 km²** (120,728 sq mi)

All lit up with Christmas decorations – St Stephen's Basilica in Budapest, the capital of Hungary.

The element polonium is named after Poland, in honour of the Polish scientist Marie Sklodowska-Curie who discovered it in 1898.

THE CENTRAL EUROPE REAL DEAL!

'HELLO' IN CZECH:
Ahoj!

HIGH TATRAS:
Slovakia's highest point is Gerlachovsky Stit in the Tatra Mountains (2,655 m, 8,711 ft)

WILD MUSHROOMS:
Every autumn Central Europeans head for the woods to search for tasty mushrooms

SCENT OF ROSES:
Bulgaria produces 70 percent of all the world's rose oil, used in making perfumes

HOT SPRINGS:
Hungary has over 1,000 hot springs and spas

FISH FOR CHRISTMAS:
In the Czech Republic, carp is the top choice for dinner on Christmas Eve

A SALT CATHEDRAL:
An underground cathedral is carved out of rock-salt at Poland's Wieliczka Salt Mine

Millions of **doughnuts** called *paczki* are eaten by **Poles** on the last Thursday before the Christian fast of Lent.

Slovakia's industry is based on the manufacture of cars, televisions and computer monitors.

The Masurian region of **Northern Poland** has over **2,000 lakes**, linked by a maze of canals and rivers. It's popular for yachting, kayaking and swimming in summer.

The novel **Dracula** (1897) tells the tale of a **vampire** from Transylvania. The character may be based on a real-life prince from Romania called **Vlad the Impaler.** He lived in the 1400s.

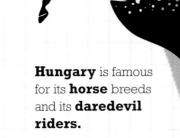

Hungary is famous for its **horse** breeds and its **daredevil riders.**

Eastern Europe

Belarus - Moldova - Ukraine

Let's travel east to the borders of Russia. Trains bound for Moscow from Berlin or Warsaw will take you via the industrial city of Minsk, capital of Belarus. Belarus is a low-lying, flat land with forests, marshes and lakes.

To the south is Ukraine. Its capital, Kyiv or Kiev, looks out over the River Dnieper and over 3 million people live in or around the city. In the south, the steppes (prairies) have a rich black soil known as chernozem. This is perfect for growing wheat, so this region is known as one of the world's big 'bread baskets'. The south of the country is warm, bordering the Black Sea around the port of Odessa. Westwards, along the River Dniester, is the small nation of Moldova, with its capital at Chisinau.

All three countries have in the past been part of the Russian empire or the Soviet Union. In the 1990s they broke away to become independent. Some of their peoples still wanted close ties with Russia, while others wanted to join up with Central and Western Europe. This has led to some big political problems.

KHOTYN FORTRESS AND RIVER DNIESTER, UKRAINE

ST MICHAEL'S MONASTERY, KIEV

GRAIN HARVEST ON THE STEPPES

MINSK

BELARUS

KIEV

KHARKIV

R Dnieper

UKRAINE

R Dniester

MOLDOVA

ODESSA

CHISINAU

Crimea

SEA OF AZOV

BLACK SEA

A PEBBLY BEACH ON THE BLACK SEA

WORLD WAR II MEMORIAL, MINSK

GOLDEN ORIOLE, MOLDOVA

SUPER STATS

The River Dnieper flows through Russia, Belarus and Ukraine on its **2,145 km (1,333 mile)** journey to the Black Sea • The Eurasian Steppe stretches all the way from Moldova and the Ukraine through Central Asia to Siberia • Wildlife of the steppes includes hamsters and ground squirrels • Moldova is the smallest – and poorest – country in eastern Europe • **40 percent** of Belarus is covered by forest.

BISON SANCTUARY

The ancient Bialowieza forest is on the borders of Belarus and Poland. A home has been created there for the very rare European bison.

? WHO OR WHAT AM I?

I am Europe's biggest rodent and have a broad, flat tail. I build dams and canals in lakes and rivers.

ANSWER: A Eurasian beaver

The **Dnieper River** is the fourth longest in Europe at **2,290 km** (1,420 miles)

WHO LIVES HERE?

Eastern Europe is the original homeland of the **Slavic peoples**, and today they make up the majority of the population. They include **Belarussians, Russians, Ukrainians** and **Poles**. Some **Tartars**, of Turkic descent, live in Ukraine, and the Moldovans include ethnic **Romanians** and **Roma**. There are followers of Eastern Orthodox Christianity and also some Roman Catholics and Protestants.

Odessa is an important naval base, oil terminal and seaport. But to many Ukrainians, Russians and other Eastern Europeans, it's simply where they go on their **holidays**. Days are spent sunbathing on the sunny beaches or paddling in the Black Sea.

STREET TRADERS

Coming up with the goods ....
Across Eastern Europe, you can trade in almost anything at one of the numerous street markets. People like to haggle over the price of everything, from spare parts for their cars to batteries, sunglasses, watches, clothes with fake designer labels, gherkins, potatoes or fresh fruit.

Modern Minsk – this city landmark houses the Belarussian national library.

Moldova is one of only three countries whose **national flags** differ depending on which side you're looking at. (The other two are Paraguay and Saudi Arabia.)

At **Easter, Ukrainians** use wax and dyes to prepare eggs, coloured in with clever designs. They even have a special **Easter egg** museum in the city of Kolomyia – partly housed inside a giant **Easter egg**, of course!

SOUP OF THE DAY:
Borscht (beetroot soup)

TOP WRESTLE:
The national sport in Moldova is traditional wrestling, known as trynta

ICE IS NICE:
In Belarus ice hockey is the most popular spectator sport

ABANDONED CITY:
Pripyat in Ukraine has been sealed off ever since a disaster at the Chernobyl nuclear power plant in 1986

DEEP METRO:
Arsenalna in Kiev is the world's deepest metro station, plunging 106 m (346 ft)

THE BLACK STORK:
Is the national bird of Moldova

FRESH FROM THE FOREST:
Belarussians like a drink made from birch sap

Belarus has about **11,000 lakes**. The biggest is Lake Narach, **80 km² (31 sq mi).**

On the move: Ukraine builds buses, trucks, trams, tractors, cars, ships and aircraft.

Ukraine grows sunflowers and is the **world's** biggest producer of oil made from the seeds.

...it is also **Europe's** top producer of **honey.**

Moldovan monks in the **1200s** built an amazing cave monastery in the cliff face at Orheiul Vechi.

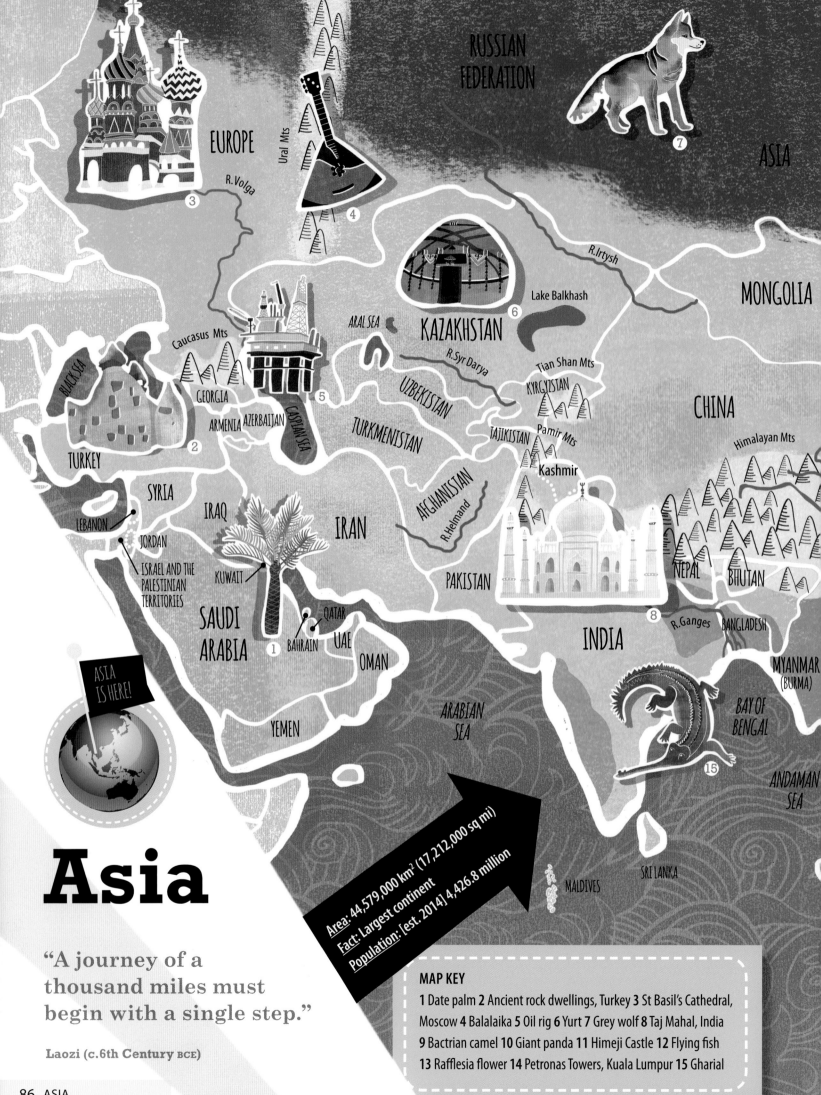

RUSSIAN FEDERATION

ASIA

EUROPE

Ural Mts

R.Volga

MONGOLIA

R.Irtysh

Lake Balkhash

ARAL SEA

KAZAKHSTAN

Caucasus Mts

R.Syr Darya

Tian Shan Mts

UZBEKISTAN

KYRGYZSTAN

CHINA

BLACK SEA

GEORGIA

ARMENIA AZERBAIJAN

CASPIAN SEA

TURKMENISTAN

TAJIKISTAN

Pamir Mts

Himalayan Mts

Kashmir

TURKEY

SYRIA

AFGHANISTAN

LEBANON

IRAQ

JORDAN

ISRAEL AND THE PALESTINIAN TERRITORIES

IRAN

R.Helmand

KUWAIT

QATAR

BAHRAIN

UAE

SAUDI ARABIA

NEPAL

BHUTAN

PAKISTAN

R.Ganges

BANGLADESH

INDIA

OMAN

YEMEN

MYANMAR (BURMA)

ARABIAN SEA

BAY OF BENGAL

ANDAMAN SEA

ASIA IS HERE!

SRI LANKA

MALDIVES

Asia

Area: 44,579,000 km² (17,212,000 sq mi)
Fact: Largest continent
Population: [est. 2014] 4,426.8 million

"A journey of a
thousand miles must
begin with a single step."

Laozi (c.6th Century BCE)

MAP KEY

1 Date palm 2 Ancient rock dwellings, Turkey 3 St Basil's Cathedral,
Moscow 4 Balalaika 5 Oil rig 6 Yurt 7 Grey wolf 8 Taj Mahal, India
9 Bactrian camel 10 Giant panda 11 Himeji Castle 12 Flying fish
13 Rafflesia flower 14 Petronas Towers, Kuala Lumpur 15 Gharial

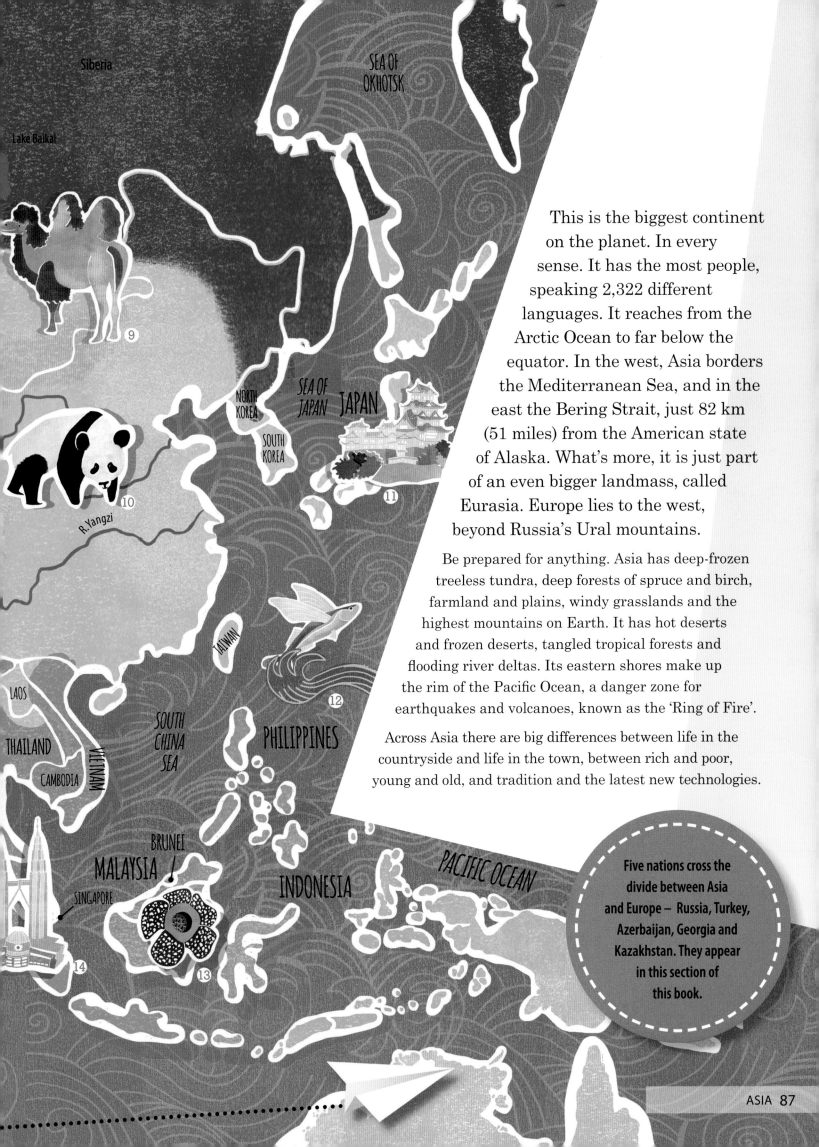

Siberia

Lake Baikal

SEA OF
OKHOTSK

SEA OF
JAPAN

JAPAN

NORTH
KOREA

SOUTH
KOREA

R.Yangzi

TAIWAN

LAOS

THAILAND

CAMBODIA

VIETNAM

SOUTH
CHINA
SEA

PHILIPPINES

BRUNEI

MALAYSIA

SINGAPORE

INDONESIA

PACIFIC OCEAN

This is the biggest continent
on the planet. In every
sense. It has the most people,
speaking 2,322 different
languages. It reaches from the
Arctic Ocean to far below the
equator. In the west, Asia borders
the Mediterranean Sea, and in the
east the Bering Strait, just 82 km
(51 miles) from the American state
of Alaska. What's more, it is just part
of an even bigger landmass, called
Eurasia. Europe lies to the west,
beyond Russia's Ural mountains.

Be prepared for anything. Asia has deep-frozen
treeless tundra, deep forests of spruce and birch,
farmland and plains, windy grasslands and the
highest mountains on Earth. It has hot deserts
and frozen deserts, tangled tropical forests and
flooding river deltas. Its eastern shores make up
the rim of the Pacific Ocean, a danger zone for
earthquakes and volcanoes, known as the 'Ring of Fire'.

Across Asia there are big differences between life in the
countryside and life in the town, between rich and poor,
young and old, and tradition and the latest new technologies.

Five nations cross the
divide between Asia
and Europe – Russia, Turkey,
Azerbaijan, Georgia and
Kazakhstan. They appear
in this section of
this book.

Awesome Asia

On top of a hill outside Kathmandu, in Nepal, there is a Buddhist temple called Swayambhunath. Monkeys climb over its walls. Coloured flags flutter in the breeze. Painted on the pinnacle are the eyes of the Buddha, looking out to the north, south, east and west. A bird flying north from here would cross the Himalaya mountains, the Tibetan plateau and the vast expanses of Siberia. A flight southwards would cross the River Ganges and India's dusty plains. Far to the east the bird might follow the winding course of the Yangzi River all the way to the East China Sea. To the west lies the valley of the River Indus, and beyond, the deserts of the Middle East.

RUB' AL'KHALI (THE EMPTY QUARTER), SAUDI ARABIA

THAILAND'S PHI PHI LEH ISLAND

Japan's highest peak is **Mount Fuji** at **3,776 m** (12,388 ft) above sea level – and it's an active volcano!

INDIAN GREAT HORNBILL

Big geography

Asia's longest river? The Yangzi at **6,300 km (3,915 miles)**. That's number 3 in the world • Asia's biggest desert is the Gobi, in Mongolia and China (covering an area of **1,295,000 km², 500,000 sq mi)** • Its biggest island is Borneo, at **748,168 km² (288, 869 sq mi)**.

BUDDHA STATUE

Cradle of religions

Many of the world's great religious faiths have their origins in Asia: the Baha'i faith, Buddhism, Christianity, Confucianism, Daoism, Hinduism, Islam, Jainism, Judaism, Shinto and Sikhism.

ASIA TOP 10

SHISH KEBAB
Tasty lamb from Turkey

JERUSALEM
City of three faiths

TOKYO
World's largest megacity

SUMO CONTEST, JAPAN
World's heaviest wrestlers

PERSEPOLIS, IRAN, 515 BC
Impressive ruins

BURJ KHALIFA, DUBAI, UAE
World's tallest skyscraper

TIGER
Biggest and stripiest cat

THE PACIFIC RIM
Indonesia's active volcanoes

RAFFLESIA FLOWER
World's biggest bloom (and it's a stinky one)

MACAU
Planet's most crowded spot

ASIANS KNOWN AROUND THE WORLD

Indian **Mohandas K Gandhi** (left) (1869-1948) was a great campaigner for freedom and non-violence. **Ban Ki-moon** (b.1944), from South Korea, has served as Secretary-General of the United Nations since 2007. **Liu Yang** (b.1978) became China's first female astronaut in 2012. Indian **Sachin Tendulkar** (right) (b.1973) is one of the greatest cricketers of all time.

ST PETERSBURG

Ural Mts

R.Irtysh

RUSSIAN
FEDERATION

R.Volga

MOSCOW

NIZHNY
NOVOGORO

CASPIAN SEA

Caucasus Mts

BLACK SEA

GEORGIA TBILISI

ARMENIA   AZERBAIJAN
YEREVAN   BAKU

NAKHCHIVAN ENCLAVE
(AZERBAIJAN)

CEILING OF ORTHODOX CHRISTIAN CHURCH, ST PETERSBURG

RUSSIA AND ITS NEIGHBOURS

ARMENIA - AZERBAIJAN - GEORGIA - RUSSIAN FEDERATION

When the sun is rising over Russia's Pacific coast, it is setting over its western borders. St Petersburg, on the Gulf of Finland, is a fine city, but Russia's capital is Moscow. This large, sprawling city is built around a medieval fortress called the Kremlin. Moscow is the centre of business, but much of Russia's wealth lies under the ground in Siberia, in the form of natural gas or metal ores.

Leave Moscow's Yaroslavsky station on the Trans-Siberian Express. You pass through the Ural mountains into Asia, and for a whole week this vast country seems to rush by your window – sunshine and snow, endless forests, villages, grimy industrial cities, frozen lakes and rivers. The train can take you to Vladivostok, or turn south into Mongolia, China or North Korea.

In 1991 many regions of Russia, then known as the Soviet Union, became independent. You can see three of them on this map. Beyond the Caucasus mountains, Georgia borders the Black Sea and mountainous Armenia, while oil-rich Azerbaijan borders the Caspian Sea.

ST BASIL'S CATHEDRAL, RED SQUARE, MOSCOW, BESIDE THE KREMLIN

Siberia

SEA OF OKHOTSK

Kamchatka Peninsula

KRASNOYARSK

Lake Baikal

IRKUTSK

ICEBREAKERS OPEN ROUTES TO THE ARCTIC PORTS

MOSCOW'S BUSINESS DISTRICT

VLADIVOSTOK

Take a look at how huge Russia is! The world's biggest nation covers one-eighth of the Earth's surface. You can see here just how far north it stretches – all the way to the Arctic circle.

Ukraine

Russian Federation

Kazakhstan

Mongolia

China

ANCIENT LANDS

With an area of over **9,653,000 km²** (3,727,044 sq mi), Siberia makes up roughly three-quarters of the total area of Russia • The Armenian capital Yerevan is an ancient city – it was founded in **782 BC** • The first known fireplace and construction in human history, which is dated back from **500,000 to 700,000** years ago, was discovered in Azikh Cave, the largest cave in Azerbaijan.

ON TRACK

The Trans-Siberian is the world's longest railway line, covering 9,289 km (5,722 miles) of track from Moscow to the Sea of Japan. It is a part of a wider network and crosses two continents and no fewer than eight time zones.

? WHO OR WHAT AM I?

I am big, brown and furry – and an emblem of Russia itself!

ANSWER: Eurasian brown bear

Many of the world's greatest **ballet dancers** have come from Russia.

WHO LIVES HERE?

Eight in 10 people are ethnic Russians, who are **Slavs**. The chief language is Russian, written in its own alphabet ('Cyrillic'). Russia is a federation of regions and peoples. These include other Slavs such as ethnic **Ukrainians** and **Belarussians,** Siberian and Arctic peoples and Turkic groups such as the **Tatars, Bashkir** and **Chuvash.** About 40 percent of Russians follow the Eastern Orthodox form of Christianity, while nearly 7 percent are Muslims. The nations to the south are home to **Georgians, Azeris, Armenians** and many others.

High leaps and **kicks** put drama into dances performed by the **Cossack** communities of southern Russia and the Ukraine.

THE FIRST BELL

It's the first day of autumn in Russia, 1st September. It is the start of the new school year, too. It is called Knowledge Day. Pupils are dressed up very smartly and carry bunches of flowers to give to their new form teacher. A first-year pupil is carried around the school, ringing 'the first bell' of the year.

St Petersburg's Hermitage museum of art contains over **3 million** precious items.

Between 1885 and 1917 **Peter Carl Fabergé** made 54 jewelled Easter eggs for the Russian royal family. Today they are worth **zillions of roubles!**

CHECK MATE!:
Russia has produced many chess Grandmasters

WHITE NIGHTS:
Midsummer party time in St Petersburg

RARE SPOTTY CAT:
The magnificent snow leopard

RUSSIAN SPRING FESTIVAL:
Maslenitsa — pancakes, sleigh rides, bonfires

HIGHEST PEAK IN RUSSIA:
Mount Elbrus (5,642 m, 18,510 ft)

WORLD'S BIGGEST INLAND SEA:
Caspian Sea — 371,000 km² (143,200 sq mi)

MOST ANCIENT CHRISTIAN STATE:
Armenia (since AD 301)

In 2012 a **39,000-year-old woolly mammoth** (ice age elephant) was found deep frozen in the soil of Siberia.

The longest river system is the **Yenisei-Angara-Selenge** at **5,539 km** (3,445 miles). Horse trotting races are held on the deep frozen river in the winter.

Mineral fuels, such as oil, account for nearly 60 percent of Russia's exports, but it also exports iron, steel and precious metals.

How would you like to live in the village of Oymyakon in Siberia? It once recorded a winter temperature of **-67.7°C (-89.9°F).** But in summer the temperature has been known to soar to **34.6°C (94°F).**

Lake Baikal is the world's deepest lake at **1,642 m** (5,387 ft). It contains about **20 percent** of all the unfrozen fresh water in the world. It is about **25 million years old.**

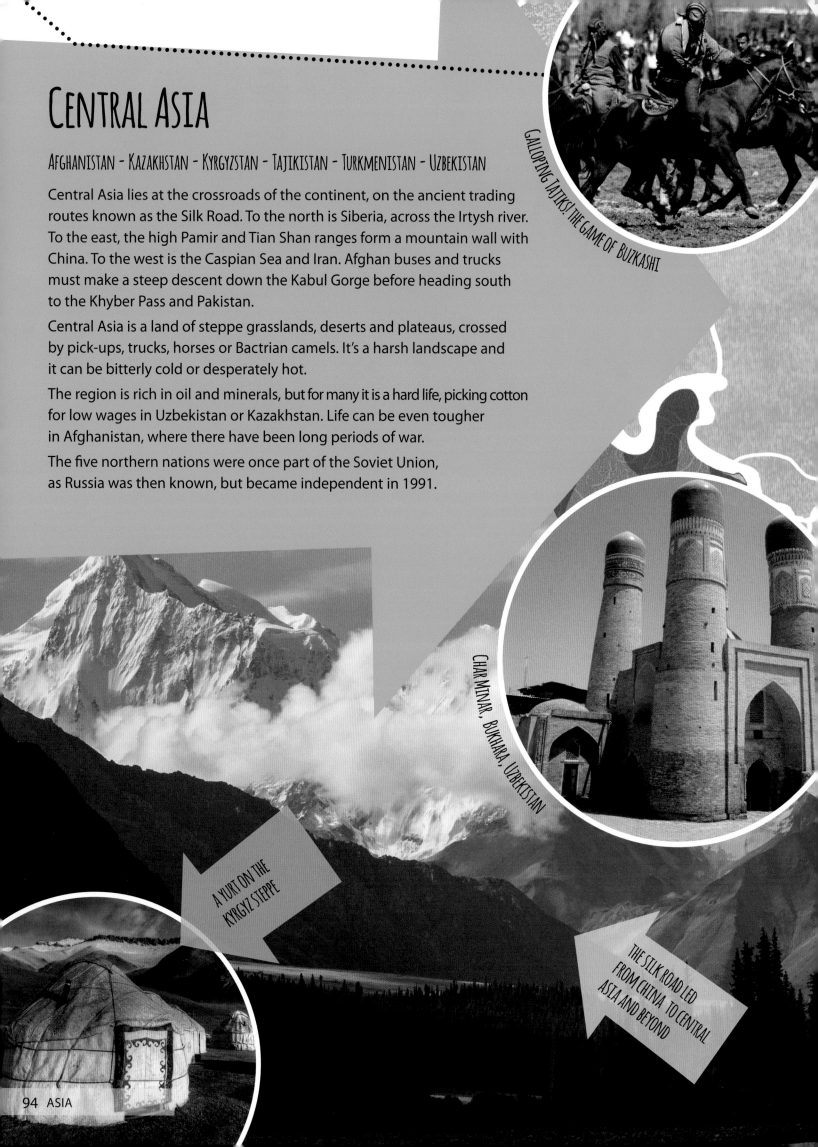

Central Asia

Afghanistan – Kazakhstan – Kyrgyzstan – Tajikistan – Turkmenistan – Uzbekistan

Central Asia lies at the crossroads of the continent, on the ancient trading routes known as the Silk Road. To the north is Siberia, across the Irtysh river. To the east, the high Pamir and Tian Shan ranges form a mountain wall with China. To the west is the Caspian Sea and Iran. Afghan buses and trucks must make a steep descent down the Kabul Gorge before heading south to the Khyber Pass and Pakistan.

Central Asia is a land of steppe grasslands, deserts and plateaus, crossed by pick-ups, trucks, horses or Bactrian camels. It's a harsh landscape and it can be bitterly cold or desperately hot.

The region is rich in oil and minerals, but for many it is a hard life, picking cotton for low wages in Uzbekistan or Kazakhstan. Life can be even tougher in Afghanistan, where there have been long periods of war.

The five northern nations were once part of the Soviet Union, as Russia was then known, but became independent in 1991.

GALLOPING TAJIKS! THE GAME OF BUZKASHI

CHAR MINAR, BUKHARA, UZBEKISTAN

A YURT ON THE KYRGYZ STEPPE

THE SILK ROAD LED FROM CHINA TO CENTRAL ASIA AND BEYOND

PEAKS OF THE TIAN SHAN, KYRGYZSTAN

ASTANA ●

KAZAKHSTAN

Lake Balkhash

R.Irtysh

ARAL SEA

R.Syr Darya

CASPIAN SEA

UZBEKISTAN

BISHKEK ●

Tian Shan Mts

KYRGYZSTAN

TASHKENT ●

Karakum Desert

TURKMENISTAN

ASHKHABAD ●

DUSHANBE ● **TAJIKISTAN**

Pamir Mts

KABUL ●

AFGHANISTAN

R.Helmand

SUPER STATS

The region's biggest city is Kabul, the capital of Afghanistan, which has a population of **3.5 million** • The highest peak in this mountainous part of Asia is Ismail Somoni in Tajikistan, at **7,459 m (24,590 ft)** • About **70 percent** of Turkmenistan is taken up by the Karakum Desert.

THE SEA THAT VANISHED

Rusting ships lie on dry land. The Aral Sea was once the fourth biggest lake in the world. When water was piped off to irrigate crops, the sea shrank to one-tenth of its size, leaving behind a salty, polluted desert.

? **WHO OR WHAT AM I?**

I have two humps and a shaggy coat to keep me warm.

ANSWER: Bactrian camel

WHO LIVES HERE?

Peoples of Central Asia have given the modern nations their names – the **Turkmen, Kazakhs, Uzbeks, Kyrgyz** and **Tajiks**. The **Uyghurs** live on both sides of the Chinese border. In Afghanistan there are other groups as well, such as the **Pashtun, Balochi, Hazara** and **Aimaq**. Dari, a form of Persian, is spoken in western Afghanistan. The religion of the region is Sunni Islam. Many Muslim women in Afghanistan wear a full robe and veil, called a chadri.

A deep blue stone called **lapis lazuli** has been mined in Afghanistan for about **8,000 years**. It is made into fantastic jewellery.

KALEIDOSCOPE OF COLOUR

At a dyeworks in Kabul, men hang out woollen yarn to dry. The colours are rich reds, oranges and purples. They will be used for making carpets with wonderful designs and patterns. For hundreds of years, Afghanistan and other countries of Central Asia have been making rugs and carpets of the highest quality.

Kazakhstan is the largest country in the world with no access to the ocean: **2,742,900 km²** (1,059,039 sq mi)

Where the **space age** began: Kazakhstan's **Baikonur Cosmodrome** (run by Russia) is the world's first and largest space launch site.

All the 'stans'...
'-stan' means 'place of', 'country' or 'land' in the **Persian language.**

One of the world's finest and most ancient **horse** breeds comes from **Turkmenistan.** The Akhal-Teke is famous for its speed, its staying power, its intelligence – and its glossy coat.

MARE'S MILK DRINK:
Kumiss, popular with the Kazakhs and Kyrgyz

THE YURT:
Round felt tent of the Steppe nomads...
Cosy in the cold!

THE MARKHOR:
Is a wild goat with massive corkscrew horns

CRAZIEST SPORT:
Afghan buzkashi, a wild horseback contest which can go on for several days

WEIRDEST NOSE:
The Saiga Antelope has a big bendy nose, which is partly dust-filter and partly air-conditioner

THE ROAD TO SAMARKAND :
In Uzbekistan — the most famous city on the old Silk Road

Top **Afghan dish**: kabuli palaw – rice, lentils, nuts, raisins, carrots and lamb.

The tomb of the **golden man** was found at Issyk in Kazakhstan. He was a Scythian **prince** from about 2,300 years ago. His coat was decorated with over **3,000 pieces of gold.**

Kazakhstan has the top economy of Central Asia. It exports oil, metals and wheat.

It's a nutty place! **Kyrgyzstan** is famous for its **almonds, pistachios** and **walnuts.**

There are **158** named mountain ranges in **Kyrgyzstan.** The highest peak in the Tian Shan, on the Chinese border, is Jengish Choqusu **(7, 439 m, 24,046 ft).**

Eastern Asia

China - Japan - Mongolia - North Korea - South Korea

China is ringed by the world's highest mountains. In the west is the Tibetan plateau, the 'roof of the world'. Long rivers such as the Yangzi wind eastwards. Most Chinese live in the east or south, harvesting wheat, maize or rice on the plains, or seeking work in crowded new megacities. Chinese civilisation dates back over 3,000 years, but these days everything in China is changing fast.

Hong Kong and Macau are Special Administrative Regions of China. The island of Taiwan is claimed by China, but has its own government.

Mongolia too is changing, with new coalmines and factories. Wind, scorching heat or severe frosts blast your face as you travel through the empty deserts and grasslands. Here and there you see the tents or gers of sheep herders, a 4 x 4 or galloping horses kicking up dust.

The Korean peninsula is divided. North Korea is a poor country, known to the outside world for its huge military parades. The wealthy cities of South Korea are famous for high-tech electronics.

HERDING GOATS, MONGOLIA

Taklimakan desert

Tibetan plateau

Himalayan Mts

THE IMPERIAL PALACE ('FORBIDDEN CITY') BEIJING

SHANGHAI
Shanghai is the world's top seaport and China's biggest city, with a population of over 24 million.

CHINESE DRAGON DANCE

ULAN BATOR ●

MONGOLIA

Gobi desert

BEIJING ●

CHINA

Yellow River

R. Yangzi

SHANGHAI ●

NORTH KOREA

● PYONGYANG

● SEOUL

SOUTH KOREA

SEA OF JAPAN

Hokkaido

JAPAN

TOKYO ●

TAIPEI ●

GUANGZHOU ●

MACAU ●

● HONG KONG

TAIWAN

SOUTH CHINA SEA

BRIGHT CITY LIGHTS, TOKYO

YAKS, TIBETAN PLATEAU

THE BIG AND THE SMALL

China has the top population stats with over **1.4 billion** citizens
• About **20 percent** of the world's population are Chinese
• **24 million** live in the city of Shanghai • Just since 1979 Shenzhen in China has grown from a small village to a city of **3.5 million**
• That's more than in the whole of Mongolia where there are only **2.9 million** people. It is the world's **least** crowded nation.

A LAND OF CONTRASTS

Japan's big-city lights, high-speed 'bullet' trains and automobile plants exist side-by-side with peaceful countryside, ancient temples and traditions. Its islands lie on the Pacific Rim, where they are at risk from earthquakes and tsunamis. The land is mountainous, with farms and large cities on the coastal plains.

?

WHO OR WHAT AM I?

I've got two black eyes and my favourite snack is bamboo shoots.

ANSWER: A giant panda

WHO LIVES HERE?

The **Han** make up over 90 percent of China's population, speaking various forms of the Chinese language. There are 55 other peoples recognised within China's borders, including the **Zhuang, Manchus, Hui, Uygur, Miao, Yi** and **Tibetans**. In the wider region are the **Japanese**, the **Koreans** and **Mongolians**. The religious beliefs of the Far East include Daoism, Confucianism and various forms of Buddhism, Shinto in Japan, Islam and Christianity.

China is the world's 3rd largest country: **9,984,670 km²** (3,855,100 sq mi) – that's slightly bigger than the USA

The Great Wall is a vast series of defences built across northern China over 1,000 years following the 600s BCE. All its parts added together come to **21,196 km (13,171 mi)**.

Chanoyu is an **ancient Japanese ceremony** for preparing and serving **tea**.

FLYING THE FISH

Colourful paper carp and streamers called *koinobori* fly in the breeze to celebrate Japanese Children's Day on 5th May. Why this fish? The carp is much admired because it uses all its strength and skills to swim upstream and leap up waterfalls. Special rice cakes filled with red bean paste, called *kashiwamochi*, are served as a treat on the day.

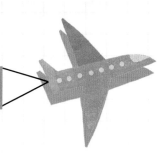

THE EASTERN ASIA REAL DEAL!

THE FORBIDDEN CITY:
The 600-year-old imperial palace in Beijing, with 980 buildings inside its walls

SHANGHAI TRANSRAPID:
This magnetic levitation train makes no contact with the track as it streaks along at 431 kph (268 mph)

HOT AND COLD:
Temperatures in the Gobi desert can vary by 35°C (63°F) in a single day

BLACK BELT:
Judo is Japan's top martial art

SPRING FLOWERS AND PICNICS:
Hanami means cherry blossom time in Japan

FEARSOME FUGU:
Fugu raw fish is a big treat in Japan, but eat the right bits —some of it contains a deadly poison!

IN A PICKLE:
Kimchi (sour and spicy vegetables), the taste of Korea

SPORT IN MONGOLIA:
Traditional archery, wrestling and horse races

Ancient Chinese inventions

- Fireworks • Acupuncture
- Cast iron • Lacquer
- Magnetic compass
- High quality porcelain
- Nail polish
- Gunpowder
- Paper money
- Printing
- Chopsticks
- Kites
- Rudders for ships
- Seismometers
  (to record earthquakes)

The **Yangzi** or Chang Jiang is **Asia's longest river** and the world's third longest at **6,300 km** (3,915 miles)

The **Yellow River** is Asia's second longest river, so called because it is so muddy. It is also known as **'China's Sorrow'** – because of its devastating floods over the ages.

Japan is made up of 6,852 islands! Most people live on the 4 biggest ones – Honshu, Hokkaido, Kyushu and Shikoku.

South Korea has the world's fastest broadband speed with an average download throughput of

33.5 megabits per second

Poached, fried or fossilised? **Dinosaur eggs** were discovered at the Flaming Cliffs site in **Mongolia** – as well as the fossils of sickle-clawed dinosaurs called velociraptors.

In 2013 Japan produced **7.9 million** cars

Southern Asia

BANGLADESH – BHUTAN – INDIA – MALDIVES – NEPAL – PAKISTAN – SRI LANKA

About 1.3 billion people live in India, the giant of Southern Asia. Its noisy city streets and railway stations swarm with crowds. Markets sell mangoes and fiery spices. Ancient Hindu temples overlook hot, dusty fields waiting for the monsoon rains. Women in brightly coloured saris wash clothes. Many Indians are poor, but India too has new high-tech industries and is changing fast.

India points southwards into the Indian Ocean, with the island nation of Sri Lanka just across the Palk Strait. To the northwest are the cities of Pakistan and the broad valley of the River Indus. Many big rivers are fed by the snowy peaks of the Karakorum range. The gigantic Himalayas run eastwards through Nepal and Bhutan along the Chinese border.

The River Ganges flows from the western Himalayas across the Indian plain, and in Bangladesh spills into a maze of waterways. The low coast of the Bay of Bengal is fertile, but often suffers from massive flooding.

THE GANGES AT VARANASI, SACRED TO HINDUS

A MAJESTIC MAUSOLEUM
The Taj Mahal at Agra in India was built in 1653. Is this marble tomb the world's most beautiful building?

PICKING TEA IN SRI LANKA

Kashmir

Karakoram Mts

ISLAMABAD

LAHORE

PAKISTAN

Punjab

R.Indus

KARACHI

NEW DELHI

Himalayan Mts

NEPAL

KATHMANDU Himalayan Mts

THIMPHU BHUTAN

R.Ganges

BANGLADESH

DHAKA

INDIA

KOLKATA

Deccan Plateau

MUMBAI

BAY OF
BENGAL

K2 – ON THE CHINA – PAKISTAN BORDER

BANGALORE

CHENNAI

SIKH GOLDEN TEMPLE, AMRITSAR

SOUTH TO THE ISLANDS
The Maldives are a group of coral
islands in the Indian Ocean. They
form the smallest nation in Asia
by area (298 km² or 115 sq mi) and
by population (393,500). They are
also the lowest lying, on average
just 1.5 m (4ft 11in) above sea level.

SRI LANKA

COLOMBO

**SUPER
STATS**

The Himalayas
have over 100
peaks higher than
7,200 m (23,600 ft)
● Mt Everest (Sagamartha or
Chomolongma) is **8,848 m** (29,029 ft)
above sea level, and climbers can reach it
from Nepal or from Tibet ● The River Ganges
travels **2,525 km** (1, 569 miles) from the
Himalayas to the sea, where it forms the world's
biggest delta covering **105,000 km²** (41,000 sq mi).

INDIA

MALDIVES

MALÉ

Battle of the colours! At the Hindu **spring festival of Holi**, people hurl brightly coloured powder or dyes at each other in the street.

India is the **largest country** in Southern Asia: **3,287,263 km²** (1,269,219 sq mi)

WHO LIVES HERE?

The fact that 447 different languages are spoken in India, 72 in Pakistan, 41 in Bangladesh and 25 in Bhutan tells you that Southern Asia is a region of many different peoples, customs and beliefs. There are great differences between city dwellers and villagers, and in India between traditional social classes called castes. Religion plays an important part in many people's lives, whether they are **Hindus, Muslims, Sikhs, Jains, Parsis, Buddhists** or **Christians**.

Legend has it that **Shah Jahan** (the Mughal leader responsible for building the **Taj Mahal**) had the hands of architects and workers chopped off once it was completed. This was to ensure they never built anything like this again.

KINGDOM OF THE CLOUDS

The secretive Himalayan kingdom of Bhutan nestles between China and India. Tourists weren't allowed here until 1974, and the kingdom has kept its traditional dress, its masked dances, its archery competitions and architecture. Wildlife includes the takin (looking like a cross between a cow and a goat), the golden langur monkey and the clouded leopard.

The bustling city of Karachi in Pakistan is home to about **23.5 million** people.

Fire dancers, drummers and illuminated elephants are all part of **Esala Perahera** (the Festival of the Tooth), a spectacular Buddhist festival in **Kandy, Sri Lanka.**

HAVEN FOR BENGAL TIGERS:
The Sundarbans region of Bangladesh and India

KULFI ICE CREAM:
Flavoured with cardamom, mango or pistachio, this treat is popular across the region

CRICKET:
Top sport in Pakistan, India and Sri Lanka

BHUTAN'S NAME:
Means 'land of the thunder dragon'

BASANT:
Pakistan's spring festival is marked by the flying of kites

INDIA-NET:
India has over 205 million internet users

TWIN TRIANGLE:
Nepal's sun-and-moon national flag has a unique shape

BOLLYWOOD BONANZA:
Mumbai is home of the super-successful Indian film industry

About **4,600** years ago the **Indus valley region** already had fine cities such as Harappa and Mohenjo-Daro, with drainage, grain stores, street grids and docks.

The world's oldest locomotive still in service is the **Fairy Queen**, built for the British East India Company in 1855. It hauls a tourist train, top speed **40 kph** (25 mph).

India is known for its farming, fishing and textiles, its call centres and IT companies.

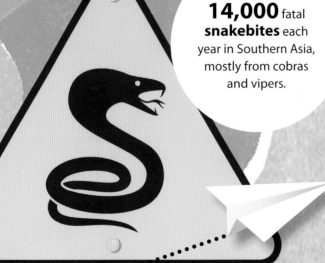

There are **14,000** fatal **snakebites** each year in Southern Asia, mostly from cobras and vipers.

More people take part in **India's general election** than in any other in the world. It takes **6 weeks** and involves **814.5 million** voters.

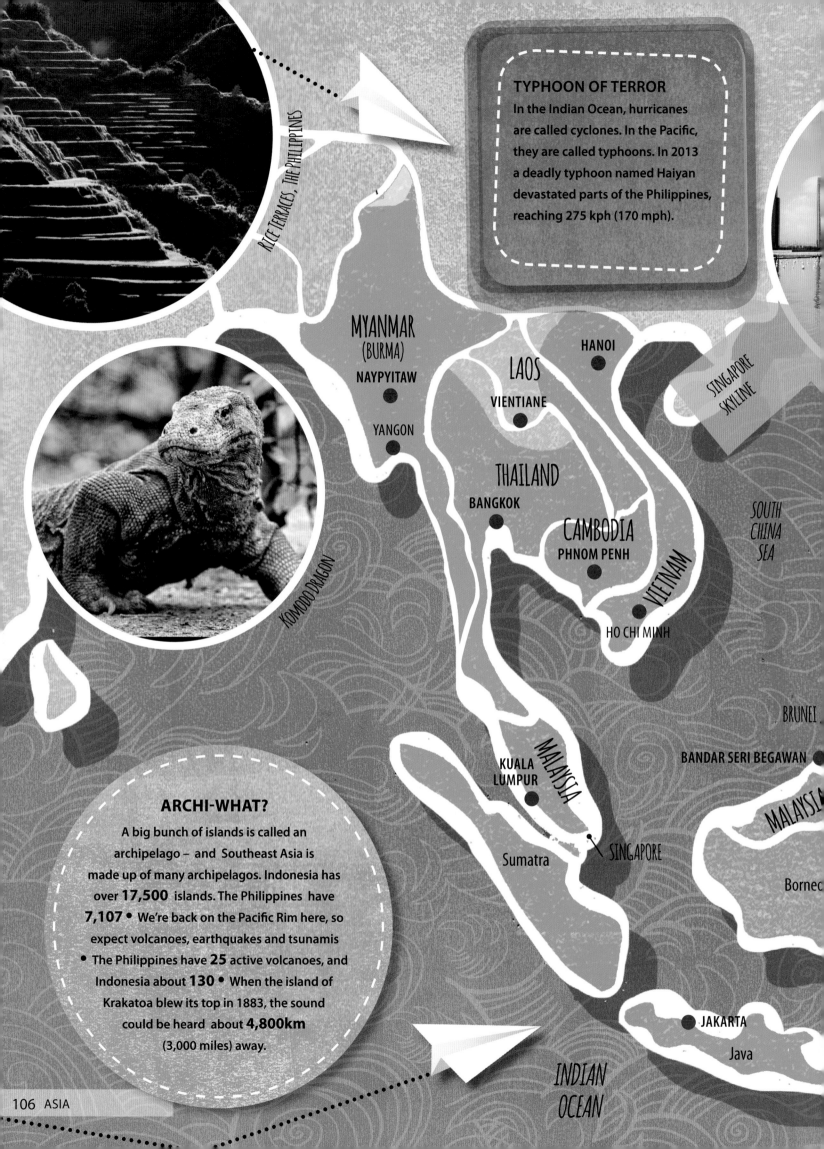

RICE TERRACES, THE PHILIPPINES

MYANMAR
(BURMA)
NAYPYITAW

YANGON

LAOS

VIENTIANE

HANOI

SINGAPORE
SKYLINE

THAILAND

BANGKOK

CAMBODIA

PHNOM PENH

VIETNAM

HO CHI MINH

SOUTH
CHINA
SEA

KOMODO DRAGON

BRUNEI

BANDAR SERI BEGAWAN

MALAYSIA

KUALA
LUMPUR

MALAYSIA

Sumatra

SINGAPORE

Borneo

ARCHI-WHAT?

A big bunch of islands is called an archipelago – and Southeast Asia is made up of many archipelagos. Indonesia has over **17,500** islands. The Philippines have **7,107** • We're back on the Pacific Rim here, so expect volcanoes, earthquakes and tsunamis • The Philippines have **25** active volcanoes, and Indonesia about **130** • When the island of Krakatoa blew its top in 1883, the sound could be heard about **4,800km** (3,000 miles) away.

JAKARTA

Java

INDIAN
OCEAN

Southeast Asia

BRUNEI - CAMBODIA - INDONESIA - LAOS - MALAYSIA - MYANMAR (BURMA)
PHILIPPINES - SINGAPORE - THAILAND - TIMOR-LESTE - VIETNAM

Between the Indian and Pacific Oceans, the Asian continent forms a long peninsula. Large and small islands enclose warm seas, where flying fish skim the waves. Laos, Vietnam and Cambodia are lands of forests and flooded rice paddies, crossed by the Mekong River.

In the west, bordered by both India and China, Myanmar surrounds another great river, the Irrawaddy. A neck of land extends southwards through Thailand, with its tropical beaches and islands, to Malaysia and Singapore. Both Singapore and Kuala Lumpur are hubs of international business.

Part of the island of Borneo also belongs to Malaysia, and part to the small nation of Brunei. The rest of Borneo's tropical forests and mountains are in Indonesia, which also includes Java and Sumatra, as well as the western region of the island of New Guinea. Timor-Leste is an independent state in the south.

Between the South China Sea and the open Pacific are the Philippines, a maze of islands with forests, ancient rice terraces and crowded cities. Manila, the capital, is on Luzon island.

Luzon

MANILA

PHILIPPINES

Mindanao

PHILIPPINE SEA

North
Maluku

INDONESIA

Maluku

Sulawesi

New Guinea

DILI
TIMOR-LESTE

Angkor Wat in Cambodia is the biggest religious monument in the world. It was built by the Khmer people in the 1100s as a Hindu temple and later became a centre of Buddhism.

WHO LIVES HERE?

Peoples of Southeast Asia include the **Thais, Tai, Annamese, Khmer, Lao, Malays, Dayaks, ethnic Chinese, Javanese, Filipino** and hundreds of other ethnic groups. In Indonesia alone 706 languages can be heard, in the Philippines 181. Many religions are rooted here – Roman Catholic Christianity in the Philippines, Buddhism from Thailand to Vietnam, Hinduism on the island of Bali. Indonesia has the world's biggest Muslim population, of about 205 million.

Indonesia is the largest country in Southeast Asia: **1,904,569 km²** (735,358 sq mi)

There are about **3 million** water buffalo in Vietnam, over **3 million** in the Philippines and **1.3 million** in Thailand. Despite their big horns, these are friendly creatures used for ploughing rice fields.

BOY MONKS OF MYANMAR

The boy monks from Myanmar (Burma) wear the simple robes of a Buddhist monk and carry a bowl for offerings. Most males in the country shave their heads and join a monastery as a trainee monk between the age of 10 and 20, and again as a full monk when they are adult. They may lead the life of a monk for just a few days – or for a lifetime.

THE NAME SINGAPORE:
Means 'lion city'

SPICE ISLANDS:
Indonesia produces the most cloves anywhere – about 57,000 tonnes a year

TALL TOWERS:
Petronas towers, twin skyscrapers, Kuala Lumpur (452 m, 1483 ft)

PINEAPPLE CHUNKS:
The Philippines are the biggest pineapple growers in the world

ORANGUTAN:
Meet the hairiest of the great apes, in Borneo or Sumatra

MUAY THAI BOXING:
Combat sport using feet, knees and elbows as well as fists

PHO BO:
Beef noodle soup, delicious street food from Vietnam

PEACH BLOSSOM:
Is used to celebrate Tet, the Vietnamese new year

FABULOUS FABRICS:
Batik patterned textiles from Java

Greater Jakarta is the most populous city area in Southeast Asia. It is home to over **28 million** Indonesians.

Thailand's top exports are computers and computer accessories, while Indonesia's are oil and gas and palm oil.

Indonesia's precious **tropical forests** are being destroyed by **illegal logging**. The burning of forest for farming often chokes the cities with smog.

The world's **biggest lizard** is the **komodo dragon** of Indonesia.

It can grow up to **3 m** (10 ft) and weigh **70 kg** (150 lb).

DO YOU FANCY A TRIP TO...

KrungthepmahanakhonAmonrattanakosinMahintharayutthaya
MahadilokphopNoppharatratchathaniburiromUdomratchaniwet
mahasathanAmonphimanawatansathitSakkathattiyawitsanukamprasit
...THIS WAY

AT THE AIRPORT THEY JUST CALL IT... BANGKOK!

The **Shwedagon pagoda** in **Yangon**, Myanmar (Burma) is covered in gold. Its crown is set with **5,448 diamonds** and **2,317 rubies.** The tip is topped with a **76 carat diamond.**

PERSIAN LEOPARD

ISTANBUL

IZMIR

Southwest Asia

Bahrain - Iran - Iraq - Israel & the Palestinian Territories - Jordan - Kuwait
Lebanon - Oman - Qatar - Saudi Arabia - Syria - Turkey - United Arab Emirates (UAE) - Yemen

Iranian herders lead their sheep and goats into the mountains through melting snows. Construction workers put the finishing touches to a gleaming new skyscraper, high above Dubai. An Iraqi man harvests the season's dates. This region, often called the Middle East, is where humans first farmed and built the first cities. Many empires and civilisations arose here over the ages. In our own times these lands have suffered from war and violence. Oil and gas have brought great wealth to some countries, but many people remain poor.

Iran lies between the Caspian Sea and the shimmering heat haze of the Persian Gulf. Iraq occupies the valleys of the Tigris and Euphrates rivers. To the south are the small but wealthy Gulf states, also Yemen, Oman and the deserts of Saudi Arabia. The sandy wilderness runs on into Jordan. Syria, Lebanon and Israel all have coasts on the eastern Mediterranean, while the Palestinian Territories include Gaza and the West Bank. The historic city of Jerusalem is revered by Jews, Muslims and Christians alike.

North of the island of Cyprus, Turkey forms a great bridge between Asia and Europe, with its largest city, Istanbul, on the divide. Many Turkish villagers are leaving the countryside, with its olive groves, rolling grasslands and mountains, to work in the growing cities.

JERUSALEM, HOLY CITY

SAND DUNES, UNITED ARAB EMIRATES

THE BLUE MOSQUE IN ISTANBUL OVERLOOKS THE BOSPORUS TO ASIA

BLACK SEA

ANKARA

TURKEY

CASPIAN SEA

OIL WELL MARMUL, DHOFAR, OMAN

SYRIA

LEBANON

BEIRUT

DAMASCUS

JERUSALEM

AMMAN

JORDAN

ISRAEL & THE
PALESTINIAN
TERRITORIES

MOSUL

IRAQ

BAGHDAD

BASRA

KUWAIT

KUWAIT
CITY

MASHHAD

TEHRAN

IRAN

Dasht-e Lut Desert

ISFAHAN

PERSIAN GULF

MANAMA

BAHRAIN

QATAR   DOHA

DUBAI

SAUDI ARABIA

RIYADH

UNITED
ARAB EMIRATES

MUSCAT

RED SEA

Arabian Desert

OMAN

YEMEN

SANA'A

ADEN

ANCIENT ASSYRIAN
CARVING, NINTH
CENTURY BC

SAND AND SALT

Fly over the Arabian desert and
it just seems to go on and on
– and on... It has an area of about
2,330,000 km² (899,618 sq mi)
• At its heart is a great wilderness of
sand called Rub'al-Khali, the Empty
Quarter • The longest rivers of the
Middle East are the Tigris (**1,899 km,**
1,180 miles) and the Euphrates (**3,596
km,** 2,235 miles) • The salty waters of
the Dead Sea lie between Jordan, the
Palestinian West Bank and Israel. This is
the lowest point on the planet, at
427 m (1,401 ft) below sea level.

WHO LIVES HERE?

The most widespread people of Southwest Asia are the **Arabs**. Other major groups include the **Iranians**, the **Turks** and the **Jews**. The **Kurdish** people live in Turkey, Iran, Iraq and Syria. There are many other minority peoples, languages and cultures. Islam is the faith with the most followers in the region. It includes Muslims of both the Sunni and the Shi'a branches. Judaism is the religion of Jews in Israel and elsewhere. There are several local Christian churches and traditions.

Saudi Arabia is the biggest country in the area: **2,149,690 km²** (83,0000 sq mi)

Over **3 million** Muslim pilgrims may attend the annual **Hajj** in **Mecca, Saudi Arabia**. It is the holiest city of Islam.

FLEEING THE WAR

Can you imagine having to leave your home at a moment's notice? You have no time to grab your favourite things. War broke out in Syria in 2011, between rebels and the government. It was terrible living in the cities as bombs were falling. Many people fled across the borders to other countries, to escape the terror. They had to live in tents. By 2014, 589,000 Syrians were living in Jordan. Another 992,000 were in Lebanon and 668,000 in Turkey. It might be years before they can go home again.

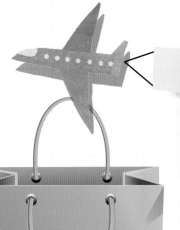

Ancient Inventions of the Middle East

- c9500 BC Farming
- c4000 BC Towns
- c3500 BC Wheeled vehicles, the potter's wheel, writing, bronze
- c2350 BC Libraries
- 2334 BC The first empire (Akkad)

Call it the original shopping mall. **Istanbul's Grand Bazaar** was founded in **1456** and it can still attract up to 400,000 visitors each day. It has 61 covered streets with over 3,000 shops.

SHADOW PUPPETS:
An ancient Turkish tradition

HIDDEN CITY OF PETRA:
Ancient desert city carved from pink sandstone, Jordan

PALESTINIAN SWEET:
Maamoul —dates or walnuts dipped in sweet semolina

MUDHIF:
Beautiful reed architecture in the marshes of Southern Iraq

'HELLO' IN KURDISH:
Say 'silaw'

NOWRUZ:
Iran's ancient spring festival

SPOTTED – BUT SELDOM SPOTTED!:
The rare Persian leopard of Northern Iran and Eastern Turkey

WORLD'S TALLEST BUILDING:
The Burj Khalifa in Dubai stands at a whopping 828m (2717 ft)

A big sport in **Saudi Arabia** is camel racing where they can reach top speeds of **65 kph** (40 mph)

Saudi Arabia has almost one-fifth of the world's proven oil reserves and is the largest producer and exporter of oil in the world.

70.7°C (159.3°F)

The **hottest** surface temperatures on Earth have been recorded by satellite and located in the Dasht-e Lut salt desert of **eastern Iran**.

Pumping fuel ... **5 of the world's top 10 oil producers** are from the Middle East – **Saudi Arabia, Iran, Iraq, United Arab Emirates, Kuwait.**

Africa

I dream of an Africa which is at peace with itself.

Nelson Mandela (1918 – 2013)

Africa is a land of big skies and fiery sunsets. Here you can see some of the last great herds of wild animals on our planet. Ancient fossils in the rocks show that this is where human beings first evolved, and where we all have our roots.

Today Africa has more young people under the age of 20 than any other continent. That means hope. You can feel the buzz and energy in school classrooms, on the busy streets of the big cities and in distant villages.

Hundreds of years ago there were great African kingdoms and empires, but most of the continents came under the control of other countries. Some Africans were sold into slavery. Today most African countries rule themselves, but many still face problems, such as poor health and lack of clean water. Droughts make life hard on farmers. Many people have been troubled by war, crime and poverty. Young Africans want another kind of future.

Most of Africa is divided into four time zones, running north to south. Two more time zones cover the Cape Verde islands in the far west, and Mauritius and the Seychelles far to the east.

MAP KEY
1 Kora harp 2 The Great Mosque, Djenné 3 Galago (bushbaby) 4 Ancient Egyptian statue of cat
5 Baobab tree 6 Mountain gorilla 7 Cocoa bean 8 Okapi
9 Red-hot poker flower 10 Ndebele painted house
11 Elephant 12 Leatherback turtle 13 Southern right whale dolphin 14 Container ship

Area: 30,221,532 km² (11,668,598 sq mi)
Fact: 2nd largest continent
Population: 1.1 billion

MADEIRA ISLANDS (PORTUGAL)

CANARY ISLANDS (SPAIN)

MOROCCO

Atlas Mountains

WESTERN SAHARA

MAURITANIA

CAPE VERDE

SENEGAL
THE GAMBIA
GUINEA-BISSAU

GUINEA

1

2

R. Niger

BURKINA FAS

SIERRA LEONE

LIBERIA

CÔTE D'IVORE

GHANA

EQUATOR

ASCENSION ISLAND

ATLANTIC OCEAN

12

ASIA

TUNISIA

MEDITERRANEAN SEA

ALGERIA

hara Desert

LIBYA

EGYPT

4

RED SEA

CHAD

SUDAN

R.Nile

ERITREA

DJIBOUTI

MALI

NIGER

BENIN

ETHIOPIA

Blue Nile

SOMALILAND

NIGERIA

White Nile

3

SOUTH SUDAN

5

EQUATORIAL
GUINEA

CENTRAL
AFRICAN REPUBLIC

CAMEROON

UGANDA

6

KENYA

SOMALIA

TOGO

BIOKO
ISLAND

R.Congo

RWANDA

R.Congo

SÃO TOMÉ
& PRINCIPE

GABON

CONGO

DEMO.
REP. OF
CONGO

EQUATOR

14

BURUNDI

SEYCHELLES

8

R.Lualaba

11

TANZANIA

COMOROS

MAYOTTE
(FRANCE)

ANGOLA

MALAWI

ZAMBIA

R.Zambezi

MOZAMBIQUE

MADAGASCAR

RÉUNION
(FRANCE)

ZIMBABWE

NAMIBIA

Namib Desert

BOTSWANA

MAURITIUS

13

9

SOUTH AFRICA

SWAZILAND

10

LESOTHO

INDIAN
OCEAN

Amazing Africa

In Kenya there is a line painted across the road, marking the Equator. You can place one foot on either side, so that you are standing on the northern and southern halves of the globe. The Equator runs right across the middle of Africa. Much of the region is warm and steamy. Its rainforests support chimpanzees, gorillas, okapi and more than 11,000 plant species. Heavy rains fill the lakes and big rivers, the home of crocodiles and hippos. To the north and south there are dry grasslands, known as savannah, where the lion is king. There are great deserts, and mountains, too. The highest ones have snowy peaks, even in hot countries.

ZAMBEZI RIVER, ZAMBIA

LIBYAN DESERT

The Nile is the world's longest river at **6,853 km** (4,285 miles)

MOUNT KILIMANJARO, TANZANIA

GREAT WHITE PELICANS, SOUTHERN AFRICA

Magnificent African animals

The African elephant is the world's biggest land mammal • A bull elephant can weigh over **6 tonnes (13,330 lb)** • The gangly giraffe is a walking skyscraper, standing about **6 m (20 ft)** tall • The ostrich is the biggest bird in the world and the fastest on land at about **70 kph (43 mph)** • All of these animals live within sight of Africa's highest mountain, Kilimanjaro, which rises to **5,895 m (19,340 ft)**.

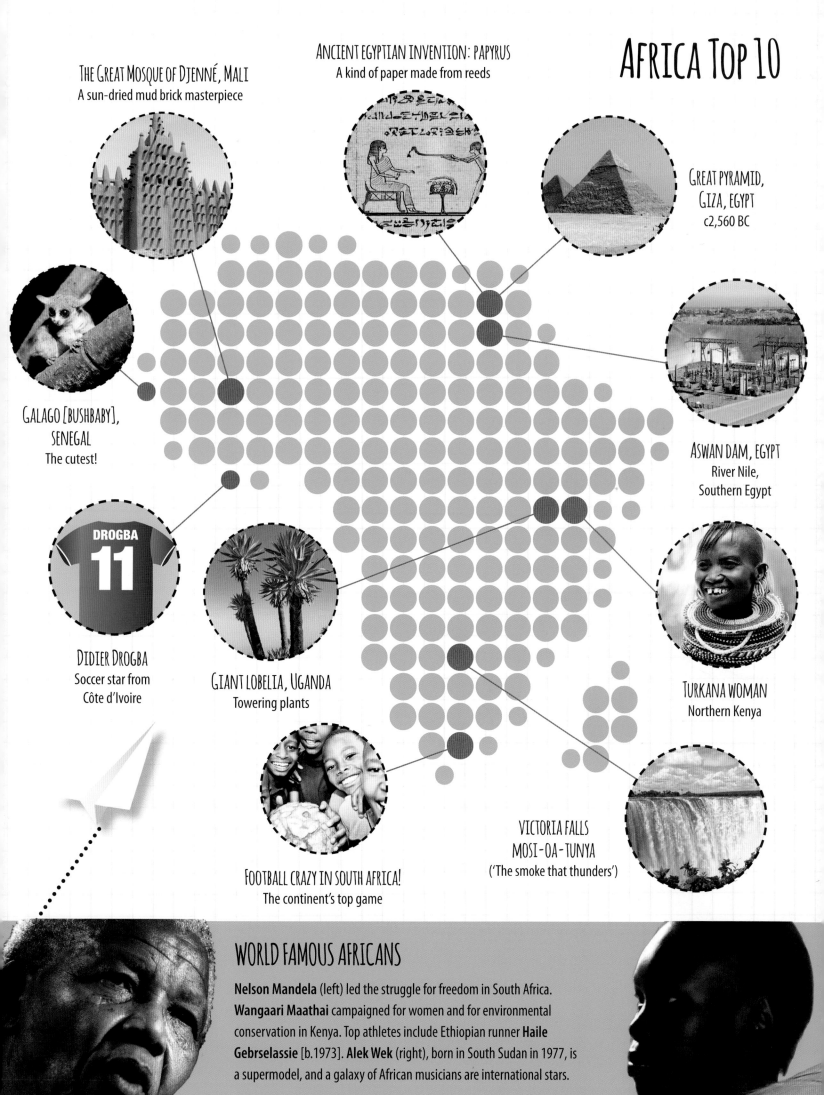

The Great Mosque of Djenné, Mali
A sun-dried mud brick masterpiece

Ancient egyptian invention: papyrus
A kind of paper made from reeds

Great pyramid, Giza, Egypt
c2,560 BC

Galago [bushbaby], Senegal
The cutest!

Aswan dam, Egypt
River Nile,
Southern Egypt

DROGBA
11

Didier Drogba
Soccer star from
Côte d'Ivoire

Giant lobelia, Uganda
Towering plants

Turkana woman
Northern Kenya

Football crazy in south africa!
The continent's top game

**Victoria Falls
Mosi-oa-tunya**
('The smoke that thunders')

World Famous Africans

Nelson Mandela (left) led the struggle for freedom in South Africa.
Wangaari Maathai campaigned for women and for environmental
conservation in Kenya. Top athletes include Ethiopian runner **Haile
Gebrselassie** [b.1973]. **Alek Wek** (right), born in South Sudan in 1977, is
a supermodel, and a galaxy of African musicians are international stars.

Northern Africa

ALGERIA - CHAD - EGYPT - LIBYA - MALI - MAURITANIA
MOROCCO - NIGER - SUDAN - TUNISIA - WESTERN SAHARA

There is an amazing square called Djemaa el-Fna in Marrakesh, Morocco. Join the crowds and you can smell delicious spices, and see dancers, storytellers, snake charmers, and water sellers in traditional clothes.
In North Africa you will also see farmers picking olives by the Mediterranean Sea, or modern city streets and busy college students and office workers in internet cafes. To the south are the mountain ranges of the Atlas and the vast wilderness of the Sahara Desert. In the south it fringes the Sahel region, often dry but grazed by goats and cattle. Eastwards, the Nile surges through the deserts of Sudan and Egypt, providing life – water for humans, animals and crops and hydro-power for cities.

SPICE MARKET, MARRAKESH, MOROCCO

MADEIRA ISLANDS
(PORTUGAL)

CANARY ISLANDS
(SPAIN)

WESTERN SAHARA

MAURITANIA

● NOUAKCHOTT

BAMAKO ●

AN ERG VIPER FROM THE SAHARA

DESERTED DESERT
Few people cross the rocks and sand dunes of the Sahara, other than oil and gas workers, or traders with their camels.

CAMELS CROSSING!!

RABAT
MOROCCO
ALGIERS
TUNIS
TUNISIA
Atlas Mountains
Sahara desert
ALGERIA
LIBYA
Libyan desert
EGYPT

MEDITERRANEAN SEA
ASIA
Suez Canal
CAIRO
Sinai
Lake Nasser
RED SEA

TRIPOLI

Ahaggar Mts.
Tibesti Mts.

MALI
NIGER
CHAD
SUDAN
R.Niger
R.Nile

NIAMEY
Sahel
Lake Chad
KHARTOUM
Blue Nile
N'DJAMENA

MANY HOUSES ARE FLAT-ROOFED AND DESIGNED TO KEEP COOL IN THE FIERCE HEAT.

AFRICAN PATTERN

PRECIOUS WATER

In some parts of the desert there is water trapped deep underground in rocks. At oases this water is brought to the surface via channels and wells. Plants can grow here and provide shade. Dates can be harvested. Goats or camels can be brought to the oases for water.

SUPER STATS

Over **9 million** people live in Cairo, the biggest city in North Africa • The pyramids at Giza were built over **4,500 years** ago as tombs for Egyptian kings, or pharaohs • The Blue Nile and the White Nile join up in Sudan and flow northwards to the Mediterranean, forming a great delta. The river pumps out **2,830 m³ (99,940 ft³)** of water every second (that's almost 19,000 full bathtubs!).

? **WHO OR WHAT AM I?**
I have eight legs, two big pincers and a nasty sting in my tail.

ANSWER: A scorpion

The **Dogon people** of Mali perfom dances and ceremonies on stilts.

WHO LIVES HERE?

Peoples of North Africa include **Arabs** and various groups of **Berbers**, such as the Tuareg. South of the Sahara are Black African peoples such as the **Fulani.** Most North Africans are **Muslims.** In Egypt there are also **Christians** of the Coptic Church.

The **Dogon** population today is around 300,000. Many live in small villages, around 700 of them with populations of less than 500. These villages are made up of caves that are carved into the **200km-long** (124 mi) Bandiagara cliffs in Mali.

GREEDY GOATS

Spring comes early to the Rif Mountains in northern Morocco. Families grow figs and maize, and many raise cattle or goats. There is plenty of green grass for the animals to eat. The trouble is, the goats strip almost every plant in sight. Herders have to keep them out of the precious forests of cedar, which grow high on the slopes.

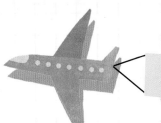

Locusts are hungry grasshopppers, which destroy crops when they swarm. There may be **50 million** of them in just **1 km²** (0.39 sq mi). That's **50 per square metre!**

THE NORTHERN AFRICA REAL DEAL!

'HELLO' IN TUNISIA:
As-salam alaykum

HIGHEST MOUNTAIN:
Toubkal, Morocco: 4,167 m (13,671 ft)

DEADLIEST SCORPION IN THE SAHARA:
The deathstalker

WORLD'S OLDEST UNIVERSITY:
Al-karouine, Fès, Morocco (founded 859)

EGYPT'S TOP BOARD GAME :
Backgammon

AMAZING ROMAN RUINS:
Leptis Magna, Libya AD c200

FABULOUS FOOD:
Steamed cous-cous

SMELLIEST PLACE:
Leather works, Fès, Morocco (hides are soaked in pigeon poo)

ANCIENT EGYPTIAN CUSTOM:
Mummified crocodiles

Egyptians own the most mobile phones in North Africa – **92,640,000.**

After a long journey in the desert a camel can gulp down **135 litres** (240 pints) of water in just **13 minutes!**

In dry lands, rainfall is a matter of **life or death.**

Egypt produces **1,374,000 tonnes** of dates every year – and that's a world record!

Morocco and Western Sahara contain three-quarters of all the world's phosphates, which are used in making fertilisers for crops.

Temperatures in the Sahara desert can soar above **50°C (122°F).**

50°

Trains in Mauritania can be up to 2.5 km (1.6 mi) long with over 200 wagons carrying iron ore through the desert.

Eastern Africa

BURUNDI · COMOROS · DJIBOUTI · ERITREA · ETHIOPIA · KENYA · MAYOTTE
RWANDA · SEYCHELLES · SOMALIA · SOUTH SUDAN · TANZANIA · UGANDA

Journeys can take you to all sorts of places – coffee farms, forests, cities or villages of thatched huts. Why not take a bus? You may be sharing it with chickens going to market... or maybe ride on a train or a truck, or a crazily crowded matatu minibus. That can be a bumpy ride, but you're sure to meet all kinds of people and hear many different languages. Inland are the deserts of Somalia, the highlands of Ethiopia, the Blue Nile and White Nile and the Great Rift Valley. To the west are Africa's Great Lakes, and the green hills and red earth of Uganda, Rwanda and Burundi.

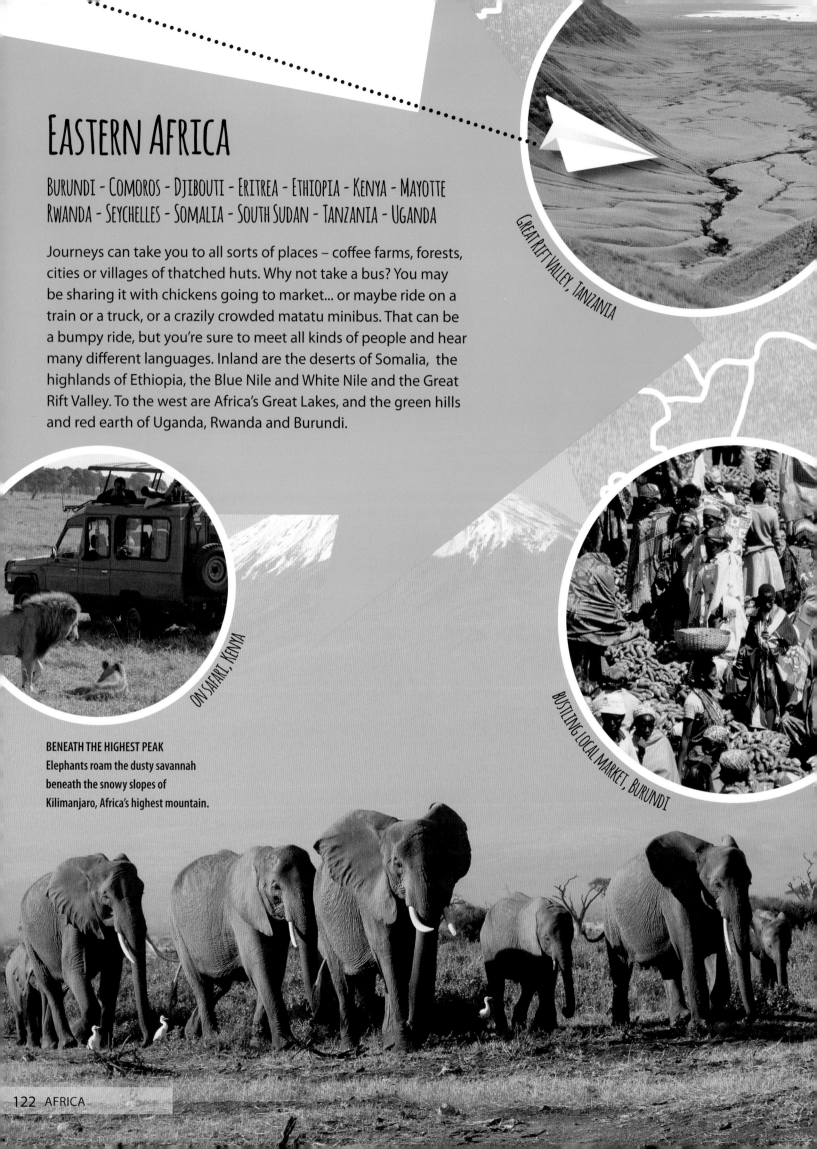

GREAT RIFT VALLEY, TANZANIA

ON SAFARI, KENYA

BUSTLING LOCAL MARKET, BURUNDI

BENEATH THE HIGHEST PEAK
Elephants roam the dusty savannah
beneath the snowy slopes of
Kilimanjaro, Africa's highest mountain.

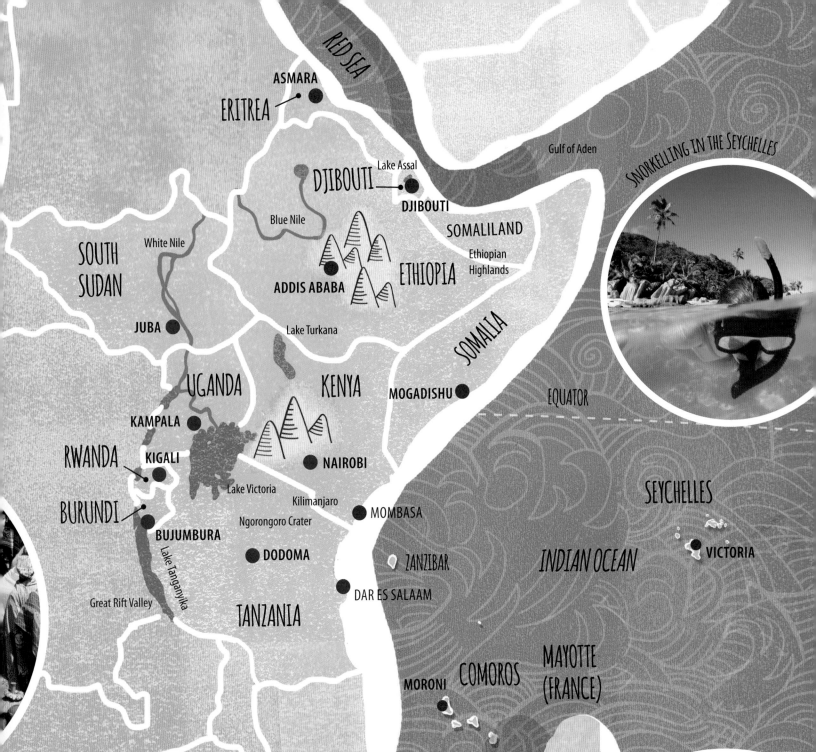

RED SEA

ASMARA

ERITREA

Gulf of Aden

SNORKELLING IN THE SEYCHELLES

Lake Assal

DJIBOUTI

Blue Nile

DJIBOUTI

SOMALILAND

SOUTH SUDAN

White Nile

Ethiopian Highlands

ADDIS ABABA

ETHIOPIA

JUBA

Lake Turkana

UGANDA

KENYA

SOMALIA

MOGADISHU

EQUATOR

KAMPALA

RWANDA

KIGALI

NAIROBI

SEYCHELLES

BURUNDI

Lake Victoria

Kilimanjaro

BUJUMBURA

Ngorongoro Crater

MOMBASA

INDIAN OCEAN

VICTORIA

Lake Tanganyika

DODOMA

ZANZIBAR

Great Rift Valley

DAR ES SALAAM

TANZANIA

MAYOTTE (FRANCE)

MORONI

COMOROS

NATURAL WONDERS

Lake Victoria is an inland sea, the biggest in Africa, with an area of **68,800 km²** **(42,750 sq mi)** • The lowest place in Africa is Lake Assal, in Djibouti, which lies **155 m (508 ft) below sea level.** Its waters are 10 times saltier than the sea • One awesome place to watch wildlife is in an extinct volcano – the **Ngorongoro crater** in Tanzania • **Footprints** found in the rocks there at Laetoli show that distant relatives of humans were walking on two feet **3.6 million years ago.**

INDIAN OCEAN SHIPPING

Small wooden dhows sail the coasts and islands, carrying mangrove timber, building materials or fresh catches of fish. Big cargo ships and tankers head for ports such as Mombasa or Dar es Salaam.

?

WHO OR WHAT AM I?

I'm big and fat, with little ears and huge front teeth. I can swim underwater and get very cross.

ANSWER: A hippo

The uniform is blue and orange at this school in Iloileri, near **Kenya's Amboseli National Park.**

The largest nation in eastern Africa is **Ethiopia**, with a total area of **1,104,300 km²** (426,373 sq mi)

WHO LIVES HERE?

Hundreds of different peoples live in these regions. Meet the **Amhara** of Ethiopia; the **Nuer** and **Dinka** of South Sudan; the **Maasai** of Kenya and Tanzania; the **Baganda** of Uganda; the **Hutu** and **Tutsis** of Rwanda... There are also **Asian** and **European** communities. There are Christians, Muslims and followers of traditional African beliefs.

Eritrea was the first country in the world to make its whole coastline of **1,347 km** (837 mi) a protected conservation zone.

HOW DOES YOUR SCHOOL COMPARE?

In Kenya, the school year starts in January and there are three terms. From 6 to 14 you have to go to primary school, although in rural and poor areas many children don't attend. You will learn English and Swahili and maths. If you pass your exams you may go on to secondary school or college.

Over **4 in every 10** Kenyans are under the **age of 14.**

Swahili saying: **Tulia tulia utakalo utalipata!** Just keep cool and you'll get what you want!

THE EASTERN AFRICA REAL DEAL!

13

Ethiopia has **13 months**. WHY? Because Ethiopia follows an ancient Christian calendar, which has an extra month of 5 or 6 days.

'HELLO' IN THE SWAHILI LANGUAGE:
Jambo!

TOP BOARD GAME:
Bao (a version of mancala)

AMAZING BUILDINGS:
Rock-cut churches, Lalibela, Ethiopia

MAKING MUSIC:
The mbira (metal keys fixed to a board)

GORILLA ID:
The nostrils of every gorilla are unique, like a fingerprint

POPULAR SNACK:
Mandazi doughnuts

DEEPEST LAKE:
Tanganyika - 1,470 m (4,820 ft)

COFFEE ORIGINS:
The coffee bush may have originally come from Ethiopia.

Flamingos get their pink colour from tiny bacteria in the water that they swallow.

The island of Zanzibar exports cloves, nutmeg, black pepper and cinnamon.

One Nile crocodile from Tanzania was nearly **6.5 m (21 ft)** long and weighed about **1,090 kg (171 st).** That's the length of **two adult swimmers!**

6.5 metres

Ethiopia is the 5th biggest producer of coffee in the world.

Clean **water** from taps is hard to come by in remote areas of **East Africa.** You may have to fetch water from a distant well, instead of going into school.

Kenya has won **25 gold medals** at the Olympics, mostly for long-distance running.

Central and West Africa

Benin – Burkina Faso – Cameroon – Cape Verde – Central African Republic
Congo – Côte D'ivoire – Democratic Republic Of Congo – Equatorial Guinea
Gabon – The Gambia – Ghana – Guinea – Guinea Bissau – Liberia – Nigeria
Sao Tomé & Principe – Senegal – Sierra Leone – Togo

Welcome to the heart of Africa – a land of great forests and rivers. There are rich company mines and oil wells in some regions, yet many people suffer from poverty and wars.

Long ago, peoples from around the Niger and Congo rivers spread out across the continent. Their wonderful masks and carvings have become classic images of Africa and highly prized by collectors all over the world.

Central Africa is warm and humid, with thunder and heavy rains. These feed the waterways that flow into the River Congo on its long journey to the Atlantic Ocean. The vast forests of the Congo region extend into West Africa, but as you travel north, they give way to grasslands and then dry and dusty plains.

CAPE VERDE

SENEGAL

DAKAR

BANJUL

PRAIA   THE GAMBIA

BISSAU

GUINEA BISSAU

CONAKRY

FREETOWN

SIERRA
LEONE

MONROVIA

RITUAL MASK, CAMEROON

CLOUD FOREST
Moisture from the clouds ensures green forests cover the mountain slopes of Central Africa.

YOUNG LOWLAND
GORILLA, GABON

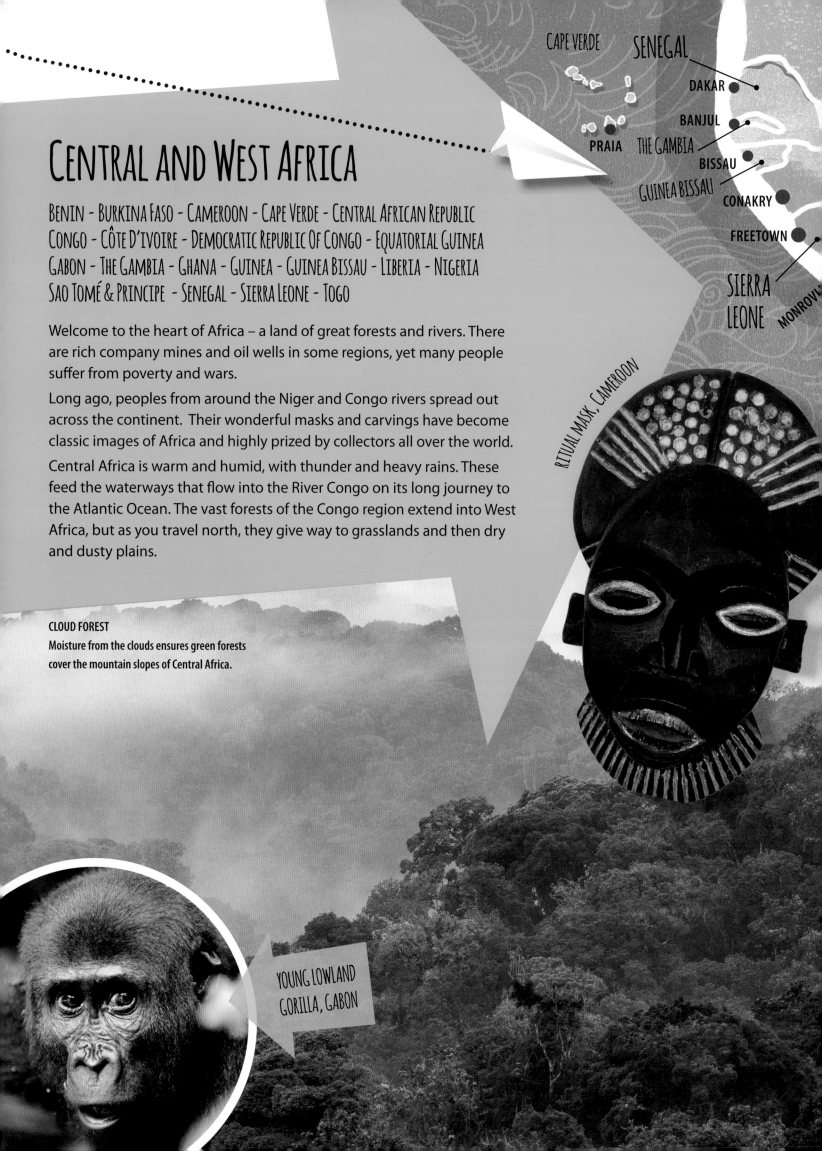

CAMEROON'S TOP SPORT - FOOTBALL!

CAMEROUN

FECA FOOT

GUINEA

BURKINA FASO
● OUAGADOUGOU

R. Niger

BENIN

GHANA

TOGO

CÔTE D'IVOIRE
Lake Volta

NIGERIA

BENUE

ABUJA

LAGOS

ABIDJAN

ACCRA

LOMÉ

PORTO-NOVO

LIBERIA

ATLANTIC
OCEAN

EQUATOR

BIOKU ISLAND — MALABO

SÃO TOMÉ
& PRINCIPE

EQUATORIAL
GUINEA

LIBREVILLE

GABON

CABINDA
(ANGOLA)

CAMEROON
● YAOUNDÉ

CENTRAL
AFRICAN REPUBLIC

BANGUI

CONGO

R. Congo

DEMOCRATIC
REPUBLIC OF
CONGO

BRAZZAVILE

KINSHASA

R. Lualaba

THE CONGO BASIN

DEADLY LAKES

Three lakes in Central Africa are killers! Lakes Nyos (right), Monoun and Kivu fill up with undergound volcanic gas. The lakes may explode or leak deadly gas into the air, killing people who live nearby.

RIVERS AND RAIN

The Congo River is the longest river in this region, at **4,700 km** (2,900 miles). In places it is also the world's deepest, at over **220 m** (720 ft). It gives its name to two countries, the **Republic of Congo** on the north bank and **DR Congo** (the Democratic Republic) on the south ● By the way, don't forget to take an umbrella to Debundscha, by Mount Cameroon – it's the wettest place in all Africa with a rainfall of **10,299 mm** (400 inches) a year.

? **WHO OR WHAT AM I?**

I can change colour, swivel my eyes and zap a fly with my long, long tongue.

ANSWER: A chameleon

Sallah is a splendid **Islamic festival** held in Nigeria. Horse riders in rich costume gallop by to honour the local ruler.

DR Congo is the largest country in the Central and West region, with a total area of **2,345,409 km²** (905,355 sq mi)

WHO LIVES HERE?

So many different peoples live in these regions – **Wolof, Fulani, Ewe, Fon, Akan, Igbo, Hausa, Yoruba, Kongo, Luba...** They may live in big cities or remote villages. They may be Christians, Muslims or follow traditional African beliefs such as Vodun. In the rainforests peoples such as the Baka and Mbuti still hunt and gather wild food.

The **Congo Rainforest** is the second largest on the planet and covers about **1,800,000 km²** (694,984 sq mi).

THE KINSUKA KIDS

White water marks the start of the Livingstone Falls, 350 km (217 mi) of rocks and swirling currents. This water is WILD! The rapids sound like thunder. Kids come here to cool off in the foam when the weather gets too hot and sticky. They are from Kinsuka, not far from the big, noisy city of Kinshasa, in the Democratic Republic of Congo.

THE CENTRAL & WEST AFRICA REAL DEAL!

'HELLO' IN THE YORUBA LANGUAGE:
Kaabo

POPULAR SNACK:
African yam chips

BIGGEST ECONOMY IN AFRICA:
Nigeria, thanks to oil

TOP FOOTBALL NATIONS:
Nigeria, Ghana, Cameroon

SMALLEST NATION IN MAINLAND AFRICA:
The Gambia (10,689 km^2, 4,127 sq mi)

MEGA LAND SNAIL:
Ghana's giant African snail is the world's biggest

UNIQUE PLANTS:
3,300 species found only in the Congo Rainforest

EYO FESTIVAL:
Costumed dancers and masquerades in Lagos, Nigeria

WEST AFRICA'S LONGEST:
River Niger (4,180 km, 2,600 miles)

A saying from Senegal: **Sahha kënz ihahayaat.** Health is a treasure.

West Africa produces about **two-thirds** of all the world's **cocoa**. 2/3

Copper and cobalt from DR Congo are used in making **mobile phones.** Some children as young as 6 or 7 have to work in the mines.

DR Congo probably has about US$24 trillion worth of minerals still to be mined. They include cobalt, diamonds, gold, copper and tungsten.

The **Akan people of Ghana** often name their children after the day of the week they were born on. The name 'Kwasi', for example, comes from 'Sunday'.

Nigeria has the biggest film industry in Africa, earning it the nickname **'Nollywood'.**

In West Africa **a kola nut** is a gift to show friendship or hospitality.

The **Gaboon viper** has the longest fangs of any venomous snake, **at 5 cm (2 in).**

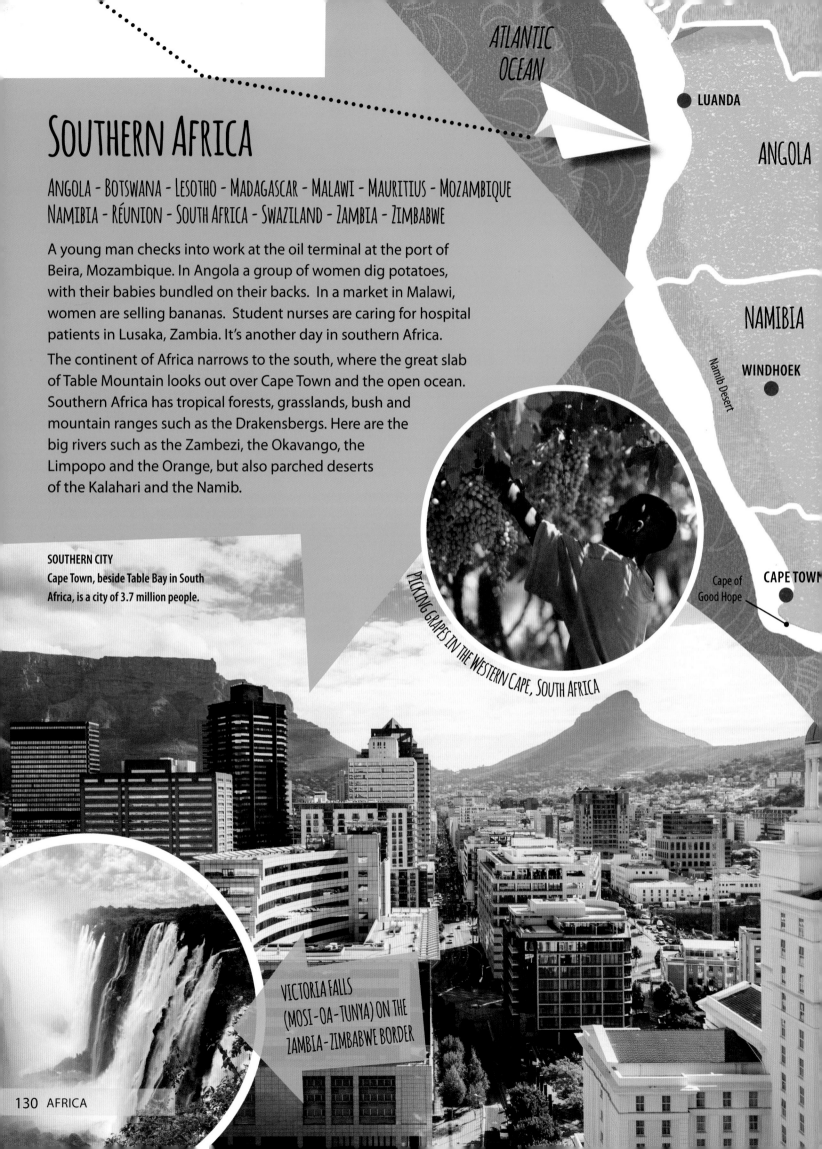

Southern Africa

Angola – Botswana – Lesotho – Madagascar – Malawi – Mauritius – Mozambique
Namibia – Réunion – South Africa – Swaziland – Zambia – Zimbabwe

A young man checks into work at the oil terminal at the port of Beira, Mozambique. In Angola a group of women dig potatoes, with their babies bundled on their backs. In a market in Malawi, women are selling bananas. Student nurses are caring for hospital patients in Lusaka, Zambia. It's another day in southern Africa.

The continent of Africa narrows to the south, where the great slab of Table Mountain looks out over Cape Town and the open ocean. Southern Africa has tropical forests, grasslands, bush and mountain ranges such as the Drakensbergs. Here are the big rivers such as the Zambezi, the Okavango, the Limpopo and the Orange, but also parched deserts of the Kalahari and the Namib.

SOUTHERN CITY
Cape Town, beside Table Bay in South Africa, is a city of 3.7 million people.

ATLANTIC OCEAN

LUANDA

ANGOLA

NAMIBIA

Namib Desert

WINDHOEK

CAPE TOWN

Cape of Good Hope

PICKING GRAPES IN THE WESTERN CAPE, SOUTH AFRICA

VICTORIA FALLS (MOSI-OA-TUNYA) ON THE ZAMBIA-ZIMBABWE BORDER

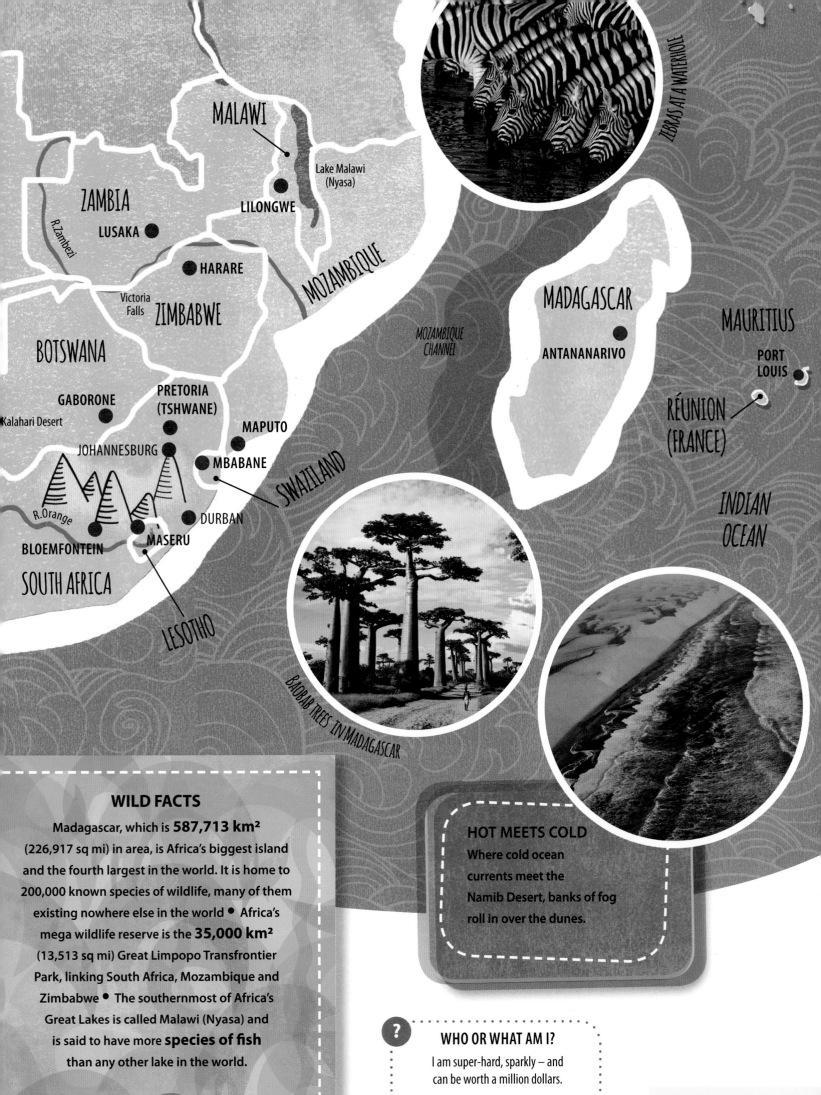

MALAWI

ZAMBIA

R.Zambezi

LUSAKA

Lake Malawi
(Nyasa)

LILONGWE

HARARE

Victoria
Falls

ZIMBABWE

MOZAMBIQUE

ZEBRAS AT A WATERHOLE

BOTSWANA

MADAGASCAR

MOZAMBIQUE
CHANNEL

ANTANANARIVO

MAURITIUS

GABORONE

PRETORIA
(TSHWANE)

PORT
LOUIS

Kalahari Desert

MAPUTO

RÉUNION
(FRANCE)

JOHANNESBURG

MBABANE

SWAZILAND

R.Orange

DURBAN

INDIAN
OCEAN

BLOEMFONTEIN

MASERU

SOUTH AFRICA

LESOTHO

BAOBAB TREES IN MADAGASCAR

WILD FACTS

Madagascar, which is **587,713 km²**
(226,917 sq mi) in area, is Africa's biggest island
and the fourth largest in the world. It is home to
200,000 known species of wildlife, many of them
existing nowhere else in the world • Africa's
mega wildlife reserve is the **35,000 km²**
(13,513 sq mi) Great Limpopo Transfrontier
Park, linking South Africa, Mozambique and
Zimbabwe • The southernmost of Africa's
Great Lakes is called Malawi (Nyasa) and
is said to have more **species of fish**
than any other lake in the world.

HOT MEETS COLD
Where cold ocean
currents meet the
Namib Desert, banks of fog
roll in over the dunes.

? WHO OR WHAT AM I?
I am super-hard, sparkly – and
can be worth a million dollars.

ANSWER: A diamond

High flying! Kids from **Soweto, Johannesburg,** make the most of the swings.

WHO LIVES HERE?

The oldest inhabitants of this region are the **Khoi-San** peoples. Hundreds of other African peoples live here, such as the **Herero, Tswana, Ndebele, Shona, Zulu** and **Xhosa**. In South Africa there are also white **Afrikaners** and other people of **European** or **Asian** descent.

The heaviest recorded white rhinoceros was **4.5 tonnes (9,900 lb)**.

SKIPPING IN SOWETO

Nearly a million people live in the huge district of Soweto, near Johannesburg. In South Africa 30 years ago, black people and white people were not allowed to live in the same parts of town. The children of Soweto protested. All that has changed today. Soweto has smartened up and is a lively place for music, dance, football and street fashion.

THE SOUTHERN AFRICA REAL DEAL!

A **braai** is a southern African **barbecue**. It might include steaks, all sorts of sausages, ribs, chicken or seafood.

Madagascar grows scented yellow flowers called **ylang-ylang**. They are used to prepare an oil used in making perfumes.

'HELLO' IN THE ZULU LANGUAGE:
Sawubona

DURBAN STREET FOOD:
'Bunny chow' (scooped out loaf filled with curry)

ANCIENT STONES:
Great Zimbabwe, 800-year-old stone city

WORLD'S BIGGEST DIAMOND MINE:
(By area) Orapa, Botswana

PEBBLE PLANTS:
Clever camouflage - lithops plants look just like real stones

HIGH JUMPER:
The Springbok (a kind of antelope) can leap 4 metres (13 ft) into the air

VANISHING RIVER:
The Okavango evaporates before it can reach the sea

Species of **lemur** are found only on **Madagascar**. The smallest of these furry animals weigh only **30 g** (1 oz) but the biggest can weigh **9 kg** (nearly 20 lb). Some of them only come out by night, and did you know that their name actually means 'ghost'?

Jewellery dating back about **75,000 years** was found in the **Blombos Cave, South Africa**. The beads were made of snail shells.

South Africa makes its money mining precious diamonds and gold.

The world's **deepest** gold mine is at Mponeng in South Africa. It burrows underground for over **4 km (2 miles).**

PHILIPPINE SEA

FEDERATED STATES OF MICRONESIA

MARSHALL ISLANDS (US)

PALAU

4

PAPUA NEW GUINEA

SOLOMON ISLANDS

MELANESIA

NEW CALEDONIA (FRANCE)

VANUATU

FIJI

Northern Territory

Queensland

5

Western Australia

3

6

New South Wales

AUSTRALIA

7

South Australia

8

2

1

Victoria

9

NEW ZEALAND

North Island

TASMAN SEA

Tasmania

10

South Island

MAP KEY

1 Shipwreck Galleries **2** Kangaroo
3 Purnululu National Park **4** Jellyfish **5** Great
Barrier Reef **6** Koala **7** Uluru **8** Eucalyptus
9 Sydney Opera House **10** Kiwi

Area: 8,600,000 km² (3,300,000 sq mi)
Fact: Smallest continent
Population: 37 million in 2013

Oceania straddles several time zones. This means that if it's midday on Tahiti in French Polynesia in the east of the continent, in Palau on the western side, it will be 7am the following morning!

SOUTHERN OCEAN

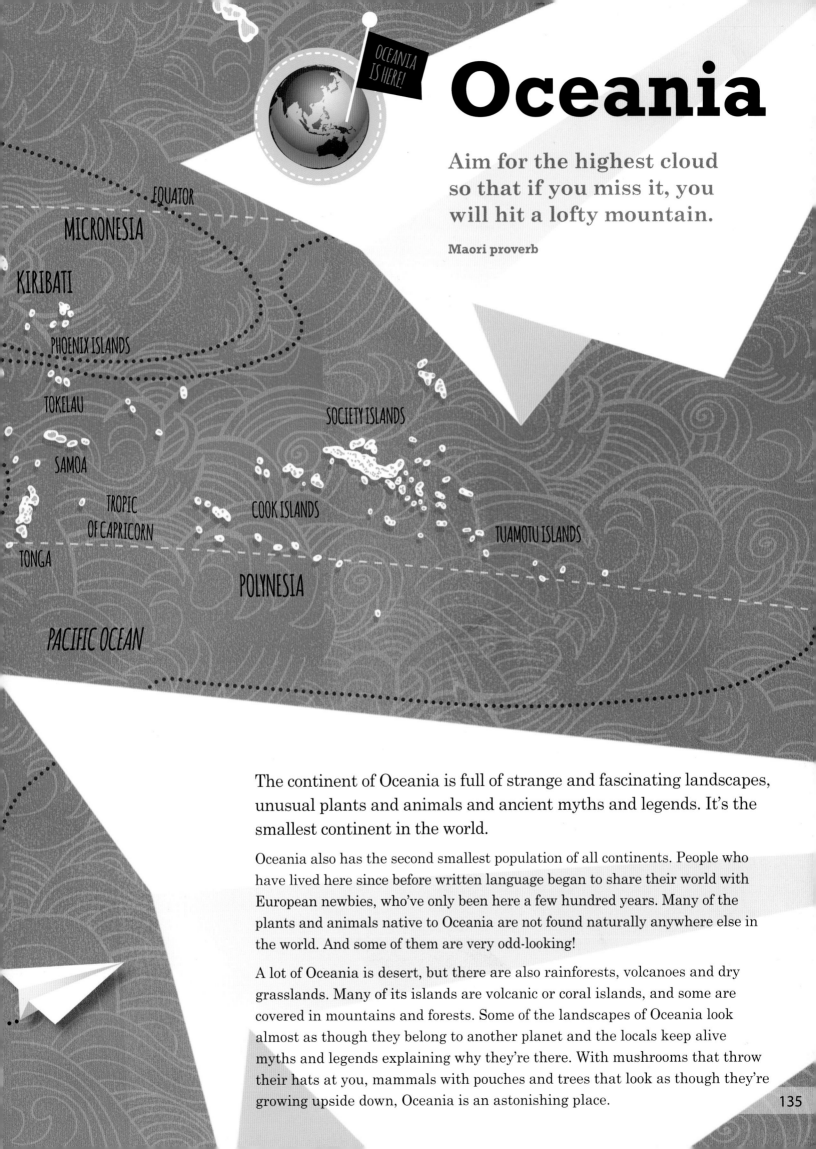

OCEANIA IS HERE!

Oceania

Aim for the highest cloud so that if you miss it, you will hit a lofty mountain.

Maori proverb

EQUATOR

MICRONESIA

KIRIBATI

PHOENIX ISLANDS

TOKELAU

SOCIETY ISLANDS

SAMOA

TROPIC OF CAPRICORN

COOK ISLANDS

TUAMOTU ISLANDS

TONGA

POLYNESIA

PACIFIC OCEAN

The continent of Oceania is full of strange and fascinating landscapes, unusual plants and animals and ancient myths and legends. It's the smallest continent in the world.

Oceania also has the second smallest population of all continents. People who have lived here since before written language began to share their world with European newbies, who've only been here a few hundred years. Many of the plants and animals native to Oceania are not found naturally anywhere else in the world. And some of them are very odd-looking!

A lot of Oceania is desert, but there are also rainforests, volcanoes and dry grasslands. Many of its islands are volcanic or coral islands, and some are covered in mountains and forests. Some of the landscapes of Oceania look almost as though they belong to another planet and the locals keep alive myths and legends explaining why they're there. With mushrooms that throw their hats at you, mammals with pouches and trees that look as though they're growing upside down, Oceania is an astonishing place.

Oceania

Oceania really is an island continent. In fact, it contains about 25,000 of them, spread over an area of ocean larger than the whole of Asia. Most of them are very small, and are the tops of underwater mountains. Only a few thousand are inhabited. Many Pacific Islanders lead traditional lives, fishing and farming for food, trading between islands on their wooden sailing boats, and living in houses thatched with palm fronds. However, there are also more modern industries, such as mining and tourism, which provide employment for large numbers of people.

The length of **Australia's eastern coastline** is **6,853 km** (4,285 mi)

RAINBOW BEE-EATER, PAPUA NEW GUINEA

GREAT BARRIER REEF

FOX GLACIER, NEW ZEALAND

POUAKAI RANGE, EGMONT NATIONAL PARK, NEW ZEALAND

Superlative Oceania

In the southern hemisphere, where Oceania is, June, July and August are the winter months, and December, January and February are the summer

• Oceania includes Australia, New Zealand (although it is not on the same continental shelf), New Guinea, Tasmania and thousands of smaller islands

• The continent straddles the International Date Line, which means that children in some countries will be complaining about having to go to school on Monday, when others practically next door are still asleep after a relaxing Sunday! That's so not fair!

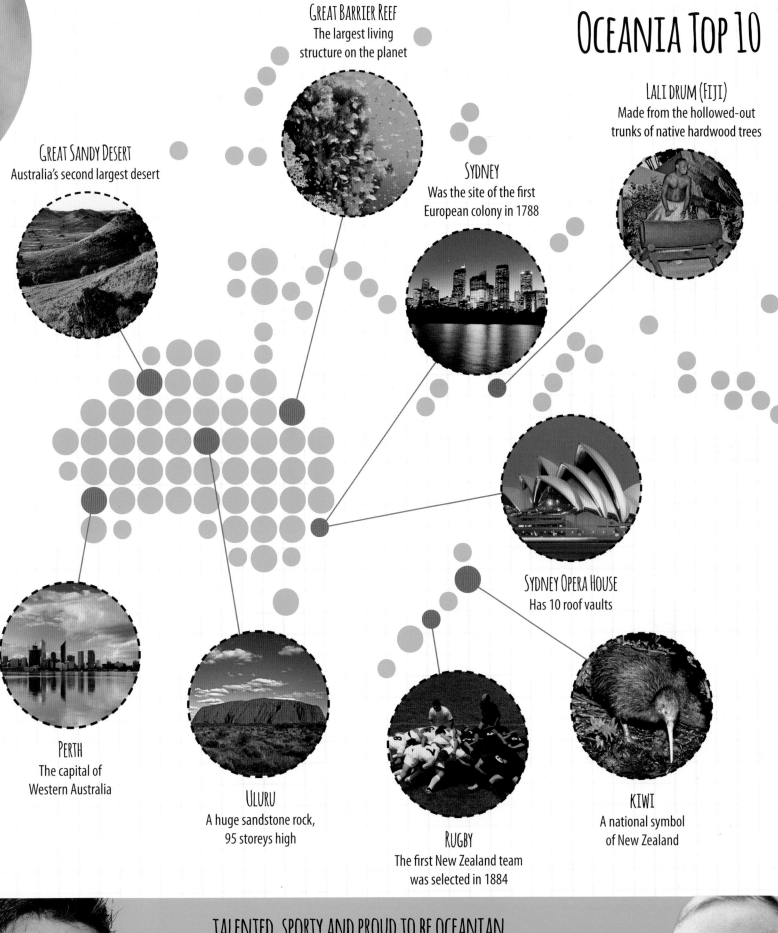

Great Barrier Reef
The largest living
structure on the planet

Lali drum (Fiji)
Made from the hollowed-out
trunks of native hardwood trees

Great Sandy Desert
Australia's second largest desert

Sydney
Was the site of the first
European colony in 1788

Perth
The capital of
Western Australia

Uluru
A huge sandstone rock,
95 storeys high

Rugby
The first New Zealand team
was selected in 1884

Sydney Opera House
Has 10 roof vaults

Kiwi
A national symbol
of New Zealand

TALENTED, SPORTY AND PROUD TO BE OCEANIAN

Oceania has given the world some amazing people and things! Actors **Mia Wasikowska** and **Hugh Jackman (left)** (*Wolverine*) are both Australian, as is director **Baz Luhrmann**. Physicist **Ernest Rutherford (right)** and mountaineer **Edmund Hillary** were both New Zealanders, while **Ricky Ponting**, ex-Australian cricket team and **Mary Donaldson**, Crown Princess of Denmark are Tasmanian, as is **Taz**, the famous cartoon Tasmanian Devil.

Australia and Papua New Guinea

The enormous country of Australia is famous for its unusual wildlife, including marsupials (mammals with pouches), such as kangaroos and wallabies, and the enormous emu, a flightless bird. Its people are famous for being tough and outdoorsy; sports and barbecues on the beach are among Australians' favourite leisure activities! Papua New Guinea is the eastern half of the island of New Guinea, and other smaller islands. Spanish and Portuguese explorers found the islands in the 16th century. The name Papua was chosen by a Portuguese explorer, and is a Malay word for frizzy hair. Later, a Spanish explorer named the island New Guinea, as its people reminded him of those from African Guinea.

THREE SISTERS, BLUE MOUNTAINS

WAVE ROCK, AUSTRALIA

PERTH

GREAT BARRIER REEF SO LARGE IT CAN BE SEEN FROM SPACE

SYDNEY OPERA HOUSE

PAPUA NEW GUINEA TRADITIONAL DRESS

PAPUA NEW GUINEA

PORT MORESBY

DARWIN

CAIRNS

Tanami Desert

at Sandy Desert

AUSTRALIA

Simpson Desert

ibson Desert

Great Victoria Desert

BRISBANE

SYDNEY

CANBERRA

MELBOURNE

SYDNEY SKYLINE

Tasmania

TASMAN SEA

EMU, SECOND LARGEST BIRD IN THE WORLD AFTER THE OSTRICH

PACIFIC OCEAN

ABORIGINAL ART

Traditional arts and crafts in Australia include painting on leaves, wood and bark carving, rock carving, sculpture, ceremonial clothing, jewellery making, basket weaving, cave painting and sand painting. Much of the art tells a story from the ancient myths and legends of the people. If the story is an important or secret one, only an artist whose family 'owns' the story can paint it.

SUPER STATS

Sydney is the **largest city** in Australia, and home to the Sydney Opera House and Sydney Harbour Bridge. The bridge is the widest single span bridge in the world, at a massive **49 m!**
• New Guinea is the second largest island in the world (Greenland is the biggest, unless you count Australia itself, which is officially a continent, not an island) • People have lived here for about **50,000** years and today there are about **850** different languages and cultures
• The **smallest town** in Australia (Cooladdi, Queensland) has a motel, train station and four-star restaurant – but only four people live there!

?

WHO AM I?

I'm a great tree climber and just LOVE eating eucalyptus. Think I'm cute? Watch my bite!

ANSWER: A koala

ABORIGINAL PAINTING

WHO LIVES HERE?

The original Australians are the **Aboriginals**, descendants of **Asian** people. The majority of Australians nowadays, however, are the descendants of Europeans who colonised the land in the **18th century**, or very recent arrivals. Papua New Guinea's people are mostly Melanesian, Papuan, Negrito, Micronesian and Polynesian.

4,509 m (14,793 ft) above sea level, **Mount Wilhelm** is the highest point in Papua New Guinea – and the whole of Oceania!

Papua New Guinea is close to the **equator**, and very warm. Yet on Mount Wilhelm and other high places, it sometimes has **snow!**

SING-SING SENSATION

Around Independence day (16th September), Sing-Sings take place across Papua New Guinea. These festivals are amazing sights with over 100 tribes showing off their music, dance and culture. You can see painted warriors with feathered headdresses dancing to the beat of the Kundu drums, while the mud men of Asaro look very fierce!

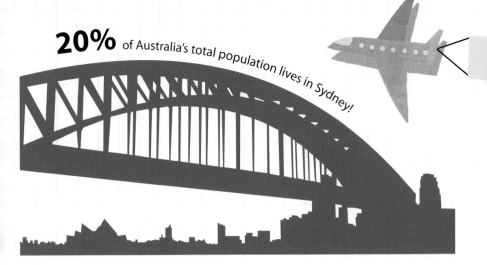

20% of Australia's total population lives in Sydney!

6,500 people speak Auslan, a sign language for deaf people. Here's how to say 'Auslan' in Auslan!

400
Australian Aboriginal languages existed when Europeans first arrived.

Only about **70** are still spoken, and about 40 of those are endangered.

One of the world's only known poisonous birds, the **Hooded Pitohul,** is native to Papua New Guinea.

At **2000 km** (1243 mi), the **Great Barrier Reef** is the longest coral reef in the world.

WHAT TO SAY:
Beaut, beudy, bonzer, ripper (they all mean 'good' in Australian English)

WHAT NOT TO SAY:
Why haven't you got corks on your hat?

FAMOUS FOR:
Tough, outdoor types

INFAMOUS FOR:
Ned Kelly

DANGEROUS ANIMALS:
Loads! Sharks, poisonous spiders and snakes, kangaroos. . .

SPORTS:
Australian rules football, surfing

JOB:
Bush ranger

HOBBY:
Going walkabout

FOOD:
Meat pies, Vegemite

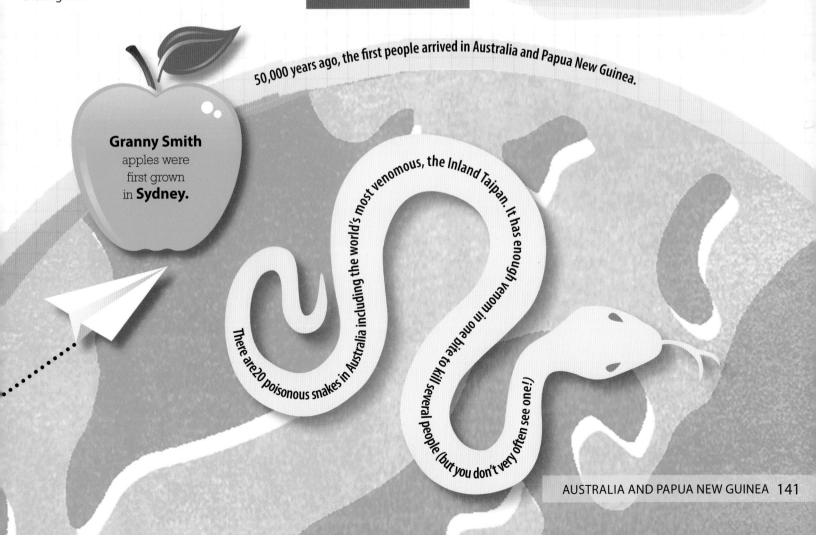

Granny Smith apples were first grown in **Sydney.**

50,000 years ago, the first people arrived in Australia and Papua New Guinea.

There are 20 poisonous snakes in Australia including the world's most venomous, the Inland Taipan. It has enough venom in one bite to kill several people (but you don't very often see one!)

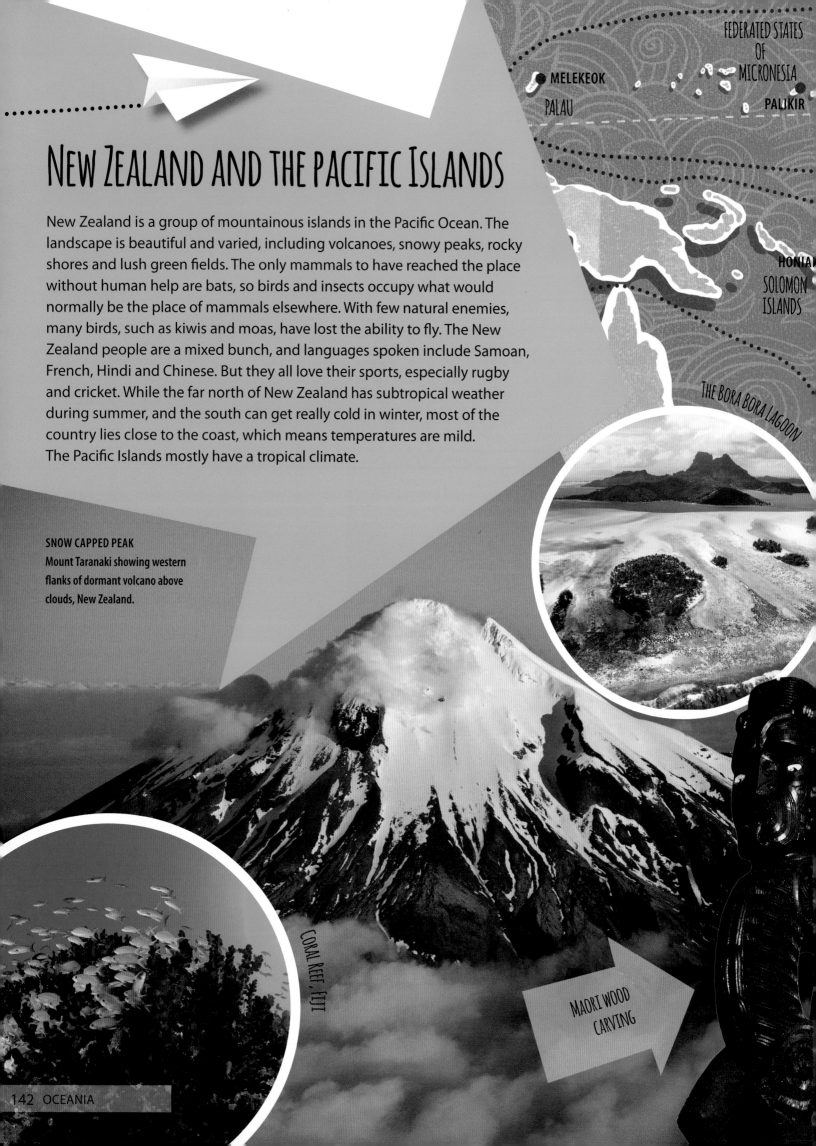

New Zealand and the Pacific Islands

New Zealand is a group of mountainous islands in the Pacific Ocean. The landscape is beautiful and varied, including volcanoes, snowy peaks, rocky shores and lush green fields. The only mammals to have reached the place without human help are bats, so birds and insects occupy what would normally be the place of mammals elsewhere. With few natural enemies, many birds, such as kiwis and moas, have lost the ability to fly. The New Zealand people are a mixed bunch, and languages spoken include Samoan, French, Hindi and Chinese. But they all love their sports, especially rugby and cricket. While the far north of New Zealand has subtropical weather during summer, and the south can get really cold in winter, most of the country lies close to the coast, which means temperatures are mild. The Pacific Islands mostly have a tropical climate.

SNOW CAPPED PEAK
Mount Taranaki showing western flanks of dormant volcano above clouds, New Zealand.

FEDERATED STATES OF MICRONESIA

MELEKEOK

PALAU

PALIKIR

HONIA

SOLOMON ISLANDS

THE BORA BORA LAGOON

CORAL REEF, FIJI

MAORI WOOD CARVING

MARSHALL ISLANDS (US)

MAJURO

MICRONESIA

EQUATOR

MOUNT COOK

SOUTH TARAWA

KIRIBATI

PHOENIX ISLANDS

MELANESIA

APIA

SAMOAN ISLANDS

SOCIETY ISLANDS

VANUATU

PORT VILA

SUVA

PAPE'ETE

FIJI

NUKU'ALOFA

TONGA

COOK ISLANDS

AVARUA

POLYNESIA

TUAMOTU ISLANDS

NOUMÉA

NEW CALEDONIA (FRANCE)

PACIFIC OCEAN

KIWI

NORTH ISLAND

AUCKLAND

NEW ZEALAND

WELLINGTON

CHRISTCHURCH

DUNEDIN

SOUTH ISLAND

EGGSTRAORDINARY

The kiwi is the national symbol of New Zealand. These shy little birds are only about the size of a chicken, but each egg laid by an adult female kiwi can reach up to a quarter of her body weight!

SUPER STATS

The Auckland Sky Tower opened in 1997 and is the tallest free-standing structure in the southern hemisphere, at **328 m (1,076 ft)** • Taveuni Island in Fiji is crossed by the International Date Line, allowing you to put one foot in today and one in yesterday! • Bungee jumping originated on Vanuatu with the inhabitants tying vines around their ankles and thowing themselves off a high tower.

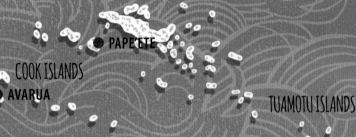

AUCKLAND SKY TOWER, NEW ZEALAND

FIRE JUGGLING IN AUCKLAND

WHO LIVES HERE?

The first people to arrive here were the **Maoris**, in about the 13th century. They named the country **Aotearoa**, which means 'The land of the long white cloud'. Dutch geographers gave it the name **Nieuw Zeeland**, after a region of the Netherlands. After James Cook sailed here in 1769, the British settled it and signed a treaty with more than **500 Maori chiefs**, from tribes throughout the country. It seems the English version of the treaty said that the Queen of England was now to rule the country, and the Maori version said that they were. The debate still rages about who should really be in control! Whatever the answer, New Zealand still attracts plenty of international immigrants, especially from nearby Asian countries.

New Zealand was the first country to give all **women** the right to vote, in **1893**.

The national day in New Zealand is **Waitangi Day**, on 6th February. It's the day the treaty between the British and Maori peoples was signed. Many local communities run events during the day, including kapa haka, the cultural dance of the Maoris.

EXPLORING ROTORUA

Rotorua in the Bay of Plenty region of New Zealand's North Island is one very smelly place! The pong, like rotten eggs, comes from sulphur in its many gushing geysers, hot springs and hissing mud pools. Here you'll find Hell's Gate (Tikitere), the largest hot waterfall in the southern hemisphere. Truly amazing!

THE OCEANIA REAL DEAL!

WHAT TO SAY:
Kia ora ('hello' in Maori language)

FAMOUS FOR:
Ernest Rutherford, the first man to split the atom, in 1919

INFAMOUS FOR:
Bungee jumping (the first commercial bungee jump in the world was a 43 m leap off Kawarau Bridge in Queenstown in 1988)

ANIMALS:
The world's smallest marine dolphin, the Hector's Dolphin, which grows to a maximum of 1.5 m (5 ft) long, is found only in the waters off New Zealand

SNAKES:
None. Not one. Not in New Zealand

FOOD:
Green-lipped mussels, supposed to be good for arthritis sufferers!

FESTIVAL:
Waitangi Day

86% of New Zealand's population live in cities. Once, the vast majority were farmers.

25% of the world's volcanoes are in the Pacific Ring of Fire.

New Zealand has more **golf** courses per person than any other country!

Rugby is the most popular sport in New Zealand, and nearly everyone strongly supports the national team, the **All Blacks.**

23 million years ago New Zealand's islands first appeared, pushed up out of the ocean by volcanic activity.

New Zealanders are often known as **'kiwis',** after the bird.

70 g (2.5 oz)
The giant weta, one of the world's heaviest insects, lives in New Zealand.

New Zealand exports lots of lamb, butter and wine. Tourism and fishing are also important for the economy.

3,754 m (12,316 ft)
Mount Cook is the highest peak in New Zealand. The Maoris call it 'Cloud Piercer'.

2 million tourists a year visit **New Zealand**. It's the country's biggest industry.

Antarctica

...the only place on earth that is still as it should be. May we never tame it.

Andrew Denton

Antarctica's landscape is barren, but beautiful. There are hardly any plants or animals on the land even in summer and, in winter, only male penguins stay there, looking after their eggs while the females go off to feed. Nobody lives here permanently, but there are scientific research bases, and researchers stay from three months to about two years to work. The only other people are visitors to the bases, tourists and explorers.

Antarctica is the only one of the continents to be permanently covered in ice and snow. It's also the windiest continent. Blizzards, like sandstorms in hot deserts, pick up snow and whirl it around so it's almost impossible to see. There are no trees or bushes, only simple plants such as mosses, lichen and algae, and the occasional small flower in summer! Penguins, seals, whales, fish and krill live in the waters around Antarctica.

SOUTH ATLANTIC OCEAN

Antarctic Peninsula

Palmer Land

Ellsworth Land

SOUTH PACIFIC OCEAN

There is so much ice in Antarctica the weight of the icesheets is pushing the land beneath them into the Earth. If all the ice melted the land would rise about 500 m (1,625 ft). But it would take 10,000 years!

Area: 14 million km² (5.5 million sq mi)
Fact: Fifth largest continent
Population in summer: About 4000 scientists
Population in winter: About 1000 scientists

MAP KEY
1 Squid **2** Fur seal **3** Leopard seal **4** Research stations from around the world are dotted all over **5** Antarctic pearlwort **6** Emperor penguin **7** Elephant seal **8** McMurdo research station **9** Minke whale **10** The ceremonial South Pole

WEDDELL
SEA

Queen Maud Land

Enderby Land

Kemp
Land

3

4

Ronne
Ice Shelf

Princess Elizabeth
Land

2

Polar Plateau

East Antarctica

Kaiser Wilhelm II
Land

West Antarctica

10

Transantarctic Ridge

6

Queen Mary Land

4

Ross
Ice Shelf

Marie Byrd Land

Wilkes Land

8

Mount
Erebus

7

Victoria Land

INDIAN
OCEAN

9

Antarctica

Scientists working at the research bases here carry out quite a range of work! Studies include how the human body and mind adapt to cold conditions. Researchers also drill ice cores to try to work out the history of the continent, and study penguins, fish, global warming, glaciology, astronomy and climatology. And it's a great spot to search for meteorites – the dark rocks stand out against the snow!

GERMAN ANTARCTIC RESEARCH BASE

Antarctica was the last of the continents to be discovered – probably in **1820,** when American seal hunter John Davis said he landed on it.

-89.6ºC (-129.27ºF) The lowest temperature ever recorded, at the Russian Vostok Station in Antarctica.

HISTORIC EXPLORERS Norwegian Roald Amundsen and his team were the first explorers to reach the South Pole, in 1911.

50 mm (2 in) of precipitation per year. Nearly all of it falls as snow.

Sunrise at the South Pole is on about 21st of September every year. Sunset is on about 21st of March the following year.

POLAR OPPOSITES
While Antarctica is a continent, or land mass, its opposite in the north, the Arctic, is a huge frozen ocean surrounded by land belonging to many different nations. For much of the year, the ice is so thick that animals and people can walk on it just as if it were land.

THE EMPEROR PENGUIN, THE BIGGEST IN THE WORLD AT OVER A METRE (3 FT) TALL, LIVES ON ANTARCTICA.

DEEP FREEZE

The ice of Antarctica is not a solid sheet. Glaciers are constantly on the move, breaking the ice and forming huge crevasses (cracks). Icebergs form along the coast, where ice shelves and glaciers break off and fall into the sea.

87% of all the **ice** on the planet is found in **Antarctica.**

ELEPHANT SEAL

WHAT TO WEAR

Because of the cold and wind, people going outside in the Antarctic usually wear several layers of clothing – a soft, breathable one next to the skin that will wick away perspiration when they're working, then two or three insulating layers they can take off if they get really warm. Two pairs of socks and gloves are also pretty crucial!

SUPER STATS

11,000km² (4,247 sq mi) above water (and ten times as big below), the largest iceberg recorded broke off from the Ross Ice Shelf in 2000 ● On Deception Island, off the Antarctic Peninsula, people bathe in warm water heated by a volcano while surrounded by ice! ● Lake Vostok, a liquid lake deep below the surface of Antarctica, may contain signs of life. Scientists are busy drilling down about **4,000 m** (13,000 ft) to reach it and find out ● Mount Erebus is Antarctica's highest mountain and the world's southernmost active volcano at **3,794 m** (12,447 ft).

In 1961 the **Antarctic Treaty** was agreed, controlling human activity in the region. Countries that have signed up to the treaty are free to carry out **scientific experiments**, but must **conserve** the environment.

WHO OR WHAT AM I?

I come to Antarctica to breed. I have a 3 m (10 ft) wing span and I can live for over 60 years. Also, I'm famous for protecting sailors.

ANSWER: An albatross

149

World quiz

1. In which country is the **Great Pyramid of Giza** located?

....

2. What is the **largest land mammal** on the planet?

a) Elephant

b) Blue whale

c) Nile crocodile

3. What is the **largest mammal** on the planet?

a) Elephant

b) Blue whale

c) Koala

4. What are the colours of the **French flag**?

....

5. **Aboriginal Australians** believe that there was a time when animal, plant and human ancestors created the world and everything it contains. What is this time called?

....

6. In Ethiopia, **how many months** are there in a year?

....

7. To the **east and west of Africa** are two oceans. Which two are they?

....

8. What is the **largest hot desert** in the world, and in which continent is it found?

....

9. What is the capital of **Egypt**?

a) Nairobi

b) Cayenne

c) Cairo

10. What are the colours of the **Chadian flag**?

....

11. What is the easternmost point of the **African continent** called?

a) Leg of Africa

b) Toe of Africa

c) Horn of Africa

12. Which is the **tallest** animal in the world?

a) Ostrich

b) Giraffe

c) Emu

13. What is the **largest country** in Africa?

a) Republic of Congo

b) Algeria

c) Rwanda

14. What was the **lowest temperature** ever recorded?

a) -45.2°C (-49.35°F)

b) -89.6°C (-129.27°F)

c) -137.7°C (-215.85°F)

15. How many different kinds of **ants** are there?

a) More than 14,000
b) Fewer than 5,000
c) More than 100,000

16. **Worker ants** are all female. **True or false**?

....

17. The **Yangzi** is the longest river in the world. **True or false**?

....

18. **Tropical rainforests** are cold and wet. **True or false**?

....

19. **Indonesian people** grow their staple food, rice, on terraces. **True or false**?

....

20. What are the colours of the **Italian flag**?

....

21. Our planet, **Earth**, is the closest planet to our Sun. **True or false**?

....

22. What is the interior region of **Australia** called?

a) The inside
b) The outdoors
c) The outback

23. How many **saunas** are there in Finland?

a) 20,000
b) 200,000
c) 2 million

24. What is the capital of **Australia**?

....

25. In which **country** are the states of Queensland and Victoria?

....

26. The **Aztecs** were an ancient people in which modern country?

....

27. What is a **bridge** that carries water called?

....

28. **Camels and llamas** are closely related. What does a camel have that a llama does not?

....

29. **Canada** is the second largest country in the world. **True or false**?

....

30. The **Caribbean** islands are also sometimes called the West Indies. **True or false**?

....

31. **Climate** is short-term, weather is long-term. **True or false**?

....

32. Which is the **largest** continent?

....

33. The **tectonic plates** carrying the continents move at about the rate of 1.5 cm (1 in) per year. **True or false**?

....

34. Where do most **earthquakes** happen?
a) Close to the edges of the tectonic plates
b) In hot countries
c) In cool countries

35. How many different **kinds of elephant** are there?

....

36. **Catfish** are covered in large scales. **True or false**?

....

37. What can **flying squirrels** do?
a) Fly
b) Jump
c) Glide

38. How many **legs** do insects have?
a) 8
b) 12
c) 6

39. What shape is an **Australian football** field?

....

40. What is the capital of **Germany**?

....

41. Approximately what percentage of an **iceberg** is under water?

....

42. What continent does the **rhea** inhabit?

....

43. What is the capital of **India**?

....

44. In which country was **Lego** first made?

....

45. How many kinds of **camel** are there?

....

46. How many humps does a **dromedary camel** have?

....

47. What is the capital of **Luxembourg**?

....

48. Which island of **New Zealand** contains its capital, Wellington?

....

49. Which **ocean** is the largest and deepest?

....

50. What is the main cause of **ocean tides**?

....

51. What is the world's largest **invertebrate**?

....

52. Where did the first **Olympic games** take place?

a) Italy
b) France
c) Greece

53. What is the world's **biggest** living bird?

a) The ostrich
b) The emu
c) The cassowary

54. What are the colours of the **Jamaican flag**?

....

55. Ostriches and emus can neither fly nor swim. **True or false**?

....

56. What colour are a **cassowary's eggs**?

....

57. About how many **Pacific islands** are there?

a) 5000
b) 15,000
c) 25,000

58. Which country is home to **pizza, pasta** and *gelato*?

a) Italy
b) Burundi
c) Australia

59. What **sweet treat** is made from the cacao bean?

....

60. What is the **largest lizard** in the world?

....

61. In which country would you find the **Taj Mahal**?

....

62. Which country is the world's largest exporter of **false teeth**?

....

63. Which was the **last continent** to be discovered?

....

64. How many tonnes was the **heaviest** white rhino ever to be recorded?

a) 0.5

b) 2

c) 4.5

65. Which country owns the **Faroe Islands**?

....

66. Which two oceans does the **Panama Canal** connect?

....

67. What do **sharks and rays** have where most other fish have bones?

a) Cartilage

b) Muscle

c) Teeth

68. Of which country was **Robert Bruce** once king?

a) Australia

b) Scotland

c) Ireland

69. Which country is famous for **flamenco music** and dance?

....

70. What is the **biggest fish** in the sea?

....

71. Which is the **longest river** in South America?

a) The Andes

b) The Aymara

c) The Amazon

72. In which continent would you find the cities of **Caracas, Bogotà and Brasilia**?

a) Europe

b) South America

c) North America

73. In which country is **Rio de Janeiro**?

a) Brazil

b) Spain

c) Bolivia

74. In which country is the island of **Java**?

....

75. Where can you find the beautiful Moorish **Alhambra palace**?

a) North Africa

b) South Africa

c) Spain

76. How many legs does a **spider** have?

....

77. What are the colours of the **Japanese flag**?

....

78. How many points are there on the **Statue of Liberty's crown**?

a) 6

b) 7

c) 8

79. What was the last state to join the **United States of America**?

. . . .

80. How many **states** are there in the USA?

a) 10

b) 50

c) 100

81. From which **three countries** did the Vikings originate?

. . . .

82. There are fewer than **200 active volcanoes** in the world. **True or false**?

. . . .

ANSWERS

19) True

18) False. Tropical rainforests are hot and wet

17) False. The longest river is the Nile, in Africa, at 6,693 km (4,159 mi)

16) True

15) A

14) B

13) B

12) B

11) C

10) Blue, yellow and red

9) C

8) The Sahara, in Africa, at over 9.4 million km² (3.3 million sq mi)

7) The Atlantic Ocean and the Indian Ocean

6) 13

5) Dreamtime

4) Red, white and blue

3) B

2) A

1) Egypt

20) Green, white and red

21) False. Mercury is the closest planet to our Sun. Earth is third closest

22) C

23) C

24) Canberra

25) Australia

26) Mexico

27) An aqueduct

28) A hump (or two)

29) True

30) True

31) False. Weather is short-term, and climate is long-term

32) Asia

33) True

34) A

35) Two; the African and the Asian elephant

36) False. Catfish are smooth-skinned.

37) C

38) C

39) Oval

40) Berlin

41) 90

42) South America

43) New Delhi

44) Denmark

45) Two; dromedary and Bactrian

46) One

47) Luxembourg

48) North Island

49) The Pacific

50) The gravity of the moon

51) The giant squid

52) C

53) A

54) Green, gold and black

55) False. They can swim, but they can't fly

56) Green

57) C

58) A

59) Chocolate

60) The Komodo dragon

61) India

62) Liechtenstein

63) Antarctica

64) C

65) Denmark

66) The Pacific Ocean and the Atlantic Ocean

67) A

68) B

69) Spain

70) The whale shark

71) C

72) B

73) A

74) Indonesia

75) C

76) Eight

77) White and red

78) B

79) Hawaii

80) B

81) Norway, Sweden and Denmark

82) False. There are more than 1500 potentially active volcanoes, and at least 500 of these have erupted in recorded history

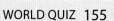

Index map

If you want to find a
particular place shown
on this map, you can
look for it in the index
on pages 158–159. Its
grid reference (a letter
followed by a number,
like 'H5') will help you
pinpoint exactly where
on this map it is located.

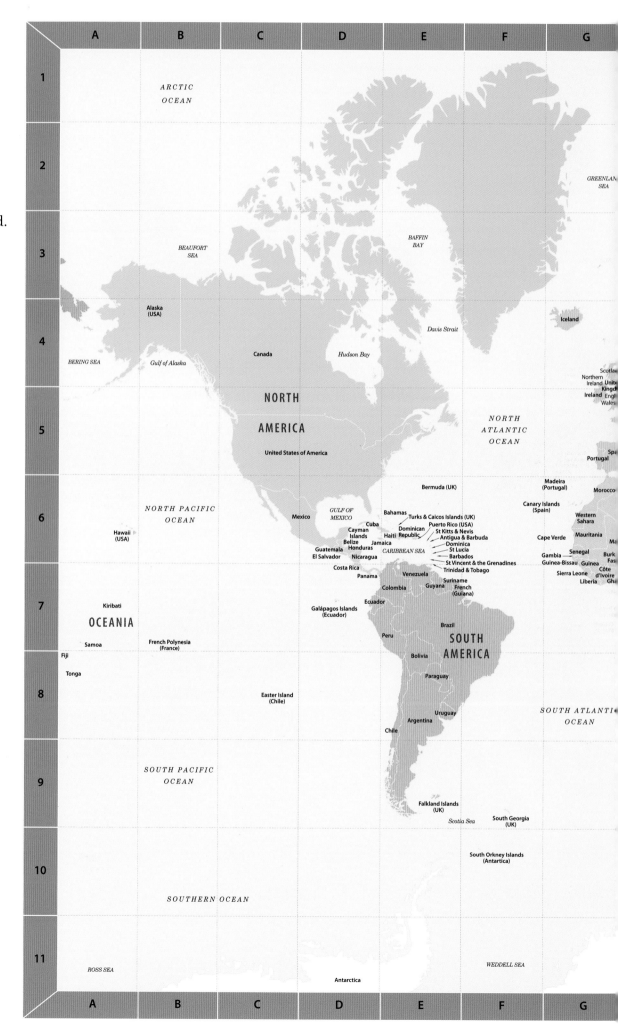

1
2
3
4
5
6
7
8
9
10
11

ARCTIC OCEAN

ARCTIC OCEAN

Svalbard (Norway)

BARENTS SEA

LAPTEV SEA

KARA SEA

NORWEGIAN SEA

Sweden

Finland

Norway

Baltic Sea

Kaliningrad (Russia)

Estonia

Latvia

Lithuania

North Sea

Denmark

EUROPE

Russian Federation

ASIA

Sea of Okhotsk

Bering Sea

Netherlands

Germany

Belgium

Czech Republic

Luxembourg

France

Switzerland

Austria

Slovenia

Slovakia

Hungary

Poland

Belarus

Ukraine

Moldova

Romania

Kazakhstan

Mongolia

Liechtenstein

Andorra

Croatia

Italy

Serbia

Kosovo

Bulgaria

Black Sea

Georgia

Caspian Sea

Uzbekistan

Kyrgyzstan

Monaco

San Marino

Vatican City

Bosnia & Hercegovina

Macedonia

Montenegro

Greece

Armenia

Azerbaijan

Turkmenistan

Tajikistan

North Korea

Sea of Japan

South Korea

Japan

Malta

Albania

Turkey

China

Tunisia

Mediterranean Sea

Cyprus

Lebanon

Syria

Iraq

Iran

Afghanistan

Israel & the Palestinian Territories

Jordan

Kuwait

Pakistan

Nepal

Bhutan

NORTH PACIFIC OCEAN

Algeria

Libya

Egypt

Bahrain

Qatar

United Arab Emirates

India

Bangladesh

Myanmar (Burma)

Laos

Taiwan

PHILIPPINE SEA

Northern Mariana Islands (USA)

AFRICA

Saudi Arabia

Oman

Nepal

South China Sea

Guam (USA)

Niger

Chad

Sudan

Eritrea

Yemen

Arabian Sea

Bay of Bengal

Thailand

Cambodia

Vietnam

Philippines

Red Sea

Djibouti

Andaman Sea

Benin

Togo

Nigeria

Central African Republic

South Sudan

Ethiopia

Somaliland

Sri Lanka

Brunei

Malaysia

Marshall Islands

Cameroon

Equatorial Guinea

Uganda

Somalia

Maldives

Singapore

Indonesia

Palau

Federated States of Micronesia

Gulf of Guinea

Gabon

Congo

Democratic Republic of the Congo

Rwanda

Burundi

Kenya

Tanzania

Nauru

Kiribati

São Tomé & Principe

Seychelles

Papua New Guinea

Solomon Islands

Tuvalu

Cabinda (Angola)

Comoros

Mayotte (France)

Timor-Leste

Vanuatu

Angola

Malawi

Zambia

Mozambique

CORAL SEA

Fiji

Namibia

Zimbabwe

Madagascar

Mauritius

New Caledonia (France)

Botswana

Mozambique Channel

Réunion (France)

Australia

SOUTH PACIFIC OCEAN

Swaziland

South Africa

Lesotho

INDIAN OCEAN

OCEANIA

Great Australian Bight

New Zealand

French Southern & Antarctic Islands (France)

TASMAN SEA

Prince Edward Island (South Africa)

Heard Island & McDonald Island (Australia)

SOUTHERN OCEAN

SOUTHERN OCEAN

Antarctica

Index

A

Afghanistan **86–89, 94–97** K6
Africa **114–133**
Alaska (USA) B4
Albania **58-61, 74-77** H5
Algeria **114–117, 118–121** H6
Andaman Sea L7
Andorra **58–61, 70–73** H5
Angola **114–117, 130–133** H7
Antarctica **146–149** D11–K11
Antigua & Barbuda E6
Arabian Sea K6
Arctic Ocean B1–N1
Arctic **148**
Argentina **46–47, 54–57** E8
Armenia **86–89, 110–113** J5
Asia **86–113**
Australia **134–141** N8
Austria **58–61, 66–69** H5
Azerbaijan **86–89, 110–113** J5

B

Baffin Bay E3
Bahamas **26–27, 42–43** E6
Bahrain **86–87, 110–111** J6
Baltic Sea H4
Bangladesh **86–87, 102–105** L6
Barbados E6
Barents Sea J2
Bay of Bengal L6
Beaufort Sea B3
Belarus **58–61, 82–85** J5
Belgium **58–61, 66–69** H5
Belize **42–45** D6
Benin **114–117, 126–129** H7
Bering Sea A4
Bering Sea O4
Bermuda (UK) **26–27** E6
Bhutan **86–89, 102–105** L6
Black Sea J5
Bolivia **46–51** E8
Bosnia & Herzegovina **58–61, 74–77** H5
Botswana **114–117, 130–133** H8
Brazil **46–53** E7
Brunei **86–89, 106–109** M7
Bulgaria **58–61, 76–81** H5
Burkina Faso **114–117, 126–129** G6
Burundi **114–117, 122–125** J7

C

Cambodia **86–89, 106–109** L6
Cameroon **114–117, 126–129** H7
Canada **26–33** C4
Canary Islands (Spain) F6
Cape Verde F6
Caribbean Islands **42–45** E6
Caribbean Sea E6
Cayman Islands D6

Central African Republic **114–117, 126–129** H7
Central America **42–45**
Central and Western Africa **114–117, 126–129**
Central Asia **86–89, 94–97**
Central Europe **58–61, 78–81**
Chad **114–117, 118–121** H6
Chile **46–47, 54–57** E8
China **86–89, 98–101** L5
Colombia **46–51** E7
Comoros **114–117, 122–125** J7
Congo (Republic of) **114–117, 126–129** H7
Coral Sea O8
Costa Rica **42–45** D7
Côte d'Ivoire **114–117, 126–129** G7
Croatia **58–61, 74–77** H5
Cuba **42–43** D6
Cyprus **58–61, 74–77** J6
Czech Republic **58–61, 76–81** H5

D

Davis Strait E4
Democratic Republic of Congo
   114–117,126–129 H7
Denmark **58–61, 62–65** H4
Djibouti **114–117, 122–125** J6
Dominica **26–29, 42–45** E6
Dominican Republic **26–29, 42–45** E6

E

East Timor *see* Timor-Leste
Easter Island (Chile) **46–49, 54–57** C8
Eastern Africa **114–117, 122–125**
Eastern Asia **86–89, 98–101**
Eastern Europe **57–61, 82–85**
Eastern United States **26–29, 34–37**
Ecuador **46–51** D7
Egypt **114–117, 118–121** J6
El Salvador **26–29, 42–45** D6
England **58–61, 66–69** G5
Equatorial Guinea **114–117, 126–129** H7
Eritrea **114–117, 122–125** J6
Estonia **58–61, 62–65** H4
Ethiopia **114–117, 122–125** J7
Europe **58–85**

F

Falkland Islands (UK) **46–47, 54–57** E9
Faroe Islands (Denmark) **58–61, 62–65** H4
Fiji **58–65** A8, O8
Finland **58–65** H4
France **58–61, 66–69** G5
French Guiana **46–53** E7
French Polynesia (France) **134–137, 142–145** B7
French Southern & Antarctic Islands (France) K9

G

Gabon **114–117, 126–129** H7
Galápagos Islands (Ecuador) **46–53** D7
Gambia **114–117, 126–129** G6
Georgia **58–61, 82–85** J5
Germany **58–61, 66–69** H5
Ghana **114–117, 126–129** G7
Great Australian Bight M8
Greece **58–61, 74–77** H5
Greenland (Denmark) **26–27** F2
Greenland Sea G2
Guam (USA) N6
Guatemala **42–45** D6
Guinea **114–117, 126–129** G7
Guinea-Bissau **114–117, 126–129** G6
Gulf of Alaska B4
Gulf of Guinea G7
Gulf of Mexico D6
Guyana **50–53** E7

H

Haiti **E6**
Hawaii (USA) **26–29, 38–41** A6
Heard Island & McDonald Island (Australia) K9
Honduras **42–45** D6
Hudson Bay D4
Hungary **58–61, 76–81** H5

I

Iceland **58–61, 62–65** G4
India **86–89, 102–105** L6
Indian Ocean L8
Indonesia **86–89, 106–109** M7
Iran **86–89, 110–113** K6
Iraq **86–89, 110–113** J6
Ireland *see* Republic of Ireland
Islas Malvinas *see* Falkland Islands
Israel & the Palestinian Territories
   86–89, 110–113 J6
Italy **58–61, 74–77** H5

J

Jamaica **26–29, 42–45** D6
Japan **86–89, 98–101** N5
Jordan **86–89, 110–113** J6

K

Kara Sea L2
Kazakhstan **86–89, 94–97** K5
Kenya **114–117, 122–125** J7
Kiribati A7, O7
Kosovo **58–61, 74–77** H5
Kuwait **86–89, 110–113** J6
Kyrgyzstan **86–89, 94–97** K5

L

Laos **86–89, 106–109** L6
Laptev Sea M2
Latvia **58–61, 62–65** H4
Lebanon J6
Lesotho **114–117, 130–133** J8
Liberia **114–117, 126–129** G7
Libya **114–121** H6
Liechtenstein **58–61, 66–69** H5
Lithuania **58–61, 62–65** H4
Luxembourg **58–61, 66–69** H5

M

Macedonia **58–61, 74–77** H5
Madagascar **114–117, 130–133** J8
Madeira (Portugal) F6
Malawi **114–117, 130–133** J7
Malaysia **86–89, 106–109** M7
Maldives **86–89, 102–105** K7
Mali **114–117, 118–121** G6
Malta **58–61, 74–77** H5
Marshall Islands O7
Mauritania **114–117, 118–121** G6
Mauritius **114–117, 130–133** K8
Mayotte (France) **114–117, 122–125** J7
Mediterranean Sea H6
Melanesia **134–137, 142–145**
Mexico **26–29, 42–45** C6
Micronesia **134–137, 142–145**
Moldova **58–61, 82–85** J5
Monaco **58–61, 74–77** H5
Mongolia **86–89, 98–101** L5
Montenegro **58–61, 74–77** H5
Morocco **114–117, 118–121** G6
Mozambique Channel J8
Mozambique **114–117, 130–133** J7
Myanmar (Burma) **86–89, 102–105** L6

N

Namibia **114–117, 130–133** H8
Nauru O7
Nepal **86–89, 102–105** L6
Netherlands **58–61, 66–69** H5
New Caledonia (France) O8
New Zealand **134–137, 142–145** O8
Nicaragua **26–29, 42–45** D6
Niger **114–117, 118–121** H6
Nigeria **114–117, 126–129** H7
North America **26–41**
North Atlantic Ocean F5
North Korea **86–89, 98–101** M5
North Pacific Ocean B6–O6
North Sea H4
Northern Africa **114–117, 118–121**
Northern Europe **58–65**
Northern Ireland F4
Northern Mariana Islands (USA) N6

Northern South America **46–53**
Northwest Europe **58–61, 66–69**
Norway **58–61, 62–65** H4
Norwegian Sea H3

O

Oceania **134–144**
Oman **86–89, 110–113** K6

P

Pacific Islands **134–137, 142–145** O7
Pakistan **86–89, 102–105** K6
Palau N7
Panama **26–29, 42–45** D7
Papua New Guinea **134–141** N7
Paraguay **46–47, 54–57** E8
Peru **46–51** E7
Philippine Sea N6
Philippines **86–89, 106–109** M6
Poland **58–61, 76–81** H5
Polynesia **134–137, 142–145**
Portugal **58–61, 70–73** G5
Prince Edward Island (South Africa) J9
Puerto Rico (USA) **26–29, 42–45** E6

Q

Qatar **86–89, 110–113** J6

R

Red Sea J6
Republic of Congo **114–117, 126–129** H7
Republic of Ireland **58–61, 66–69** G5
Réunion (France) **114–117, 130–133** J8
Romania **58–61, 78–81** H5
Ross Sea A11
Russia **58–61, 82–85, 86–89, 90–93** L4
Rwanda **114–117, 122–125** J7

S

Samoa A7
San Marino **58–61, 74–77** H5
São Tomé & Principe **114–117, 126–129** H7
Saudi Arabia **86–89, 110–113** J6
Scotia Sea E9
Scotland **58–61, 66–69** G4
Sea of Japan N5
Sea of Okhotsk N4
Senegal **114–117, 126–129** G6
Serbia **58–61, 74–77** H5
Seychelles **114–117, 122–125** K7
Sierra Leone **114–117, 126–129** G7
Singapore **86–89, 106–109** M7
Slovakia **58–61, 76–81** H5
Slovenia **58–61, 74–77** H5
Solomon Islands O7
Somalia **114–115, 122–123** J7
Somaliland **114–115, 122–123** J7
South Africa **114–117, 130–133** H8
South America **46–57**
South Atlantic Ocean G8
South China Sea M6
South Georgia (UK) **46–47, 54–57** F9
South Korea **86–89, 98–101** M6
South Orkney Islands (Antarctica) F10
South Pacific Ocean B9
South Sudan **114–117, 122–125** J7

Southeast Asia **86–89, 106–109**
Southeast Europe **58–61, 74–77**
Southern Africa **114–117, 130–133**
Southern Asia **86–89, 102–105**
Southern Ocean B10–O10
Southern South America **46–49, 54–57**
Southwest Asia **86–89, 110–113**
Southwest Europe **58–61, 70–73**
Spain **58–61, 70–73** G5
Sri Lanka **86–89, 102–105** L7
St Kitts & Nevis E6
St Lucia E6
St Vincent and the Grenadines E7
Sudan **114–117, 118–121** J6
Suriname **46–53** E7
Svalbard (Norway) H2
Swaziland **114–117, 130–133** J8
Sweden **58–61, 62–65** H4
Switzerland **58–61, 66–69** H5
Syria **86–89, 110–113** J6

T

Taiwan **86–89, 98–101** M6
Tajikistan **86–89, 94–97** K5
Tanzania **114–117, 122–125** J7
Tasman Sea O9
Thailand **86–89, 106–109** L6
Timor-Leste **86–89, 106–109** M7
Togo **114–117, 126–129** G7
Tonga A8
Trinidad & Tobago E7
Tunisia **114–117, 118–121** H6
Turkey **58–61, 82–85, 86–89, 110–113** J5
Turkmenistan **86–89, 94–97** K5
Turks & Caicos Islands (UK) E6
Tuvalu O7

U

Uganda **114–117, 122–125** J7
Ukraine **58–61, 82–85** J5
United Arab Emirates **86–89, 110–113** K6
United Kingdom **58–61, 66–69** G4
United States of America **26–29, 34–41** C5
Uruguay **46–47, 54–57** E8
Uzbekistan **86–89, 94–97** K5

V

Vanuatu **O7**
Vatican City **58–61, 74–77** H5
Venezuela **46–51** E7
Vietnam **86–89, 106–109** M7

W

Wales **58–61, 66–69** G5
Weddell Sea F11
Western Sahara **114–121** G6
Western United States **26–29, 38–41**

Y

Yemen **86–89, 110–113** J6

Z

Zambia **114–117, 130–133** H7
Zimbabwe **114–117, 130–133** J8

Acknowledgements

Published in October 2014 by Lonely Planet Publications Pty Ltd

ABN 36 005 607 983
www.lonelyplanet.com
ISBN 978 1 74360 389 5
© Lonely Planet 2014
© Photographs as indicated 2014
Printed in Singapore   10 9 8 7 6 5 4 3

Publishing Director	Piers Pickard
Publisher	Mina Patria
Art Director	Beverley Speight
Project Manager	Jessica Cole
Authors	Deborah Murrell, Philip Steele
Illustrator	Alice Lickens
Layout Designers	Kevin Knight, Lisa McCormick
Image Researcher	Shweta Andrews
Cartography	Wayne Murphy, Anita Banh, Corey Hutchinson
Pre-press production	Tag Response
Print production	Larissa Frost

Thanks to Joe Bindloss, Jo Cooke, Laura Crawford, Megan Eaves, Helen Elfer, Lisa Eyre, Jen Feroze, Sue Grabham, Gemma Graham, Alex Howard, Nigel Longuet, Andy Mansfield, Kate Morgan, MaSovaida Morgan, Matt Phillips, Dee Pilgrim, Sarah Reid, James Smart, Dan Tucker, Anna Tyler, Branislava Vladisavljevic, Tasmin Waby, Dora Whitaker, Clifton Wilkinson

PHOTO CREDITS

KEY: t -top, tc-top centre, tr-top right, tl-top left, tcr- top centre right, tcl- top centre left, c-centre, cr-centre right, cl-centre left, ca-centre above, cb-centre below, cla-centre left above, cra-centre right above, clb- centre left below, crb – centre right below, b-bottom, bc-bottom centre, br-bottom right, bl-bottom left, bg-background.

Corbis: 11tc, 29bl, 63t, 80c, 91br, 96, 102 – 103c, 102bg, 127br, 139tr, 142bg, 142bl, 143cb, 148tr, 148cr, 149cr.

Getty images: 11cl, 11crb, 18b, 19t, 19c, 28bg, 28t, 29tc, 29tr, 29cra, 29crb, 29cb, 29clb, 29cl, 29tl, 29tcl, 30t, 40, 42cr, 43tr, 43c, 43cl, 44, 48bg, 48tr, 48cra, 48c, 48clb, 49tr, 49cr, 49crb, 49c, 49cb, 49clb, 49cl, 49cla, 49tl, 49bl, 50cr, 50bg, 51tr, 51crb, 52, 54bg, 54bl, 55cl, 56, 60bg, 60tr, 60cra, 60c, 60bc, 61tc, 61tr, 61cr, 61crb, 61cb, 61clb, 61cl, 61cla, 61tl, 62t, 62cr, 62bg, 62bl, 63br, 64, 64cb, 66tr, 66cr, 66crb, 66bg, 66bl, 67crb, 68, 70bl, 70 – 71bg, 70 – 71b, 71tr, 71cr, 71cl, 72, 74tr, 74cr, 74bg, 75tr, 75br, 75bc, 76, 76c, 78tr, 78cr, 78 – 79bg, 78bl, 79br, 80, 81clb, 82tr, 82cr, 82bg, 83tr, 83cr, 83bc, 84, 88bg, 88tc, 88crb, 88br, 89tc, 89tr, 89cra, 89cr, 89crb, 89cb, 89clb, 89cl, 89tl, 89bl, 90cr, 90bg, 91c, 92, 94tr, 94cr, 94bg, 94bl, 95tr, 95cr, 98tr, 98cr, 98bg, 98bl, 99cr, 99bc, 100, 102tr, 103tr, 103br, 104, 106tl, 106cl, 107tl, 108, 110tr, 110bl, 111tr, 111bc, 112, 116bg, 116br, 118tr, 118cr, 118br, 118bc, 119cl, 119br, 120, 122cr, 122bg, 122cl, 123cra, 124, 126cr, 126, 127tr, 127cl, 128, 130cr, 130bl, 131crb, 131c, 132, 136bg, 136tr, 136cra, 136br, 137tc, 137tr, 137ca, 137cra, 137crb, 137cb, 137clb, 137cl, 137tl, 138tr, 138cr, 138br, 138bg, 139br, 140, 142cr, 143bc, 143br, 144, 148 – 149bg, 149cl.

Indiapicture: 29br, 49tc, 49br, 61br, 61bl, 82bl, 84c, 88ca, 89br, 102bl, 117bl, 117br, 137br, 137bl.

MIX
Paper from responsible sources
FSC™ C021741

iStock: 6c, 8cr, 13tl, 13tr, 13cra, 13cb, 13clb, 15br, 16bcl, 16bcr, 19b, 20b, 28cr, 28b, 28clb, 30bg, 30bl, 30crb, 31crb, 32, 34cla, 34crb, 34bg, 35tr, 35br, 35bc, 36, 37c, 37cr, 38tr, 38cr, 38bg, 39tc, 39cl, 39b, 42bg, 43cr, 43b, 48bl, 50tr, 50bl, 54tr, 54cr, 54br, 74 – 75b, 90c, 105cl, 110bg, 116tr, 116ca, 116cr, 117tc, 117tr, 117cra, 117cr, 117crb, 117clb, 117cl, 117cla, 117tl, 118bg, 118bl, 119c, 122tr, 123br, 126bl, 130bg, 131tc, 136cr, 139c, 139clb, 142br, 143tr, 143crb, 152bc, 154bc.

National Aeronautics and Space Administration (NASA): 37cb.

Shutterstock: 33tl, 65cla, 70tr, 70tr, 93t, 110cr.

LONELY PLANET OFFICES

AUSTRALIA
90 Maribyrnong St, Footscray, Victoria, 3011, Australia
Phone 03 8379 8000 Email talk2us@lonelyplanet.com.au

USA
150 Linden St, Oakland, CA 94607
Phone 510 250 6400 Email info@lonelyplanet.com

UNITED KINGDOM
240 Blackfriars Road, London SE1 8NW
Phone 0203 771 5100 Email go@lonelyplanet.co.uk

POTTED

ANDY STURGEON

PHOTOGRAPHY BY THOMAS STEWART
STYLING BY LYNDSAY MILNE

conran
OCTOPUS

Thanks to Tom and Lyndsay, Muna and Megan, Stephen Reilly, Charlotte Barton for the beginning, Jim Knight at Chessington Nurseries and most of all Sarah, for never giving up hope that I'd eventually finish, and Luke for not making too much noise.

The author and publishers would like to thank the following for allowing us to photograph their homes and premises: Melanie Barnes and Nicholas Nasmyth, John Stevenson, Georgia Sion and Kevin McGuinness, Tom Lloyd and Polly Richards, Adam and Isabelle Sodowick, Anna Malni, Jo Hagan, Kew Gardens, Bow Wow, CA1, Out of Time, Bowles and Linares, Vessel and Palm House Nurseries. Also Sarah Hollywood for the styling on p47, 139, 144 (left) and Christian Siekmeier for the picture of the spider plants on p41.

First published in 2001 by
Conran Octopus Limited
a part of Octopus Publishing Group
2–4 Heron Quays, London E14 4JP
www.conran-octopus.co.uk

Commissioning Editor Claire Wrathall
Senior Editor Muna Reyal
Editor Karen Collier
Creative Director Leslie Harrington
Executive Art Editor Megan Smith
Production Controller Alex Wiltshire
Proofreader Rosie Hankin
Indexer Ingrid Lock

British Library Cataloguing-in-Publication Data.
A catalogue record for this book is available from the British Library.

ISBN: 1 84091 174 3

Colour origination by Sang Choy International, Singapore

Printed in China

CONTENTS

INTRODUCTION 7

THE PLANTS 11
bright dark **warm** cool
kitsch pariahs **plain peculiar**
climbers + trailers **big** office
unkillable challenging **damp**
scented **feng shui**

KEEPING THEM HAPPY 92
light + artificial light water
pests, diseases + problems
temperature + humidity
potting + repotting hydroponics
feeding propagation **pruning**
while you're on holiday
bringing them back from the dead

GROUPS OF PLANTS 118
herbs + edibles citrus
bromeliads orchids **cacti**
succulents ferns bulbs
carnivorous conservatory
outside in

BUYER'S GUIDE 170
SUPPLIERS 173
INDEX 174

INTRODUCTION

PLANTS ARE GOOD NEWS. THEY'RE GOOD
FOR YOUR HEALTH AND GOOD FOR YOUR SOUL.
THEY CAN BE COOL, STYLISH, SEXY EVEN, BUT
THEY SHOULD BE PART OF YOUR ROOM DESIGN
NOT SOME APOLOGETIC AFTERTHOUGHT.

For me the whole gardening thing began with a packet of seeds. Well, to be precise, two packets of seeds, because when I was a child, I grew both kinds. Mustard *and* cress. It starts that way for most people, a small tray on the window-sill, some soggy loo paper and a scattering of seeds. Coming home from school each day to inspect the rapid progress of my miniature field of green ranked right up there with Action Man, Lego and making the stuff they showed us on Blue Peter. Fortunately, I seem to have shaken off the urge to construct space ships from loo rolls and dress male dolls up as soldiers, but the fascination for plants has endured.

Plants are good news. They are good for the environment and good for the soul. Now I don't want to sound like an old hippy, but plants do have an incredibly calming, spiritual effect on people. We use the care of plants as a shield to protect us from our stressful, hectic lifestyles and growing plants either indoors or in the garden satisfies a deep-rooted human instinct to nurture. They're an incredible medicine for both mental and physical health.

Businesses have sussed out the positive effects plants have on people and the spaces they inhabit. They reap the benefits by landscaping their office interiors to increase worker productivity and reduce absenteeism while restaurants and hotels use plants to bring in customers. They invest a lot of money in greenery and not without good reason.

But indoor plants are currently languishing in the midst of a major image crisis which they don't deserve. Unfortunately even the phrase 'house plant' conjures up horrid images of dusty yellow leaves, and sad little spider plants barely clinging onto life, so I won't be using it again.

But where did it all go wrong? We've become obsessed with design and yet we can't get it right in the indoor plant department. Plants should play a vital role in our homes and our places of work. They should be included in the design of a room and not plonked in as an afterthought. A plant should have its own space like a piece of furniture or artwork and be chosen in the same way. Plants with an architectural quality are in vogue, big barrel cacti or graceful trees, but it doesn't end there. The type of container in which it sits is absolutely crucial. Get that wrong and you might as well not bother. A sublime succulent in a grotty plastic pot standing in an old saucer is taboo. After all, it doesn't matter how much you

spend on a dress if you tuck it into the back of your knickers when you come out of the loo.

But, first and foremost, the plants need to be healthy because an ugly plant is worse than no plant at all. The first thing to do is to pick the right plant for the right place and decide on the amount of care you're prepared to give it. Then all you've got to do is keep your plant happy. But as luck would have it, most indoor plants are extraordinarily easy to look after. You just need to follow these five basic rules:

1 Water and feed them correctly. Most indoor plant deaths are caused by overwatering.
2 Most plants need a winter rest with less water, less feeding and less heat.
3 Treat any trouble immediately. Bad doses of pests and diseases are hard to cure.
4 Choose the right plant for the right place. Put it where it grows best not just where it looks best.
5 Avoid extremes or sudden changes in temperature and light.

I've put the common name of each plant first but any one plant can have several different common names. So to clarify this I've also used the Latin name afterwards. Unfortunately a clever bunch of botanists somewhere are constantly renaming plants so your particular plant may be labelled with an obsolete but more familiar moniker. To confuse things even more, some of the big nurseries in Europe have a rather annoying habit of making up their own variety names. What I'm trying to say is don't worry too much about the name of a plant, if it doesn't match up exactly with the one in the book, you're probably quite safe following those care instructions anyway.

The basic tenet of this book is organic. Spraying powerful insecticides indoors is clearly not going to be good for your health or that of your pets so I've offered alternatives. When it comes to organic solutions, there is far less choice in far less fancy packaging because the big chemical companies can't make fat profits out of them, but they do work. And then there are environmental issues like the use of peat which is the main ingredient of most 'off the shelf' indoor plant composts. Peat bogs are ancient habitats and once they are drained are lost for ever. There are plenty of peat-free alternatives on sale and I urge you to use them instead.

Experts now believe that a lot of the stuff we surround ourselves with in our homes and workplaces emits harmful gases. Building materials like plywood, chipboard and paint, carpets, furniture, photocopiers and computers, and the glues and resins that hold them all together give off formaldehyde and all sorts of other nasties. As you are reading this you could be sitting in a self-created haze of 150 horrible things including carbon monoxide, hydrogen, methane, ammonia and nitrogen oxide. To that unpleasant cocktail add low air humidity, exacerbated by heating in winter and we're in all sorts of trouble.

With all that in mind, some experts consider that indoor air pollution is an even greater threat to health than outdoor pollution due to the amount of time we are exposed to it. In our so-called 'advanced societies' we spend a staggering 90 per cent of our lives indoors. Sick Building Syndrome has sidled into our vocabulary and is allegedly responsible for allergies, asthma, eye, nose and throat irritations, fatigue, headaches and respiratory problems.

Good ventilation can improve indoor air quality, but that isn't a realistic option in hermetically sealed office buildings with air conditioning, or even in the home when leaving all the windows open in winter has a rather alarming effect on your heating bills.

Thankfully, in 1980, the good people of NASA started doing extensive research sparked off by the problem of air quality aboard Skylab and they've decided that plants are the answer. After all, in nature, plants clean the atmosphere, and the rainforests are the world's lungs. It's no different indoors. Photosynthesis replenishes the oxygen used up by people, but plants also take in toxins from the atmosphere and break them down with the help of microbes in the compost.

NASA has discovered that some of the best plants are Boston fern, chrysanthemum, gerbera and miniature date palm, but you'll come across details of other excellent air purifiers in this book.

For many people, this book may be the first step of a lengthy gardening odyssey, but for others it could be as far as they'll ever travel on the horticultural road. But however far you journey and no matter how far you've already come, *Potted* should be able to take you wherever you want to go. I don't want this book to be only for flat-dwelling, frustrated gardeners who don't have their own piece of outdoors, I also want it to be useful to people who have no interest in the process of caring for a plant and just want something to look fantastic without any hassle.

I've included lots of plants that are easy to get hold of and easy to look after and I've also included a few new ones that may take a bit of extra trouble and care, but are well worth it. This book will let you dip into it at will and get as little or as much info out as you choose. If you only have one plant then it will tell you how to look after it and maybe, just maybe, encourage you to have more.

MOST PLANTS ARE INCREDIBLY EASY TO LOOK AFTER. BUT THE MAJORITY ARE KILLED BY OVERWATERING. IRONICALLY, THEY'D DO MUCH BETTER IF TOTALLY NEGLECTED.

THE PLANTS

BRIGHT

BRIGHT

In most homes 'bright' translates as 'a window-sill that doesn't get direct midday sunshine' and it is the perfect home for many flowering plants which basically like lots of light all year. If a window is east- or west-facing it will avoid the strongest midday sun, but if it does get direct sunlight it has to be filtered by a translucent blind or a sheer curtain. Or if the sun shines on it all day in summer, you'll need to pull the plant back about 60cm from the glass or there'll be trouble. The healthy greenness can get bleached out of the leaves, dry scorched patches will appear and if you mist them with water they'll discolour. Too far back into the room and the plants won't flower as well and growth gets all leggy. You'll see there are a couple of exceptions here which can benefit from a few hours of direct sunshine, and in winter, when the sun is far less intense, most plants will relish a couple of hours of direct sun a day, which will improve their chances of flowering well.

YESTERDAY, TODAY, TOMORROW PLANT (far left)

Brunfelsia pauciflora/calycina

Slowly reaching about 60cm it flowers in spring and summer. Yesterday the flower was purple, today it's violet and tomorrow it's white. On the fourth day it's had enough and dies. But it will only flower if it has a winter rest.

light bright light, but needs three to four hours of direct sunlight every day in winter.

temperature average warmth except during the winter rest period when it must be moved to a cool room at around 12 or 13°C for six weeks.

water moderately in the summer and feed every two weeks but keep fairly dry in winter.

special needs replace the compost each year but don't increase the pot size, they flower best in small pots. Pinch out the tips to keep it bushy.

problems mealy bug and whitefly.

GOLDFISH PLANT (left)

Columnea x banksii

This one with dark green leaves and red flowers is the easiest variety to grow and, like 'Carnival' (pictured) with red-edged yellow flowers, will bloom nearly all year. All are fairly hard to kill but need a lot of love and affection in order to do well. Cuttings root in four weeks and flower while really young. Put three or four in a pot.

light bright but never direct sun.

temperature average warmth but keep the humidity as high as possible by spraying and standing on a pebble tray.

water moderately. They hate having wet roots. Feed with high-phosphate liquid fertilizer at a quarter of the recommended strength.

special needs every other year trim off the bottom third of the roots with a knife, replace with fresh compost and repot.

problems watch out for aphids.

MADAGASCAR PERIWINKLE

Catharanthus rosea (page 12)

This easy-to-grow plant with shiny green leaves gets covered in pink flowers from mid spring to early autumn. There is a white form 'Albus'. The pharmaceutical trade uses this plant in the fight against childhood leukaemia.

light although bright light is fine, a few hours a day of unadulterated sunshine won't go amiss.

temperature it likes normal room temperatures, but never below 10°C.

water plentifully but don't stand in water and feed with liquid fertilizer every two weeks.

special needs you get really good flowering plants if you grow them from seed in spring.

problems they are best chucked away once they've flowered.

ROSE OF CHINA (page 13)

Hibiscus rosa-sinensis

The trumpet-shaped flowers are outrageously exotic and come in all sorts of colours including white, yellow, pink, orange and crimson. They mostly appear through late spring and summer. Plants happily reach 60cm or more in height.

light a bright window-sill is ideal but a few hours of direct sun each day is appreciated.

temperature average warmth but during the winter move it to somewhere cooler at about 13°C.

water moderately during the active period with a fortnightly high-potash liquid feed. Keep it fairly dry in winter and cut out the feeding.

special needs in spring prune all the stems and branches down to a neat framework about 15cm high.

problems whitefly.

LOLLIPOP PLANT (above)

Pachystachys lutea

It's not to everyone's taste this one. Little white flowers pop out of the lollipop-like cluster of yellow bracts which last for about three months in summer.

light bright filtered light but never direct sun.

temperature Average warmth all the time.

water moderately all year but slightly less in winter.

special needs give a liquid fertilizer every other week from spring to summer.

problems it should flower by the time it reaches 30–40cm. If it doesn't, switch to a high-potash, tomato-type fertilizer.

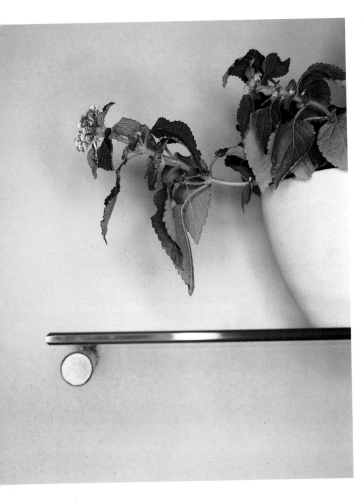

YELLOW SAGE (left)
Lantana camara

It's a bit of a weed over much of the sub-tropical and tropical world but it looks good indoors. The clusters of tubular flowers open yellow, then turn red. There are forms that have white, orange or pink flowers. Watch out because it's poisonous.

light a few hours of direct sunlight every day all year makes them flower well.

temperature it likes average warmth with a break in winter in a cool room at anything between 5 and 10°C.

water plentifully while in flower with a liquid fertilizer every two weeks and provide high humidity. In winter let it almost dry out.

special needs prune back to about 15cm high in winter. Cuttings taken in spring will flower better than old plants.

problems whitefly.

SHRIMP PLANT
Justicia brandegeeana/ Beloperone guttata

The common name comes from the salmon-coloured sort of prawn-shaped flowers (if you half close your eyes). It's quite common and very easy to grow, flowering for most of the year. An exception to the rule, a sunny window-sill is ideal for this plant, especially if shut behind curtains at night which keeps it nice and cool.

light bright light with a little direct sun.

temperature average warmth, cooler at night.

water moderately, allowing the top to dry out a bit between watering. Water sparingly in winter.

special needs pinch out the tips of young plants to keep bushy. Mature plants can be chopped back by half in mid spring.

problems none in particular.

LIPSTICK VINE (right)
Aeschynanthus lobbianus

A long-stemmed trailer with striking red flowers between June and September. Sadly it's a bit temperamental and if you don't give it a proper winter rest it won't flower the following year. Ideal for hanging pots.

light lots of bright light all year but never direct sun.

temperature a room on the cool side of warm is best but they absolutely must have a cooler winter rest at around 13 or 14°C.

water plentifully while in flower and give an extremely weak liquid feed. In winter it's essential to keep it on the dry side. High humidity is a must.

special needs Repot every two or three years.

problems watch out for aphids.

GOOSEFOOT
Syngonium podophyllum

The immature leaves of this tropical vine are shaped like arrowheads but as the plant gets a few years older they develop first two and then four additional pointy lobes. The creamy yellow variegated form 'Emerald Gem' is the most common variety available.

light bright filtered light but absolutely no direct sun which damages the leaves. The green form will grow in medium light but all the variegated ones need bright light or growth slows down and they get a bit leggy.

temperature average warmth with high humidity.

water moderately and sparingly in winter.

special needs liquid feed every two weeks.

problems it may get red spider mite if the air is dry.

Other bright plants *umbrella plant (p80), guatemalan rhubarb (p47/48), dumb-cane (p36/37), begonia (p31)*

SILK OAK
Grevillea robusta

This fast-growing tree with fern-like leaves can easily put on 50cm a year if happy. The young leaves are tinged a beautiful coppery brown. They don't flower indoors and are ideal for cool, bright spots.

light bright is best, but they also like direct sun, especially in winter.

temperature cool to average warmth if the humidity is raised.

water moderately in active growth and sparingly in winter.

special needs repot in spring using azalea compost which is acidic. Feed every two weeks from spring to summer.

problems central heating and dry air can make the leaves drop off.

DARK

Take a trip down to a flower shop or a garden centre and you'll be faced with all kinds of plants, but sadly most will need to be kept near a window or they'll start to look rubbish several weeks after you get them home. The leaves get a bit lacklustre, the stems get leggy and spindly and the plants will begin a long and painful journey to the other side. Flowering plants are non-starters in dimly lit rooms so foliage plants are the way forward. Nothing will grow in total darkness but the plants here will be ok in the inner recesses of your room away from windows. In the Light and Artificial Light section on page 95 this is described as medium or dim light. Generally they will tolerate bright light as well. You can also use other plants in dim or dark rooms and rotate them by giving them a few weeks on and a month or two off.

DARK

PAINTED DROP-TONGUE

Aglaonema crispum (below left)

This is a brilliant plant for dingy rooms and if you treat it right it will look good for ages. The 30cm long leaves are several shades of green and there are a number of varieties. In summer or early autumn barely noticeable hooded flower spikes appear.

light medium, never direct sun.

temperature average warmth all year. For extra humidity stand on a pebble tray.

water moderately allowing top half to dry out between waterings. It doesn't really have a winter rest. Feed monthly.

special needs repot mature plants once every few years. They never need large pots.

problems cold air and draughts make the leaves curl.

RHUBARB (below right)

Rheum rhaponticum

Rhubarb will actually grow in a windowless room like a hallway. Buy a crown or dig up a lump from the garden in spring. Put it in a big pot and the new leaves will shoot up searching for light.

light doesn't need any, but if it gets some light the leaves will be more green rather than yellow. The pot will need turning so the plant doesn't grow lopsided.

temperature room temperature right down to freezing.

water keep it moist.

special needs plant in soil-based compost with some well-rotted manure. Cut the stems and discard the poisonous leaves. Put it outside in late summer.

problems watch out for aphids on young growth.

IVY TREE

x *Fatshedera lizei*

A cross between ivy and a glossy leaved plant, *Fatsia japonica*. It will grow outside so can put up with cold rooms and entrance halls. The leaves are about 15cm across and shaped like a hand with five pointed fingers. There is a variegated form with cream margins.

light bright or medium light. Variegated forms need the most.

temperature cold is fine. But they will live in heated rooms if the humidity is kept up.

water moderately and then sparingly in winter.

special needs pinch out the tips in spring to keep it bushy. The stems need staking or they'll flop over.

problems watch out for aphids, scale and red spider mite in dry warm air.

PEACE LILY (page 18)
Spathiphyllum 'Mauna Loa'

In spring and summer the 60cm tall clump of glossy green leaves is crowned by a knobbly white flower sheathed in a white spathe. It slowly turns green and lasts about five or six weeks. *S. wallisii* is the more common, smaller variety. Some varieties are fragrant.

light prefers medium light. Too much sun scorches the leaves.

temperature grows well in normal room temperatures, however is sensitive to dry air, so stand pot on a pebble tray. Keep warm and humid to encourage flowering.

water moderately but if you let it dry out, the leaves collapse. Dunk in a bucket of water to revive it. Too wet and the roots rot.

special needs liquid feed every other week from spring to summer.

problems attacks from red spider mite when humidity is low.

PHILODENDRON (page 19)
Philodendron

Philodendrons, which are related to the cheese plant, come in lots of different shapes but most of them have big, lush, glossy leaves. Some of the climbing ones, like the variety 'Red Emerald' have a burgundy tinge to the foliage. *P. selloum* and *P. bipinnatifidum* make a massive clump of huge deeply lobed leaves and are probably a bit big for the average room.

light actually prefer bright light, but do grow well in darker corners. If the leaves become small and pale, move towards the window.

temperature average warmth, never below 14°C.

water moderately, just enough to keep soil moist. In the winter, let compost dry out.

special needs use a moss-covered pole to support climbers, spray the moss daily with water and poke the aerial roots into it.

problems yellow leaves are caused by overwatering.

PARLOUR PALM (above)
Chamaedorea elegans

This slow-growing palm will eventually reach about 90cm and is virtually indestructible. After about three years sprays of small bobbly yellow flowers appear.

light grows well in anything from dim to bright light.

temperature tolerates a wide range, but does best in normal room temperatures. Can stomach dry air but becomes prone to red spider mite and brown leaf tips.

water plentifully during the active period to keep the compost moist. In winter keep it barely moist.

special needs give a liquid feed once a month during spring and summer.

problems yellowing, mottled leaves are probably caused by red spider mite.

CARDOMOM
Elettaria cardomomum

Probably not the prettiest plant in the world, but its ability to thrive in extremely poor light makes it very useful. If you can't get anything else to grow try this. The pointed leaves are over 30cm long on stalks as high as 75cm. Flowers rarely appear indoors. The leaves are aromatic if crushed.

light very poor to bright light. Can survive anything except direct sunlight.

temperature average warmth.

water moderately in active growth and sparingly in winter. Liquid feed every other week.

special needs to propagate, clumps can be divided or it can be grown from seed.

problems leaf edges turn brown if it's too cold.

Other dark plants *prayer plant (p32), goosefoot – green (p16), ivy (p53), cast iron plant (p71)*

WARM

Most popular indoor plants are only popular because they like the same sort of living conditions as we do. But this can cause a few problems for anyone who likes to set the thermostat on their heating a little higher than normal because a lot of plants won't like it. The plants in this category won't mind those few extra degrees, but the golden rule is: the hotter the room, the higher the humidity must be. In most cases standing pots on a layer of pebbles in a saucer of water will do the trick. As the water evaporates, the humidity around the plant is increased, but the pot mustn't actually be in the water. Standing a container of water on a radiator near the plants also makes a difference.

DIPLADENIA (page 22)
Mandevilla sanderi

This is really a twining climber but it flowers when it's quite young, which is a bonus. The trumpet-shaped blooms are pink with a yellow throat and some are almost red, and last from late spring to early autumn. The glossy green leaves remain all year.

light bright light is essential. Direct sunlight will damage it, but too little light and it won't flower.

temperature average warmth but it needs a cooler rest period in winter. Keep the humidity up.

water sparingly and keep slightly drier in winter.

special needs liquid feed every two weeks in active growth.

problems they only flower on the current year's growth so once the blooms have finished, trim back all this growth to the main stems.

GOODLUCK PLANT (left)
Cordyline fruticosa

Cordylines and dracaenas are very similar and need roughly the same conditions. This one with red-splashed leaves grows to about 60cm tall. It develops a bit of a cane as the lower leaves yellow and naturally drop off.

light bright light. Direct sun bleaches dry patches in the leaves.

temperature average warmth or warm rooms but you must raise the humidity.

water plentiful with a liquid feed every two weeks, but ease off in winter or you'll kill it. Severe underwatering causes brown spots.

propagation propagate with cane cuttings in spring.

problems it will die in cold rooms.

VELVET PLANT (page 23)
Gynura sarmentosa

Aptly named, the hairy leaves of this little trailing plant are iridescent and shimmer in a peacock's tail-sort-of-way.

light give bright light, with some direct sunlight.

temperature average warmth is fine but they'll grow in warm rooms as long as you stand in a pebble tray to raise the humidity.

water moderately in active period, do not wet the foliage. Liquid feed once a month except in winter.

special needs nip out the tips to keep it bushy and remove the small revolting-smelling dandelion-like flowers in spring.

problems watch out for aphids.

SILVER NET LEAF (right)
Fittonia verschaffeltii argyroneura

This plant has a nasty habit of kicking the bucket a couple of weeks after you've got it home. The solution to this is lots of warmth and humidity around the leaves. The dwarf varieties are strangely easier to grow. The most common type with pink veining is a little tasteless.

light medium light in summer but move to a brighter place in winter.

temperature quite warm is best, but watch the humidity.

water little and often is best with a liquid feed every other week. Keep the compost just moist and let it get a bit drier in winter.

special needs plants get straggly so trim them back in spring.

problems if it gets a bit cold or the compost ever dries out, the plant is history.

EMERALD TREE (below)
Radermachera sinica
What sets this plant apart from the others is its tolerance of dry air and therefore centrally heated rooms. Otherwise it has to be said that despite its elegant name this plant is not much of a looker. It just sort of grows into a small green tree but people seem to like it.
light bright but detests midday summer sun.
temperature likes average warmth, but it will be happy in quite warm rooms.
water plentifully but don't let it get soggy.
special needs feed every other week in active growth. Propagate with stem cuttings in the summer.
problems none really, but very occasionally whitefly.

ANGEL'S WINGS
Caladium hortulanum
Papery thin, arrow-shaped leaves about 40cm long rise up on stalks of the same length between late spring and autumn. These spectacular plants may be white with green veining or marbled red, pink or green. Because they need unusually high temperatures and humidity they are best treated as temporary plants but they can be kept and brought back into leaf the following year.
light bright light but not direct sun.
temperature above average warmth with a very high humidity.
water moderately but as the leaves die down reduce watering and keep fairly dry for about five months. Liquid feed at half strength every other week.
special needs use a peat substitute compost.
problems leaves go brown and dry if humidity is too low.

TEMPLE BELLS
Smithiantha
The dangling bell-like flowers in late autumn may be orange or red, often with a speckled yellow throat depending on which variety you have. The heart-shaped leaves have a curious mottling and plants themselves can be around 60cm tall. They have a completely dormant winter rest.
light medium to bright light away from direct sun.
temperature warm and humid. Don't let it drop below about 18°C. Conservatories are best.
water moderately to keep it moist except in winter rest period.
special needs after flowering the plants die down. Let the compost dry out and remove the short scaly brown rhizomes from the pot and store in vermiculite until repotted in spring.
problems brown leaves are caused by dry heat and overwatering.

WARM

FALSE ARALIA (below left)
Schefflera elegantissima/
Dizygotheca elegantissima
Check out any film or TV show that was made before about 1995 that featured cannabis plants and you can bet that it was actually this or its stumpier-leaved cousin, often sold as *D. veitchii*. In fact, the almost black leaves are far too dark, but that never seemed to bother anyone.
light bright but never direct sun.
temperature warmth is absolutely vital. So is humidity.
water sparingly, but it walks a very thin line between over- and under-watering. Give little and often.
special needs being slow-growing they only need moving into a larger pot every other year. Put three plants per pot to make them look bushier.
problems leaf drop is caused by cold, underwatering and sudden changes in temperature.

CALATHEA (below right)
Burle-marxii
These plants are very closely related to ctenanthes and can be a little petulant but the leaves have amazing patterns which makes them worth it.
light bright light. Direct sun curls the leaves.
temperature keep it warm, at least 20°C and preferably higher. Keep the humidity up.
water moderately to keep it moist and then sparingly in winter. Don't use cold or hard water. Feed every two weeks in spring and summer.
special needs never feed until at least four months after repotting.
problems stems go limp and rot if plants are too cold or overwatered in winter.

MONKEY PLANT
Ruellia makoyana
The velvety green leaves have a tinge of purple and silver veining, and in winter it has 5cm long rose pink trumpet flowers. The stems tend to flop making it a good plant for a hanging basket.
light bright light, especially in the winter months or else flowering period is shortened.
temperature must be kept warm with a high humidity.
water moderately but give them a two-month rest after flowering and only water sparingly.
special needs repot if necessary in spring.
problems watch out for aphids on the shoot tips.

Other warm plants *kris plant (p78), glory lily (p163/165), bromeliads (p132–135), allamanda (p164)*

COOL

If you've got somewhere in your home that gets a bit chilly, you may have trouble growing a lot of the usual indoor plants. The trick is to choose tough things that don't mind the lack of warmth. These plants are particularly useful for barely heated or seldom-used rooms, communal stairwells and corridors, porches and even cool conservatories. Just remember that they like cool not cold, so most won't appreciate freezing conditions.

PORCELAIN BERRY

PORCELAIN BERRY (page 28 left)
Ampelopsis brevipedunculata 'Elegans'
Normally sold as an outdoor plant, this little climber has green leaves splashed white and pink with pinky red stems. It can be trained as a climber or left to trail.
light bright filtered light is essential.
temperature cold and unheated rooms are best but will grow in ordinary room temperatures.
water moderately. Never let it dry out. Sparingly in winter.
special needs prune at any time of year to keep it to a manageable size and to stop it from getting straggly.
problems too much humidity can encourage mildew.

GUM TREE (page 28 right + 29)
Eucalyptus
There are many different varieties; just choose one that looks good when it's young. Cool bright rooms like unheated stairwells are ideal. Some can also be used as temporary indoor plants and put outside after a month or two.
light as much as possible.
temperature they grow best in cool rooms. Average room temperatures can make them go crispy after a short while.
water moderately with a fortnightly liquid feed. Water sparingly in winter.
special needs might need some pruning to make it bushy rather than tall and thin.
problems they will only last a year or two at most indoors.

FLOWERING MAPLE (below)
Abutilon x hybridum
These shrubby plants can be anything up to about 1.5m, but flower when quite young in white, yellow, red and orange. There are also some with variegated leaves splashed with yellow. It is happy as an indoor plant or in a cool greenhouse or conservatory.
light bright with at least three to four hours of direct sunlight.
temperature a cool room. The warmer it is the higher the humidity needs to be.
water moderately, keep quite dry in winter. Liquid feed fortnightly in spring and summer.
special needs may become tall and spindly so cut back to about 30cm in early spring.
problems whitefly, greenfly and red spider mite.

COOL

BEGONIA (below)
Begonia

There are loads of different begonias, some grown for their outrageously gaudy leaves, some for their pretty flowers and others (which make the best indoor plants) for both. There are tiny ones and huge climbing ones too numerous to mention.

light a bright spot but no direct sun except in the depths of winter.

temperature no higher than 20ºC. Avoid really cold nights. Keep humidity high during the growth period.

water moderately while active and feed every two weeks. Water sparingly in winter. Begonias hate overwatering.

special needs repot foliage types every spring or they'll lose colour.

problems rots and mildews.

CAPE COWSLIP
Lachenalia aloides

This is a beautiful plant but unfortunately can't live in heated rooms. The speckled green strap-like leaves arise from a bulb which flowers in winter. Small hanging bells of yellow flowers that fade to scarlet at the tips are carried on stalks about 30cm tall.

light bright with some direct sun.

temperature really cool, as low as 5ºC in winter.

water moderately, keeping moist while in flower.

special needs slow down watering after flowering and stop after about a month. Keep it dry and repot in autumn. Start watering once shoots appear.

problems warm rooms are a killer.

GENISTA
Genista x spachiana

You'll see these small bushes for sale in spring and early summer. Yellow, slightly fragrant pea-like flowers virtually obscure the thin pale green leaves. They really are temporary plants that look rubbish for 11 months of the year, so chuck them after flowering.

light bright with some sunlight.

temperature cool rooms make the flowers last for much longer.

water plentifully before and during flowering.

special needs if you really want to keep them, cut back the shoots after flowering, stand outside and then bring into a cool room in autumn. Increase the watering in mid winter.

problems only what they look like for most of the year.

COOL

ROSE (left)
Rosa chinensis
Often known as miniature roses or patio roses, these are the only ones suitable for indoors. They are about 30cm tall, usually flower between early spring and autumn, come in a range of colours, but are rarely scented. Some people keep them all year but they should be put in the garden once they are past their best or chucked away.
light bright light.
temperature cool window-sills are best, but they will be happy in ordinary room temperatures.
water moderately and never let it dry out. Liquid feed once every two weeks.
special needs prune by half in early spring before bringing them back indoors. Deadhead regularly.
problems watch out for aphids and red spider mite.

KAFFIR LILY
Clivia miniata
Dark green strap-shaped leaves, as much as 7cm wide, fan out from the centre and plants can be 90cm across. In late winter a flower spike about 45cm tall pushes up from near the middle of the plant. Yellow-tinged orange bell-shaped flowers open at the top.
light bright light but no direct sun.
temperature they need a cool, preferably unheated, room for about two months in winter but are happy in average warmth while actively growing.
water moderately from spring to autumn and then sparingly, just enough so it doesn't dry out.
special needs liquid feed every two weeks from when the flower stalks start showing until early autumn. Only repot if it's bursting out of its pot. Remove seed pods after flowering.
problems too much winter warmth causes small, short, early flowers.

PRAYER PLANT
Maranta leuconeura kerchoveana
The common name comes from this little plant's nocturnal habit of curling its leaves up and raising them to the heavens. The pale green foliage has dark brown blotches either side of the mid rib.
light medium light. Strong light browns the edges and leaves fade.
temperature it only just sneaks into this category because it really prefers cool bordering on warm, but definitely not cold. Anything between about 18 and 21°C is good, any higher and the humidity must be increased.
water plentifully, but sparingly in winter.
special needs propagate by dividing clumps in spring. Feed every two weeks in active growth.
problems stems go limp if plants get too cold.

LADY'S EARDROPS (right)
Fuchsia
There are thousands of varieties, most of which have these pod-like flower buds. You can either buy small plants in spring and discard them after flowering or you can overwinter the plants somewhere very cool and put them back on show in spring.
light bright light, with a couple hours of strong sunlight every day.
temperature likes cool conditions.
water plentifully but in winter keep fairly dry. Feed every week when in flower.
special needs in spring trim back by a third. Take cuttings in late summer or spring.
problems attacks from aphids and whitefly.

Other cool plants *rhubarb (p20) cape leadwort (p53), buddhist pine (p59), lapageria (p164), oleander (p164)*

'Ostentatious, art of worthless pretentiousness' is the dictionary definition for kitsch and these plants definitely fit the bill. Ostentatious without a doubt, some people would consider them so gaudy and tasteless as to also be completely worthless but they have their admirers. Many seem to belong to another time and are for ever trapped in a previous decade, but they all have a certain something. It's just hard to figure out what it is.

KITSCH

KITSCH

HERRINGBONE PLANT
Maranta leuconeura var. *erythroneura* (below left)

The unbelievably exotic leaves are a luxurious deep velvety green with pink herringbone veins and paler green markings. Underneath they are a purple colour.

light medium light, but in the winter give them a well-lit, sunless spot. Too much light gives the leaves brown edges.

temperature it likes average warmth, but keep the humidity up by standing the pots on moist pebbles.

water plenty in the active months, less in winter. Avoid splashing the leaves.

special needs liquid feed once every two weeks. Repot in spring.

problems sensitive to direct sunlight and dislikes draughts with a passion.

SWISS CHEESE PLANT
Monstera deliciosa (below right)

There can't be many people who don't know this plant. The mature leaves can be 60cm across with lots of holes and perforations but in normal room conditions they stay on the smaller side. Like many philodendrons, they naturally grow up tree trunks so need some sort of support.

light bright to fairly dim conditions.

temperature average warmth, keep the humidity up if you can.

water moderately during active growth and sparingly in winter. Overwatering turns leaves yellow.

special needs liquid feed once every two weeks during active period. Repot in spring.

problems not enough light causes leggy growth and leaves without holes. Dry air causes brown leaf tips.

DUMB-CANE (right)
Dieffenbachia amoena

The big leaves are splashed with a creamy white and the plant can get to 1.5m in height, but as it ages the lower leaves naturally fall to reveal a cane. *D. Seguine* 'Tropic Snow' is a particularly good one and there are smaller clumpier varieties like *D. picta* 'Camilla'. These plants are toxic and in their native South America the men of certain tribes brew a potion which freezes the vocal chords of their womenfolk. Hence dumb-cane. It's also a good air purifier.

light bright filtered light. Direct sun bleaches leaves.

temperature warm conditions, it doesn't like cold rooms at all. High humidity is important.

water moderately and then sparingly in winter.

special points feed every two weeks with liquid feed in its active period.

problems cold and draughts make lower leaves yellow and wilt. Watch out for red spider mite and wash your hands after touching it as the plant is poisonous.

COCKSCOMB/PLUME FLOWER
Celosia

Usually grown outside as a bedding plant, there are two types. One, *C. argentea* var. *cristata*, has colourful velvety cockscomb flowers that look totally artificial and the other, with spiky, fluffy plumes, is *C. Plumosa* group. They both come in reds, pinks and yellows.

light lots of light but be sure to avoid baking sun.

temperature cool temperatures make the flowers last longer.

water moderately, keeping the compost always moist.

special needs buy in bud or flower, keep on a window-sill and chuck out after flowering.

problems none really.

URN PLANT (page 34 + 35)
Aechmea fasciata
This bromeliad has thick leathery grey leaves with a whitish bloom which smudges if touched. The gaudy pink flower head is actually made up of bracts or modified leaves and lasts for six months.
light growth in full sunlight is essential for flowering.
temperature average warmth with high humidity.
water keep the central vase topped up with water, refresh it every few weeks. Water the compost moderately and let it dry a bit between waterings. Feed with half-strength liquid feed every other week while active.
special needs trim away parent plant after flowering and allow offsets to develop.
problems parent plants die off after flowering.

CHENILLE PLANT
Acalypha hispida
There are two types: those with 45cm long tassels of tiny bright red flowers in late summer and autumn, and those grown for their patterned leaves mottled coppery green and streaked with red and purple. The flowering sort are definitely the most kitsch with their funny rat-tail flowers. In a conservatory, both plants can reach the height of a person.
light bright light.
temperature always warm but with a high humidity.
water plentifully and then sparingly in winter.
special needs they branch naturally; pruning will only remove flower buds.
problems watch out for mealy bug and red spider mite especially in dry air.

CALATHEA (above)
Calathea crocata
Most calatheas are grown for their colourful leaves but this one has curious orange flowers on erect stems. The dark green leaves have a purple tinge beneath and make a neat clump about 40cm high.
light medium. Bright light tends to spoil the leaf colouring.
temperature average warmth with good humidity.
water plentifully during the active growing period, but go easy during the rest period.
special needs a liquid feed every other week is important during active growth.
problems limp stems are caused by cold air and wet compost in winter months.

KITSCH

TUBEROUS BEGONIAS
Begonia (below left)

These plants are temporary visitors which make a splash of colour and then die back down. They flower in summer and autumn and are bought in bloom or raised by planting the tubers (the knobbly rooty things) in spring in moist compost.

light bright light is essential.
temperature average warmth, store somewhere cool in winter.
water freely when in flower but keep the tubers dry in winter.
special needs after flowering, withhold water and cut off shoots. Lift tubers and store in compost.
problems non-tuberous types can be chucked after flowering.

CAPE PRIMROSE (below right)
Streptocarpus

There are all kinds of varieties and colours of this little plant. The crinkly green leaves just sort of sit there not doing much but they flower almost non-stop. There are some extraordinarily beautiful types like *S. pentherianus* which have only one large leaf.

light bright light when active and medium light in the winter.
temperature average warmth. Raise humidity in warm rooms.
water moderately when active and sparingly in winter especially if there is a non-flowering rest period.
special needs apply a high-phosphate liquid feed at half strength every two weeks in the active period. Remove seed pods and flowers as they fade to encourage further blooms.
problems avoid cold draughts. Single-leaved types normally die after flowering.

COCK ON A PLATE (right)
Anthurium scherzerianum

Not the easiest plant to grow but well worth it. The waxy red 'flowers' with their flower spikes appear between spring and late summer and last for some time. They have dark green leathery leaves. There are also white and pink varieties.

light medium light, put them near a slightly shaded window.
temperature average warmth. Keep humidity levels up to encourage flowering.
water plentifully when active but sparingly in winter.
special needs liquid feed every two weeks in spring and summer.
problems dislikes fluctuations in air temperature. Leaves get dusty.

Other kitsch plants *croton, flame nettle, zebra plant and devil's ivy (all p44)*

PARIAHS

Some plants are unquestionably vile. Laws should be passed to prevent their sale in the shops and they should be made unwelcome in our homes. There are plenty to choose from: brash gaudy things that totally lack style and plain ugly things without any obvious merits. Many were popular in a bygone era and quite frankly should have been left there. But, of course, fashion goes in circles and it's inevitable that today's pariahs will become tomorrow's essentials. So what you'll see here is an indictment of the past and doubtless a prediction for the future.

REX BEGONIA (above left)
Begonia rex 'Vesuvius'
These foliage begonias come in
a veritable rainbow of colours –
extraordinary combinations of
pinks, gold, yellows and anything
else you can think of. To add insult
to injury they sort of shimmer
which makes them also look
totally artificial.
light bright light, but never direct
sun. Turn the pots occasionally.
temperature average warmth but
never below about 15°C. They like
high humidity.
water moist from spring to
autumn and then sparingly in the
winter months.
special needs propagation is
unfortunately very easy from
leaf cuttings.
problems pot-bound plants lose
their colour.

RUBBER PLANT (above right)
Ficus elastica 'Decora'
The problem with rubber plants is
that they just grow straight up so
you end up with a tall thin plant
that's bashing its head on the
ceiling. They were real seventies'
plants and went hand in hand
with the rest of the awful fashions
of that decade. The variegated
ones, like 'Tricolor' which is
splashed with pink and cream,
are particularly unpleasant.
light dingy rooms make them
a bit leggy but they do seem able
to grow anywhere.
temperature again not fussy.
water keep it fairly dry.
special needs air layering is your
best bet for propagation.
problems overwatering will cause
lower leaves to fall. The leaves get
very dusty.

PEPPER ELDER
(below left and right)
Peperomia caperata 'Red Luna'
You're probably wondering why this is here because it does look rather good. The heart-shaped leaves and rat-tail flowers add up to a stylish little 10cm plant so what's the problem? The problem is that it rapidly dies, but not before losing its leaves and becoming very ugly.
light bright, but shade from sun.
temperature average warmth, but if it's too warm they'll lose their leaves unless the humidity is raised.
water compost must dry a little between waterings, cut right down in winter, use tepid water and don't get it on the leaves.
special needs propagate in spring with 5–7cm tip cuttings or try your hand at leaf cuttings.
problems cold makes the leaves drop off, overwatering makes leaves wilt and stems rot, and draughts cause brown leaf edges.

POLKA-DOT PLANT (page 40)
Hypoestes phyllostachya
Most varieties of this objectionable little thing have spots of pink like someone's spilt a can of paint. There's one called 'Splash' which is particularly nasty. On top of that, they tend to get straggly with age.
light bright filtered light.
temperature average warmth, slightly cooler in winter.
water moderately, keep the compost just moist and feed every two weeks in active growth. If it dries out, the plant may die. Oh well.
special needs propagate by taking 10cm cuttings, remove the lower leaves and root them in a glass of water.
problems they aren't as easy to kill as they should be.

AFRICAN VIOLET (page 41)
Saintpaulia ionantha
These are old people's plants. When you reach a certain age you get a bus pass, a pension and an African violet.
light a bright window-sill. They won't flower if they don't get enough light in winter.
temperature like their owners they need a nice warm room and don't like draughts. They love high humidity.
water moderately. Too much water makes the roots rot. Use tepid water and don't get it on the leaves or they'll get brown spots. At every watering give a one-quarter strength liquid feed during active growth.
special needs take leaf cuttings for propagation.
problems apart from generally being horrid, they can get mealy bugs, aphids and botrytis.

PARIAHS

DEVIL'S IVY
Epipremnum aureum/
Scindapsus aureus
Perhaps its only saving grace is its ability to purify air. A climber or trailer, it can grow several metres or more. The usual form has bright green, heart-shaped leaves splashed with yellow, but there are others with white marbling. All look artificial. People really love this ugly plant, perhaps because it's easy to grow. They seem to do really well in chip shops.
light bright filtered light.
temperature average warmth.
water moderately during active growth and just enough in winter to stop it drying out.
special needs liquid feed every two weeks. Repot, if necessary, each spring. Pinch out tips to keep bushy.
problems in low light levels, leaf colour fades. Avoid draughts.

CROTON (right)
Codiaeum variegatum var. *pictum*
The one pictured is possibly the most acceptable form of this plant. Most of the others have broader leathery leaves with all kinds of spots and blotches in red, orange and yellow, often all at once. They look like plastic.
light lots of light is essential on an east- or west-facing window, otherwise you get leaf loss and poor colour.
temperature average warmth with a high humidity.
water plentifully, but go easy in winter. Liquid feed every two weeks from spring to autumn.
special needs move into a pot one size bigger each spring.
problems red spider mite and scale may cause problems. Brown leaf edges are caused by low temperatures.

BUSY LIZZIE (above)
Impatiens walleriana
There are plenty of these plants in our gardens so there's no need to bring them inside as well. Some have vivid pink or red flowers and then there are the New Guinea hybrids with splashes of yellow on the leaves. They tend to become leggy, lose their leaves and flowers and develop stem rots. All in all, they're remarkably fussy indoors.
light lots of bright light.
temperature average warmth.
water keep it moist, water a little almost every day in summer. Liquid feed every two weeks.
special needs they won't flower when you repot them.
problems avoid hot dry air, too much light, too little light, overwatering and underwatering.

FLAME NETTLE
Coleus/Plectranthus
Brighter leaves and a greater range of colours is probably impossible to find. But why even look? They all have the appearance of the aftermath of a technicolor yawn or some bad psychedelic experience. In their defence they are quick and easy to grow and make bushes 30–60cm high. They are often used outside for bedding.
light as much as possible, including some full sun.
temperature average warmth but raise the humidity in higher temperatures.
water plentifully. Plants quickly wilt if they're too dry and although they virtually recover they will then shed a few leaves.
special needs regularly nip out the growing tips to keep them bushy and never let them flower.
problems watch out for red spider mite in dry rooms.

ZEBRA PLANT
Aphelandra squarrosa
The zebra plant could also have gone into Kitsch because it looks the part, but it's hard to care for so really does belong here. The glossy green leaves with startling ivory markings are about 20cm long and in spring there are cone-shaped flower spikes of yellow bracts. The plants reach about 40cm high.
light bright light.
temperature average warmth with high humidity.
water plentifully in active growth and barely moist in winter.
special needs these greedy plants need liquid feed every week while in growth.
problems leaves always seem to fall off as a result of underwatering, cold air, draughts or too much sun. It's really hard to get them to flower again. Watch out for aphids, mealy bug and scale at the shoot tips.

Other pariahs *none because they are intentionally left out.*

PLAIN PECULIAR

Some plants look weird. They just aren't what we expect and don't conform to our image of what an indoor plant is: pretty flowers, perhaps some heart-shaped leaves and maybe a nice trunk. There are probably many other plants in these pages that could fall into this category but these ones are definitely quite odd or just not usually grown as indoor plants.

BEAD PLANT

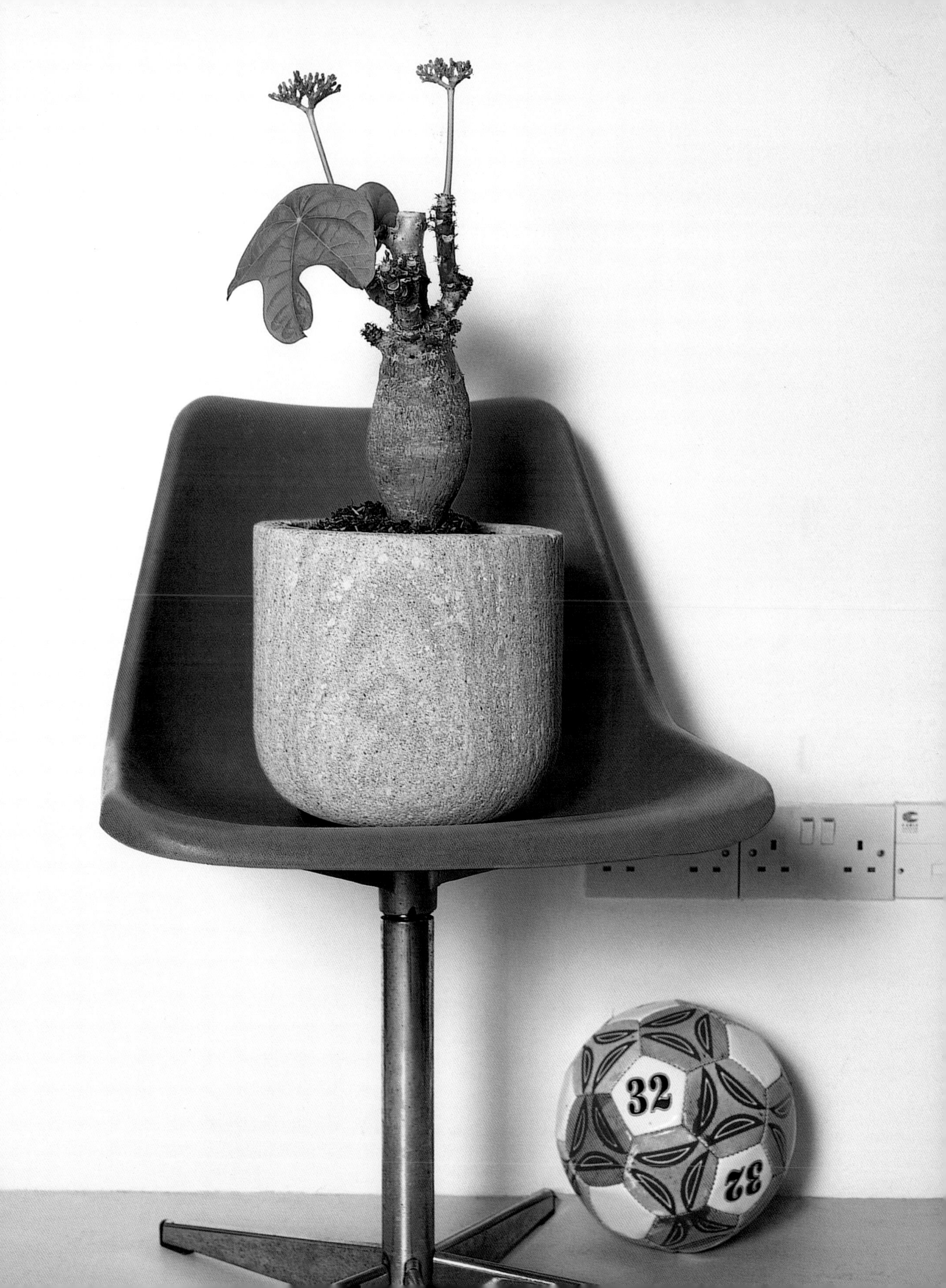

GUATEMALAN RHUBARB

PLAIN PECULIAR

SAGO PALM (far left)
Cycas revoluta
Like a palm but not a palm, this plant was around when the dinosaurs roamed the earth. Very slow growing, it may only put on one stiff green leaf a year and lives for ages. It won't flower indoors.
light give them loads of bright light with or without direct sun.
temperature average warmth. It will tolerate a range of temperatures and low humidity.
water moderately in summer and in the winter only enough to stop compost from drying out.
special needs liquid feed monthly from early spring to early autumn.
problems too much water will eventually kill the plant.

DEVIL'S ROOT (left)
Zamioculcas zamiifolia
This succulent has shiny fleshy stems and leaves that look like they've come out of a mould.
light bright or direct sunlight.
temperature average warmth.
water moderately, sparingly in winter. Overwatering tends to rot the roots and the base of the stem.
special needs liquid feed every other week in active growth.
problems very easy to keep with enough light. Don't overwater.

BEAD PLANT (page 46)
Nertera granadensis
This plant used to be very fashionable but its 1970s' appeal left it on the style scrap heap. Watch out because it's due for a comeback. A low mat of creeping green leaves is covered in orange berries the size of small peas. They are fully developed by late summer and last a few months.
light bright light with at least three hours of direct sunlight every day.
temperature cool to average warmth. Keep humidity high.
water moderately, just enough in winter so it doesn't dry out.
special needs put outside in late spring if you can until the berries start to form. Liquid feed now and then during the summer.
problems not always worth coaxing back into 'berry', it is often binned afterwards.

GUATEMALAN RHUBARB
Jatropha podagrica (page 47)
A weirdo of a plant from Central America, the swollen bottle stem is naked in winter but in early spring, flower stalks appear and are topped by tiny coral-red flowers which last for ages. Several deeply lobed leaves will appear later which the Mayans boil and eat. *J. curcas*, a close relative, was used for high-octane fuel trials in Sri Lanka. Reaches about 60cm tall.
light bright light. Avoid direct summer sun.
temperature average warmth.
water sparingly with very little in winter. Overwatering leads to blackened shoot tips.
special needs when necessary, repot in spring or the lower leaves will yellow or drop in summer.
problems mealy bugs.

TURF (GRASS)
An ordinary piece of turf makes an unusual indoor plant. Cut it into strips or any shape you want and put in containers on the window-sill. It can also be easily grown from a thin scattering of seed.
light bright or full sunlight is essential. Turn the container round every day so it doesn't grow bendy.
temperature cold to average. The warmer it is the faster it will grow.
water plentifully. Keep moist.
special needs feeding isn't necessary. Grow in shallow trays or pots with 3 or 4cm of compost. Trim once or twice a week.
problems watch out for mould and spray with a fungicide.

MALABAR NIGHTSHADE
Basella rubra (this page)
This twining climber with waxy green, purple-tinged leaves is probably best in a conservatory, but it will grow in a bright room. The pink and white flower buds on the shoot tips never really open and just swell to form small black berries. It grows over a metre a year.
light bright filtered light and even a little direct sunshine. Put outside in summer if you can.
temperature average warmth.
water plentifully in active growth and then cut right down in winter.
special needs liquid feed every two or three weeks in active growth. Cut back at any time if growth is excessive.
problems none in particular.

INDOOR BONSAI
All the best sorts have to be kept outside but there are a few fairly decent ones grown from familiar indoor plants. The older the plant, the more expensive it is, but some of the ones for sale are basically just tree seedlings so watch out. Look up the growing conditions for the particular plant but here's a basic guideline.
light bright light.
temperature average warmth.
water always moist but not wet, this can mean a daily soaking. Humidity is important.
special needs continually pinch out the growing tips and train branches where you want them by loosely winding stiff wire around them. Repot established plants every two years in spring in the same shallow container. Cut away a third of the roots and pull away the old compost. Liquid feed every six weeks.
problems they aren't easy and hate draughts and radiators.

Other peculiar plants *stag's horn fern (p153), cock on a plate (p38), the devil's backbone (p147)*

CLIMBERS
+ TRAILERS

Trailing plants are mostly just climbers without any support that are allowed to go floppy. They don't need much special care and if they get long and leggy, just chop back the stems to make them a bit tidier. Climbers, on the other hand, need training because they don't really do it on their own so you have to give them a helping hand. Wind new shoots in before they become too long and woody and, if necessary, tie branches in with a loop of green garden string. Don't tie it too tightly though or you'll garrotte the stems and chop the plant in half.

Climbers can be trained up anything including something permanent like banisters, shelves or vertical wires fixed to the wall. But if you're shoving a support into a pot, place it towards the outer edge so you don't damage any roots. Moss poles should probably be banned. Basically a bamboo cane with a load of moss wrapped around it, they are useful for holding up heavy plants like philodendron and cheese plants, and aerial roots can be poked into them, but they aren't pretty.

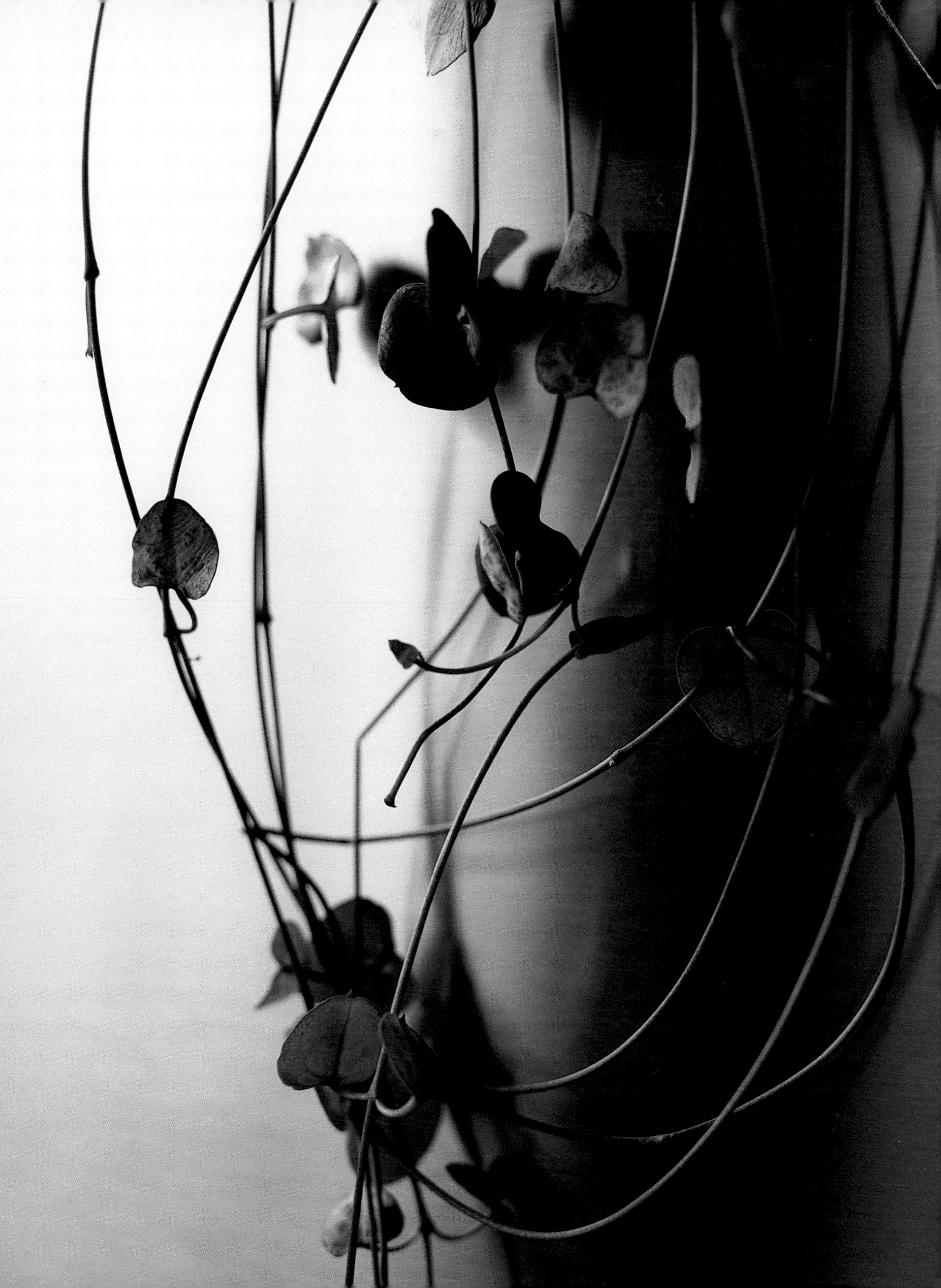

SWEETHEART PLANT (page 50)
Philodendron scandens

You can't really go wrong with this climbing or trailing plant which is perfectly happy in most homes. The pointy heart-shaped leaves are a bronzy colour at first and then turn deep green. Keep it bushy by pinching off the shoot tips every now and then.

light bright light is best but it will survive in darker corners.

temperature average warmth. It won't be happy below 13°C.

water moderately in spring and summer, enough to keep soil moist, and give a fortnightly liquid feed. In winter, let compost dry out a little.

special needs to propagate, take 7.5–10cm tip cuttings in late spring or early summer.

problems avoid direct sun. If it's too warm in winter it produces weedy leaves which must be cut off.

ROSARY VINE (page 51)
Ceropegia linearis woodii

This weird trailing succulent is very easy to grow. It produces thin dangling stems with fleshy dark green marbled leaves which are silvery white on top and purple beneath. From late summer to early autumn, happy plants will produce lots of dull pink tubular flowers.

light thrives in bright light.

temperature does well in any normal room temperatures but it will live down to 5°C.

water sparingly, it is best to allow top half of compost to dry out before next watering. Feed monthly in spring and summer.

special needs plant up tuberous growths which are produced along the stems.

problems if it's too wet in winter it will rot.

CREEPING FIG (below)
Ficus pumila

This pretty little thing is normally a trailing plant but if it's happy it will grow up a wall, sticking to it with aerial roots. The 2cm heart-shaped leaves are slightly puckered and there is also a variegated form (pictured). They look good grown at the base of other larger plants.

light bright light, avoid direct sun.

temperature flourishes in cooler temperatures, almost capable of withstanding frost. In centrally heated rooms, you must keep the humidity up.

water always keep moist and never allow roots to become dry or its leaves will shrivel.

special needs give a liquid feed fortnightly between spring and autumn.

problems red spider mite if the humidity is low.

CAPE LEADWORT (below)
Plumbago auriculata

This climber is normally trained over a hoop of wire when young. Wind in new shoots, but it's quite speedy so you'll then need to train it up something. It flowers from spring to autumn and comes in pale blue or occasionally white.

light loves full sunlight.

temperature cool to average, but in winter a cool rest at 8–10°C.

water loads during the active period, but don't stand in water. In winter give just enough to stop it drying out.

special needs feed fortnightly from spring to summer with a high-potash tomato-like fertilizer.

problems flowers are only produced on the current year's growth so trim the old stems back in spring to encourage new shoots and therefore flowers.

BLEEDING HEART VINE
Clerodendrum thomsoniae

An excellent 3–4m high climber for the conservatory, it can also be kept pruned as a pot plant for the house. The 12cm long leaves are corrugated and not particularly pretty but in spring, summer and early autumn there are clusters of white puffed-out flowers with scarlet tips.

light bright filtered light for flowers.

temperature average warmth. It will only flower if kept humid during active growth and given a cool winter rest.

water plentifully in active growth and sparingly in winter.

special needs liquid feed every two weeks except winter. In spring prune stems back by half and pinch out tips regularly if you want a small plant.

problems none in particular.

IVY
Hedera helix

There are loads of these green and variegated fast-growing small-leaved ivies. They have little aerial roots that cling onto anything so they're great climbers, yet they can also be left to trail or be trained round hoops of wire and regularly trimmed.

light bright or medium light.

temperature cool or even cold rooms. Raising the humidity is very important in warm, heated rooms.

water moderately and slightly less in winter. Don't let compost dry out.

special needs liquid feed every other week in active growth. Cut shoots back occasionally to keep it bushy and use them for cuttings.

problems Red spider mite is very common in warm rooms. Chuck the plant away rather than trying to cure bad infestations.

GRAPE IVY (above left)
Cissus rhombifolia

This is a tough old plant that is extremely tolerant of poor conditions. It can climb or trail and can grow at least 50cm a year. It will soon reach about 3m if it's got something to grow up. The leaves are silvery beneath and deep glossy green on top.

light ideally bright light, yet will tolerate anything but strong sun.

temperature average warmth but during the winter prefers a rest at a much cooler 13°C.

water moderately during the active period and feed fortnightly. In winter only keep the compost just moist.

special needs to propagate, take young tip cuttings, 7.5–15cm, long in spring.

problems strong sunlight will scorch the leaves and mildew is common especially if the compost is too soggy.

CHESTNUT VINE (above right)
Tetrastigma voinierianum

This is the mother of all vines with each leaf measuring more than 30cm in length once it's unfurled. The only drawback is that it's quite rampant, so you need loads of space to accommodate it. High ceilings or a tall conservatory is essential.

light needs bright light.

temperature average temperature, but not hot centrally heated rooms. They hate warm, dry air and dramatic fluctuations in temperature.

water moderately from spring to autumn, but ease off a bit in winter.

special needs feed fortnightly from spring to autumn. To propagate, take 25cm long tip cuttings any time except winter.

problems it grows so fast you'll have to prune it a lot.

PAPER FLOWER (right)
Bougainvillea glabra

Ubiquitous in the Mediterranean and the sub-tropical world, this climber will flower well in spring and summer of its first year, but it is difficult indoors. You need a conservatory for further flowering.

light the sunniest place you've got.

temperature average warmth, but in the winter months keep cool – down to about 10°C.

water water moderately so it's just moist, but keep almost dry in winter. Feed fortnightly while in flower.

special needs stem cuttings in summer are quite easy.

problems too much heat in the winter months makes it suffer.

PASSION FLOWER
Passiflora

There are hundreds of different passion flowers, but not all are suitable for growing indoors. *P. citrina*, with yellow flowers, can be kept as a small vine less than a metre high and it can flower all year except the winter months. *P. sanguinolenta* has pinky red flowers, *P.* x *allardii*, the purple-flowered *P.* 'Amethyst' and the red-fruited *P. rubra* are all scented. The one drawback is that flowers only last for a day or two.

light lots of light, even a south-facing window.

temperature average but keep the humidity up. Spray leaves daily.

water moderately, although they are thirsty plants and in summer usually need daily watering.

special needs when they get overgrown, unravel and prune out as much as half the shoots to within 15cm of the main branches. Feed regularly while in active growth.

problems red spider mite.

Other climbers and trailers
philodendron (p19/21), devil's ivy (p44), wax flower (p87), jasmine (p84)

BIG

Big is beautiful and some species only look good once they reach stately proportions. Because most plants grow quite slowly indoors, it's worth investing a bit of cash in something magnificent. Large plants should be treated as pieces of furniture or artworks and incorporated into room designs rather than stuck in as an afterthought. So don't just go out and buy a huge palm and then figure out where to put it when you get home. Big plants can be quite pricey so, to protect your investment, make sure you choose the right plant for the right place and give it some space so it doesn't get bashed into and damaged.

BIG

COCONUT PALM (page 56)
Cocos nucifera
This is probably the best value-for-money plant there is. The nursery just shoves a coconut in a pot, it sends up a few 1.5m leaves and then they sell it. You can expect to keep it looking good for a couple of years and then it should really be binned.
light bright filtered light near a window is best.
temperature average warmth.
water moderately all year but it doesn't seem to mind neglect.
special needs put it into a bigger pot so it doesn't topple over and a fortnightly feed won't go amiss.
problems none really.

TUFTED-FISHTAIL PALM
Caryota mitis (page 57)
These unusual palms are slow growing, but they will reach a couple of metres high and develop a spreading crown. Small plants look rubbish so pick a big one. Lots of light is the key to success.
light bright or filtered light.
temperature average. The warmer it is, the more humidity is needed.
water plenty of water in summer, but go easy in the winter just enough to stop the soil drying out.
special needs feed every other week except winter.
problems red spider mite can be a problem. Lower fronds naturally go yellow and drop off.

BANANA PLANT (below)
Musa acuminata 'Dwarf Cavendish'
Bananas grow really fast, about a metre a year, with plenty of warmth, water, food and light. The leaves are easily damaged so wrap it up well before you take it home.
light bright with some direct sun.
temperature average warmth, but give it good humidity.
water needs plenty in the active period, add liquid feed every time. In winter water sparingly.
special needs propagate in the spring by removing suckers and planting up.
problems watch out for red spider mite under the leaves.

DRACAENA (above left)

Dracaena deremensis 'Warneckii'
Dracaenas have long, strap-shaped, often, stripy leaves. They are mostly erect plants that develop a single cane or trunk as the lower leaves fall off with age. All are pretty easy to keep and basically have the same requirements. This particular variety has white and green stripy leaves and reaches about 1.8m high.
light bright but not direct sunlight.
temperature average warmth protected from draughts. They don't like the cold at all.
water plentifully so the compost is always moist but never ever soggy. Water sparingly in winter. Feed every other week in active growth.
special needs repot every two years using a soil-based compost because it is heavier and stops tall plants from falling over.
problems overwatering is a big killer. Dry air or soil makes leaf tips go brown.

CANARY DATE PALM (above)

Phoenix canariensis
This classic palm tree will do well indoors if it gets plenty of light. The fronds are quite stiff so give it lots of space to make sure it won't poke people's eyes out. It is quite slow growing but it will eventually get to about 2m tall. The miniature date palm *P. roebelenii* is less than a metre high with more feathery, wide-spreading fronds and is an excellent air purifier.
light direct sunlight although *P. roebelenii* prefers bright filtered light.
temperature average warmth, but a cool winter rest as low as 10°C is best.
water plentifully in the growing period, but sparingly in winter, so the compost is barely moist.
special needs feed once every two weeks from spring to summer.
problems keep out of cold draughts. Yellowing fronds may be a result of irregular watering and low light.

BUDDHIST PINE

Podocarpus macrophyllus
Unheated rooms are really best for this conifer, cold hallways and porches are ideal. As it gets older, the branches start to droop and it becomes a fairly graceful little tree. They can reach several metres indoors if the pot is big enough. The tough flat green leaves are about 8cm long and not easily damaged.
light bright filtered light.
temperature cool to average warmth is best.
water moderately but allow to become fairly dry in winter unless in a warm room.
special needs some form of staking might be required. If a plant gets too open, trim back side shoots in spring to make it bushier. Repot each spring with a soil-based compost.
problems fairly trouble-free.

PONY TAIL PALM (left)
Beaucarnea recurvata

This is a really easy plant to grow. The plume of grassy leaves give the plant its common name but it's also called elephant's foot because of the swollen base of the usually single grey stem. Fairly slow growing, it's a good idea to buy big.

light bright with a little sun.

temperature average warmth, dry air isn't a problem.

water give it a good soak, then leave it until it becomes moderately dry. Avoid overwatering.

special needs repot every other year in spring.

problems for some reason cats like chewing the leaves which doesn't seem to harm the cats but it doesn't do a lot for the plants.

UMBRELLA TREE
Schefflera actinophylla

This stately tree-like plant can reach a couple of metres high. There are between five and seven tough shiny leaves that radiate out from a central point like the spokes of an umbrella. They are quite easy plants to grow and are excellent air purifiers.

light bright light.

temperature ideally a cool room between 15–18°C, but they'll survive higher if the humidity is kept up. If it falls to below about 13°C, then leaves will drop.

water moderately in active growth but keep on the dry side in winter.

special needs feed every two weeks in active growth. Repot every other spring – small pots keep the plants small. Clean the leaves regularly with a sponge.

problems mealy bug and scale.

FIG (right)
Ficus 'Audrey'

Most of the different figs are pretty tough plants that are happy in most indoor environments. This one is similar in habit to the more common fiddle leaf fig, *Ficus lyrata*. Like the closely related rubber plant, *F. elastica* they grow very upright and very quickly, 30 or 40cm a year is normal.

light anywhere between medium and bright. Avoid direct sun.

temperature average warmth. Raising the humidity is only necessary in very warm rooms.

water sparingly so the compost is barely moist.

special needs sponge the leaves to remove dust.

problems overwatering makes the lower leaves drop.

NORFOLK ISLAND PINE
Araucaria heterophylla

This turns into a proper tree in a big conservatory, but is a bit more manageable indoors growing about 10–15cm a year. A feathery conifer, it has bright green needles on branches arranged in tiers.

light medium to bright light. If it's too dark the needles drop.

temperature they'll be happy in a really wide range from cool to warm but increase the humidity at the upper end.

water plentifully in active growth but only moderately in winter.

special needs repot every two years with a soil-based compost. Liquid feed every two weeks.

problems excessive central heating can make the needles crispy and eventually kills the plant. Keep away from radiators.

Other big plants *kentia palm (p68), rubber plant (p42), weeping fig (p71), philodendron (p63/65)*

OFFICE

Plants in offices are said to reduce absenteeism and improve worker output but they need to be fairly tough and low maintenance in order to thrive. In foyers, they must be able to survive draughts and perhaps an accumulation of cigarette butts in the pot. Elsewhere they need to have rugged leaves that won't get damaged by people brushing past them. They need to be able to put up with a fairly dry air-conditioned atmosphere and the occasional cup of coffee being chucked on their roots. On the plus side, most offices have fairly constant temperatures and the only problems are likely to arise if the offices get too cold at night when no one is there.

NARROW-LEAVED FIG (left)
Ficus barteri 'Variegata'
This is that little bit more resilient than the popular weeping fig *F. benjamina* and is less prone to shedding its leaves.
light bright, but not as much for the non-variegated sort.
temperature average warmth.
water moderately, allow compost to dry out a bit between waterings. Too much water makes the lower leaves fall.
special needs feed fortnightly in active growth, wash dust off leaves.
problems the milky white sap can be an irritant so don't get it in your eyes. Watch out for scale and mealy bug. Avoid radiators and draughts.

CORN PALM (page 62)
Dracaena fragrans 'Massangeana'
This is a particularly rugged plant and is good for removing toxins from the air. It can reach between 2–3m high. The closely related *D. deremensis* is just as good.
light prefers bright light but also grows in dimmer conditions.
temperature average warmth.
water keep moist, reduce in winter.
special needs repot every two years and feed every fortnight during active growth.
problems fairly trouble-free.

ARECA PALM
Chrysalidocarpus lutescens/ Dypsis lutescens
A feathery palm several metres high with lots of yellow stems. It does well near office windows, shaded by blinds or tinted glass.
light bright filtered light.
temperature average warmth. They don't seem to mind minor fluctuations and put up with low humidity better than kentias.
water somewhere between plentifully and moderately.
special needs liquid feed every two weeks in active growth.
problems draughts can make leaves dull greeny brown.

PHILODENDRON (page 63)
Philodendron
There are loads of philodendrons and they are all good in offices. There are some, like *P. selloum* and *P. bipinnatifdum,* with rosettes of massive leaves which need a lot of space and then there are the climbing sorts like *P. scandens* (p50/52) and the one pictured.
light bright filtered light. They'll survive dimmer conditions but plants get leggy.
temperature average warmth.
water moderately and then sparingly in winter.
special needs climbers need a moss pole or something for support. Poke the stubby aerial roots into the moss.
problems overwatering causes yellowing leaves. Leaves can be damaged by excessive battering.

ASPARAGUS FERN (right)
Asparagus setaceus
Not really a fern at all. It starts off bushy with its almost horizontal, almost triangular fronds but then turns into a twining climber sending out long winding shoots. These can be allowed to trail or be chopped off. *A. densiflorus* 'Sprengeri' is even tougher with drooping stems covered in needle-like leaves.
light bright light is essential, but not direct sunlight.
temperature average warmth.
water plentifully to keep it moist but sparingly in winter.
special needs liquid feed every two weeks during active growth. Repot in spring.
problems underwatering and low humidity can cause yellowing and dropping foliage. Pale leaves may also be due to red spider mite. Beware the tiny thorns on the stems.

JAPANESE ARALIA
Fatsia japonica
This green glossy leaved plant can be grown like the Ivy tree (page 20).

ADONIDIA PALM
Veitchia merrillii
This palm from the Philippines has a bright green trunk, swollen at the base. The chunky fronds are strongly arched. Reaching as much as 5–6m, this is a plant for foyers and large spaces. The Alexander palm, *Ptychosperma elegans*, is similar but often grown as a clump.
light bright, filtered light.
temperature average, above 15°C.
water moderately, less in winter.
special needs liquid feed every fortnight in growth. Yellowing of fronds may be magnesium deficiency, apply liquid seaweed.
problems red spider mite, mealy bug.

Other office plants *grape ivy (p54), kentia (p68), peace lily (p18/21), painted drop-tongue (p20)*

SPINELESS YUCCA

UNKILLABLE

UNKILLABLE

Some people just can't keep plants alive no matter how hard they try. Others don't have the time or simply can't be bothered. But whether you've got green fingers or not, the simplest solution is to choose plants that refuse to die. There's nothing worse than a suffering plant that sits in the corner looking sad. So pick something indestructible that thrives on neglect, puts up with draughts or darkness, massive leaps in temperature and no affection whatsoever. Of course, nothing is totally indestructible; if you deprive anything of light or water it will eventually die, the only difference is that some die much faster than others. Cacti and succulents are classic examples – they only thrive if you give them lots of sunlight, water and fertilizer, but they'll cling onto life for ages without much of anything. The biggest killer of indoor plants is overwatering, so it's always safest to be stingy with it, but the plants here will mostly put up with extremely erratic watering by hopeless gardeners.

KENTIA PALM
Howea forsteriana
Probably the most popular indoor palm because it's so tough. It's actually several plants in one pot so it never forms a proper trunk.
light bright or medium light is fine. It can be kept in darker corners as long as you move it near to a window every other day.
temperature average. Low humidity isn't really a problem but very dry air makes leaf tips brown.
water plentifully but never stand in water. In darker cooler conditions water sparingly.
special needs small pots are fine, but repot every two or three years.
problems pale leaves and fine webbing underneath is caused by red spider mite.

SPINELESS YUCCA (page 66)
Yucca elephantipes
These familiar plants have a knobbly brown trunk with two or three clumps of green leaves at the top. As these clumps grow they also develop canes as the lower leaves fall off.
light bright light, if they don't get enough they will stop growing but still survive. Too much sun bleaches and scorches the leaves.
temperature average warmth but they'll survive down to 10°C.
water plentifully, keep the compost moist but much drier in winter. Fairly long periods without water don't cause much damage.
special needs if they get too tall chop through the cane and new shoots will appear just below the cut. Use the cane for cuttings.
problems trouble-free.

WANDERING JEW
Tradescantia zebrina/Zebrina pendula
This almost trailing plant has iridescent oval leaves about 5cm long with two broad silver stripes. Underneath they are purple. In spring and summer it produces small purple, three-petalled flowers. Other cream and green (and sometimes pink) tradescantias are very similar but trail a bit more.
light bright light is best. They'll survive in less but get leggy and the leaf colour fades a bit.
temperature cool or average warmth. The warmer it is the faster they grow.
water moderately in active growth and sparingly in winter. They don't seem to mind a bit of neglect.
special needs If they get leggy chop them back. The cuttings root easily in compost or in a glass of water. Put at least five in a pot. Regularly pinch out shoot tips to keep compact.
problems none really, apart from getting leggy.

MADAGASCAR DRAGON TREE
Dracaena marginata (page 67)
This plant actually improves with neglect. The narrow green leaves with red edges are gradually replaced by thinner, prettier leaves if deprived of bright light and the stems grow a bit crooked.
light likes bright light but is happy well away from windows.
temperature average warmth.
water moderately in the growing season, but go easy in winter. Doesn't mind underwatering, but too little can cause brown leaf tips.
special needs feed occasionally.
problems none really.

MOTHER-IN-LAW'S TONGUE (right)
Sansevieria trifasciata 'Laurentii'
This succulent was once incredibly popular and has since been out of favour but it's set for a comeback. Perhaps its greatest asset is its unkillability for which it scores 9.5.
light bright light but can also withstand direct sunlight.
temperature average warmth but won't grow in cold rooms.
water moderately but keep fairly dry in winter.
special needs propagate by leaf cuttings. Feeding isn't important.
problems overwatering makes the base of the stems rot and leaves go yellow.

SPIDER PLANT
Chlorophytum comosum 'Vittatum'
Barely a toilet in the land has eluded the humble spider plant. Cascading stems with small white flowers turn into tiny plantlets – miniature imitations of the green-and-white striped parent.
light really adaptable. Anything except extreme sun or shade.
temperature warm or fairly cold rooms. Doesn't mind dry air.
water plentifully in the active period, moderately in winter.
special needs feed fortnightly, but it isn't essential.
problems excess heat or dark makes leaves pale and limp.

UMBRELLA PLANT
Schefflera arboricola
Also called *Heptapleurum arboricola* this is a smaller relative of *S. actinophylla* (p60). Very hard to kill, it will reach nearly 2m in ordinary room conditions and keeps growing almost year round. Each leaf is made up of about ten leaflets each on a stalk like the spokes of an umbrella. There is a fairly garish variegated form.
light bright, but medium is ok.
temperature average warmth.
water moderately but will cope with a bit of forgetfulness.
special needs pinch out the growing tips to encourage branching otherwise they just keep going straight up and eventually topple over. They seem to grow happily in a tiny pot but repotting each year is preferred. Liquid feed every few weeks in active growth.
problems sudden changes or hot dry air can cause a bit of leaf drop but they won't die.

WEEPING FIG (left)
Ficus benjamina
Probably the best indoor plant in the world. It only manages to get in here by a nose on account of its penchant for dropping all its leaves. But even if that does happen, it won't die and they'll grow back. There are lots of different varieties around these days and the various variegated ones are good but need a little more light.
light bright light is best.
temperature average warmth but it acclimatizes well to most rooms.
water moderately. Erratic watering isn't too much of a problem. Liquid feed fortnightly in active growth.
special needs moving the plant around and sudden changes in conditions can make the leaves drop but new ones grow back.
problems scale insects, and overwatering will cause lower leaves to fall.

FLAMING KATY (below left)
Kalanchoe blossfeldiana
You can't actually kill this flowering succulent, even if you try. They flower for months and months but once they've finished they are best chucked away. They grow to between 15 and 20cm high and flower in red, pink and yellow.
light a sunny window-sill is ideal.
temperature average warmth but is happy in colder rooms.
water it doesn't need much water so keep it on the dry side.
special needs feed every two weeks while in flower, but it isn't essential. Remove the flowers when they fade if you can be bothered.
problems none really.

CAST IRON PLANT (below right)
Aspidistra elatior 'Milky Way'
The Victorians named this plant because it put up with their gas-light rooms and coal-fire fumes. It seems to do best if you don't do anything to it. Grown for its leaves, it does also produce inconspicuous little purple flowers at ground level.
light will survive in dark corners but prefers medium light. Variegated ones need medium to bright light.
temperature very adaptable.
water moderately and not very often. Allow top two-thirds of the compost to dry out between waterings. Liquid feed every two weeks in the growing period.
special needs aspidistras do best when they are left alone. Repot only if it needs it after three or four years.
problems generally trouble-free but watch out for red spider mite.

Other unkillable plants
ivy (p53), ivy tree (p20), philodendron (p19/21), peace lily (p18/21), parlour palm (p21)

CHALLENGING

If you think about it, plants aren't meant to be grown indoors anyway and quite frankly it's a miracle that so many different ones will do so well in your living room. Sadly, it's human nature for us to want things that we can't have and people try to grow plants that just don't want to be inside and yearn for the great outdoors, or at the very least a conservatory. But for anyone who likes a challenge, here are a few plants that are worth a bit of extra hassle.

JUNGLE FLAME (below left)

Ixora coccinea

They won't put up with much deviation from their ideal growing conditions. This evergreen shrub, with glossy green leaves, flowers when it's very small but it can get to over a metre high. There are varieties with orange, yellow, pink and red flowers which appear in summer.

light bright light on a window-sill is best.

temperature average warmth with high humidity.

water moderately and then sparingly after flowering.

special needs liquid feed every two weeks in spring and summer. Repot each spring but just topdress older plants.

problems scale insects can appear and all the leaves fall off if you don't get the watering right.

ROSE GRAPE (below right)

Medinilla magnifica

A warm greenhouse or conservatory only makes it slightly easier to grow this tricky customer. They can reach a metre tall and, in late spring, the pink flower heads extend to 45cm long. To have any hope of getting them to flower, however, you must pamper them continually.

light bright filtered light is essential for this plant.

temperature they must be kept constantly warm, between 20 and 26°C, with a consistently high humidity. A winter rest at about 18°C is needed.

water moderately with a fortnightly liquid feed in spring and summer. Water sparingly in winter.

special needs immediately after flowering in early summer cut all branches back by half.

problems red spider mite loves it.

DUTCHMAN'S PIPE (page 72)

Aristolochia gigantea

A warm conservatory or greenhouse is really needed for this evergreen twining climber which can reach 10m but, in theory, it could be grown in a large, warm, bright room. In summer it has bizarre chocolate-purple flowers, sometimes the size of a head. Flowers are borne on old stems.

light bright filtered light.

temperature average warmth.

water freely and apply liquid feed monthly from spring to autumn. In the winter months, water sparingly.

special needs softwood cuttings in early spring. Prune after flowering.

problems mostly trouble-free, but can get rampant so needs plenty of space.

MAIDENHAIR FERN (page 73)
Adiantum raddianum

This beautiful feathery fern has black wiry stems and delicate pale green fronds. Sadly, they are so delicate that a little too much heat or a missed dose of water and the fronds shrivel and die. Brightly lit bathrooms seem to be the best place for them. They also love bottle gardens.

light bright sunlight, never full sun.

temperature very cool conditions. Raise the humidity in warm rooms. Cold rooms aren't a big problem.

water keep the compost always just moist but never soggy. Never let it dry out. Give a monthly liquid feed at half strength except in winter.

special needs trim off damaged or dead fronds. Repot occasionally in spring.

problems hates fluctuations in temperature.

BIRD OF PARADISE
Strelitzia reginae

Keeping them alive is easy but getting them to flower in ordinary room conditions is nigh on impossible unless you move them around. You really need a conservatory. Normally growing to around a metre high, the paddle-shaped leaves are on the end of long stalks with orange and blue flowers in late spring and early summer. Plants only flower when about six years old.

light bright light with a little direct sun (although not at midday) is essential for flowering.

temperature average warmth while in active growth but in winter, a cool, possibly unheated room at about 13°C. Without this rest, they won't flower.

water moderately in active growth and sparingly in winter.

special needs liquid feed every two weeks in active growth. Repot in spring.

problems scale insect on the undersides of the leaves.

AFRICAN HEMP (right)
Sparmannia africana

This large-leaved plant can reach several metres tall and it isn't hard to keep alive. But it is difficult to get it to flower and then keep it flowering. The double-flowered 'Flore Pleno' and the basic species are notoriously hard to coax into bloom so if you can, get the dwarf form 'Nana' and treat it as best you can.

light bright filtered light.

temperature constant cool temperatures of about 15°C.

water moderately and give a fortnightly liquid feed from spring. In the winter water sparingly.

special needs remove the flowers once they've finished because on their own, they won't fall for ages.

problems whitefly and red spider mite are very common in normal room conditions.

FIRECRACKER FLOWER
Crossandra infundibuliformis

It's hard enough to pronounce its name let alone keep it alive. Growing to about 60cm tall with glossy green leaves, in spring and summer they produce orangey-red tubular flowers, flared at the ends. Even very young plants flower. The problem is they absolutely must have a very high humidity which is difficult in your living room.

light bright light but no direct sun.

temperature average warmth. They don't like the cold.

water moderately so the compost is always moist. In winter, sparingly.

special needs keep that humidity up. Slotting it amongst other plants helps, daily misting and a pebble tray are essential.

problems red spider mite is common.

Other challenging plants *some orchids (p137–139), jewel plant (p78), gardenia (p82/84), wax flower (p87)*

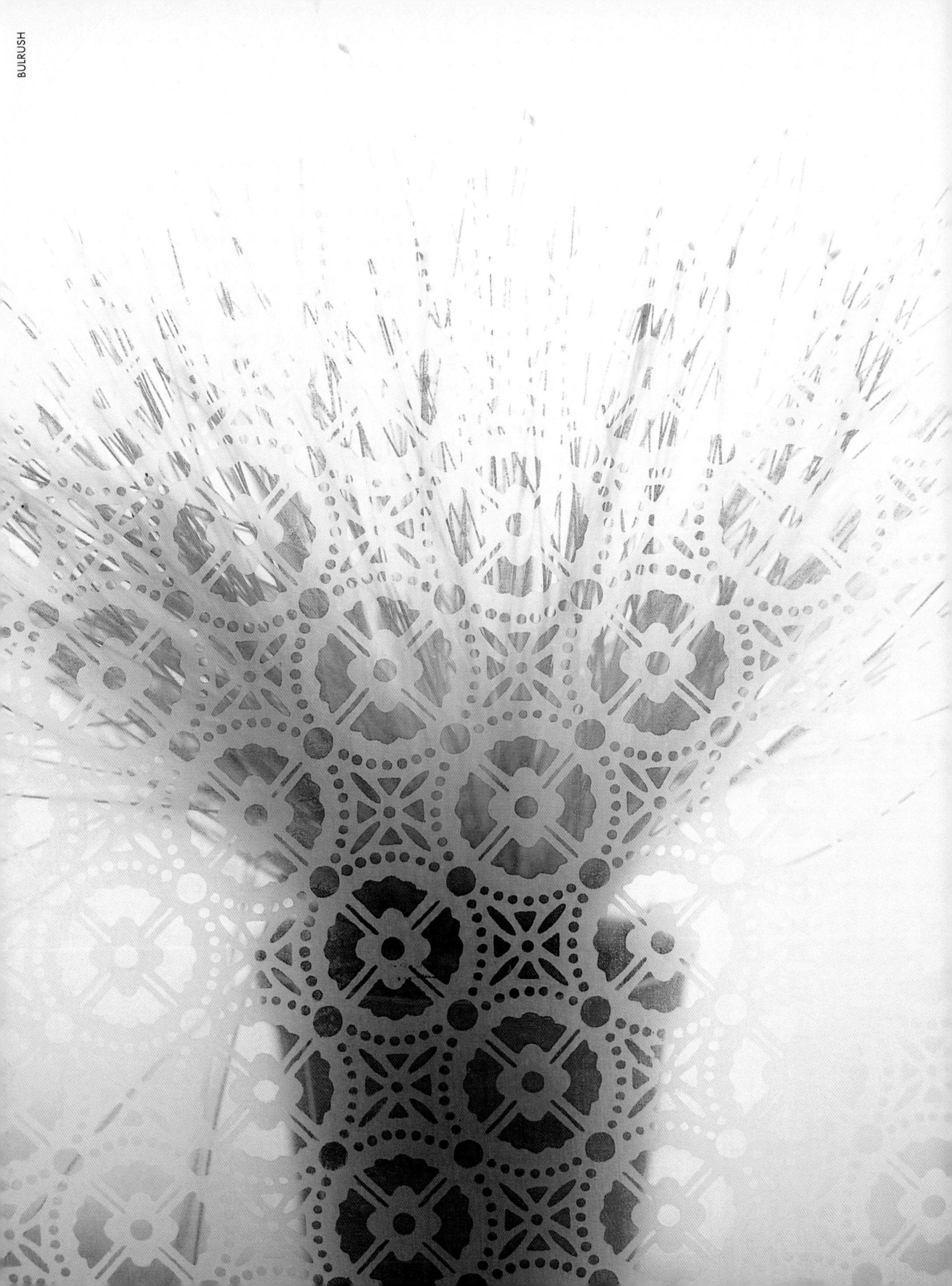

DAMP

Most indoor plants are killed because their owners give them too much water. So it's nice to have a few plants that like to get their feet wet and won't suffer a soggy end. Some like to be permanently moist but not waterlogged. Others can even be stood in a saucer or other container of water during the growing season. One advantage is that you can go off on holiday and not have to worry. The deeper the saucer, the longer you can go away for. You also don't have to fuss about accurate watering techniques because you can see when you've given it enough.

KRIS PLANT (above left)
Alocasia x amazonica
This amazingly beautiful waxy leaved plant is unfortunately a bit tricky to grow as an indoor plant as it likes to be very warm and humid. It's better off in a conservatory but as it's so striking give it a go anyway. Smaller plants are best for indoors.
light bright light, but away from direct sun.
temperature likes it warm, at least 20ºC. Avoid cool rooms. Humidity must be permanently high. Keep away from radiators.
water keep compost permanently wet but only just moist in winter.
problems temperature fluctuations, cold and draughts can cause yellowing and spotted leaves. Watch out for mealy bugs. Contact with sap may cause skin irritation.

FAIRY MOSS (above right)
Azolla filiculoides
This is a pond plant really but the tiny delicate fronds look pretty good floating around in a bowl on the window-sill or a centrepiece for a table. It keeps the water clear on its own.
light give it bright light.
temperature puts up with a whole range of conditions.
water grow in a bowl of water and never let it dry out.
special needs even a tiny piece of plant will quickly spread to cover the whole surface of a bowl, so propagating is easy.
problems ducks like eating it, but that shouldn't be too much of a problem in your kitchen.

JEWEL PLANT
Bertolonia marmorata
This is a tricky plant to look after in the home and consequently not very common. High humidity is essential. They form a low clump of shimmering dark green heart-shaped leaves about 15cm long with five silvery lines running lengthways. Small purple flowers occasionally appear.
light bright or medium light.
temperature warm rooms but with a high humidity.
water plentifully during active growth but only sparingly in winter.
special needs be careful not to get water on the leaves which can cause brown marks.
problems lack of humidity encourages red spider mite and brown-edged leaves.

DAMP

MIND YOUR OWN BUSINESS
Soleirolia soleirolii
A perfect common name for this creeping plant that spreads everywhere. Even in the confines of a pot it will sort of pour over the sides. It has tiny green leaves and doesn't flower. It's very good for growing at the base of large plants. There is a silvery variegated form and a golden yellow one.
light bright or medium, but it is adaptable. It will get straggly if it's too dark and tends to grow towards the light so rotate pots weekly.
temperature cold to average warmth, it can even live outside.
water plentifully from underneath, never let the compost dry out but don't stand plants in water.
special needs trim leggy plants with scissors. Liquid feed every four weeks. Easily propagated by pushing little bits into compost.
problems variegated plants sometimes turn green.

BULRUSH (page 76)
Scirpus cernuus
This graceful little plant looks like a clump of grass and has tiny whitish flowers on the tips of the bright green leaves. Small plants are upright at first and, as the leaves reach their full 25cm, they flop over but in a good way.
light medium or bright light, put them on a north-facing window-sill
temperature average warmth, but will be happy down to about 8°C in winter.
water stand in water unless kept at lower winter temperatures.
special needs liquid feed once every four weeks. Propagate by division, pull clumps apart in spring.
problems change water regularly, if stale water is left in the saucer, especially in cooler temperatures, it starts to stink.

CLUB MOSS (below + page 77)
Selaginella
These plants look like sort of ferny mosses. Some are only a few centimetres high while others get to a stately 30cm tall. They like the humidity of bathrooms and are at home in shallow pots of free-draining compost.
light they hate direct sun. Keep in medium light away from windows.
temperature average warmth but keep the humidity up. They aren't good with central heating and dry air is fatal.
water give it plenty, but don't ever let the pot stand in water.
special needs give them a trim in spring to neaten them up a bit if they need it. A weak liquid feed once a month is fine.
problems plants yellowing then turning black is due to bad watering. Make sure they aren't waterlogged and don't water the leaves.

DAMP

ARUM OR CALLA LILY (left)
Zantedeschia

The white-flowering type is quite common but now there are some smaller more colourful soft pink, yellow and carmine varieties. They flower in early summer and grow to about 40cm. In winter, the leaves die down.

light bright light with some direct sunlight.

temperature when it is starting into growth in the early spring months keep cool at a temperature of 10–13°C for about two months. Raise to average warmth when flowering.

water sparingly from early spring and as growth increases so should the water. Once in full leaf, stand the plant in a saucer of water. When the plant stops flowering reduce the water again and keep the compost fairly dry in winter. Liquid feed every two weeks in full leaf until flowering stops.

problems susceptible to fungal diseases and prone to aphids.

FLAME VIOLET
Episcia cupreata

In summer, red and yellow flowers are produced in groups of three or four on these low spreading plants. The leaves are a wonderful coppery green with silvery markings around the central vein.

light bright light with a bit of direct sun but not at midday.

temperature average warmth with essential high humidity.

water plentifully to keep compost constantly moist. In cooler temperatures ease off a bit.
E. 'Cygnet' can be stood in water.

special needs liquid feed at a quarter strength every time you water it.

problems watch out for aphids on young leaves.

UMBRELLA PLANT (right)
Cyperus alternifolius

This easy rush has straight stems about a metre tall topped by a tuft of grassy leaflets. *Cyperus papyrus* is a magnificent, majestic plant of biblical fame, but much harder to grow. The pith of the stout 2m triangular stems has been used for making paper since ancient times. *C. involucratus* 'Gracilis' is a much shorter 30cm variety.

light grow in bright light.

temperature average warmth, but slightly cooler in winter.
C. papyrus likes to be a bit warmer than the others all year.

water impossible to overwater, stand the pots in any watertight container and liquid feed every fortnight.

special needs crowded plants can be repotted in spring and divided at the same time to make more plants.

problems the water may start to smell so change it every now and then.

SWEET FLAG
Acorus gramineus 'Variegatus'

This grassy plant makes clumps of green and white striped leaves about 40cm tall. Quite a tough little plant, it doesn't mind cold, draughts or waterlogging.

light bright light.

temperature cool rooms are best, preferably unheated in winter.

water stand them in water; if they dry out the leaf tips go brown.

special needs propagate by dividing the plants at any time.

problems red spider mite can be troublesome in warm rooms.

Other damp plants *cock on a plate (p38), blechnum fern (p153), tufted-fishtail palm (p57/58), bleeding heart vine (p53)*

SCENTED

Smell is the most powerful and evocative of all the senses and is hugely important indoors when even the slightest perfume can fill a room. But it's a very subjective thing. What may smell fantastic to me may be revolting to you. Different times of day and different temperatures will also play their part, so what you'll find here are things that I think have a wonderful perfume but the best advice is try before you buy. Some of these plants are hard to coax into bloom for a subsequent year so they should all be bought in bud or in flower. That way, you're guaranteed to get your money's worth.

SCENTED

SCENTED GERANIUM (left)
Pelargonium

It's the leaves of geraniums that are scented. They can smell of lemon, peppermint, apple and all sorts of things. There are even some unpleasant ones that smell of fish and the London Underground. They are really easy to grow and can survive neglect.
light as much light as possible, direct sunlight would be great.
temperature average warmth. A cool winter rest is preferable in a cold room.
water thoroughly, then not again until compost looks dry. Keep almost dry in winter.
special needs pinch out tips in spring to keep plants bushy. Remove faded flower heads and yellow leaves. Stem cuttings in late summer are very easy.
problems excess water and humidity causes a black rot at the base.

JASMINE
Jasminum polyanthum

The pink-tinged, sweet-smelling flowers of this climber look good even in bud and it is more popular than the white- and yellow-flowered varieties because it flowers when it's quite young. If left to grow it will reach several metres high but it can be trained around a hoop of wire and kept to about 70cm high. The flowering period is mid-winter to mid-spring.
light bright, with some direct sun.
temperature cool conditions are best. They'll survive average warmth but won't flower as long.
water plentifully while it is in active growth.
special needs after flowering, cut plants back to keep them under control. Propagate by stem cuttings in spring and pinch out the tips of young plants.
problems warm rooms make plants struggle.

GARDENIA
Gardenia jasminoides (page 82)

Waxy white fragrant flowers appear in summer on this slow-growing bush. The mound of glossy green leaves usually gets to between 30–45cm high as an indoor plant. The smell is sweet and powerful. They are easy to keep but hard to get to flower.
light bright light, but never in direct sunlight.
temperature keep it at a steady 16–17°C with a high humidity when flower buds are forming. Once the buds have formed keep at average room temperature, up to a maximum of about 23–24°C, but keep it steady.
water moderately while in growth and very slightly less in winter.
special needs nip out long shoot tips in early spring to keep bushy. Feed every two weeks from spring to early autumn with azalea fertilizer.
problems sudden changes in temperature make buds drop off.

ANGELS TRUMPET (page 83)
Brugmansia/Datura

The curled buds unfurl into huge dangling 25cm long trumpet flowers. The most common are white, but yellow and orange are available. The scent, particularly in the evening, is overpowering to some. Ideally they are conservatory plants or can be put outside in the summer and kept somewhere cool indoors in winter.
light bright with some sun.
temperature average warmth but keep cool in the winter. An unheated room is best. They can be grown in a warm or cool conservatory.
water give it plenty from spring to autumn, sparingly in the winter.
special needs prune the plant almost to the ground in winter to save space. Feed every other week in spring and summer.
problems whitefly and red spider mite are common. All parts of the plant are poisonous.

STAR JASMINE
Trachelospermum jasminoides

An evergreen climber growing several metres tall indoors, it is really an outdoor plant (see Outside In, pages 166/169). From spring to summer, it has sweet-smelling jasmine-like flowers. The glossy leaves are green, but there is a prettier, less rampant variegated form.
light constant bright light, but shade from direct sunlight.
temperature always keep it cool.
water plenty in the growing season, just enough in the winter months to stop it drying out.
special needs liquid feed fortnightly from spring to autumn. Needs bamboo canes for support.
problems a bit of a rampant grower, but generally trouble-free.

CHERRY PIE

Heliotropium arborescens
This easy-to-grow plant has usually purple but sometimes blue or white flowers that do smell exactly like a cherry pie. It's uncanny. They flower in summer.

light lots of bright light, but avoid hot sun.

temperature average warmth but must be kept cool in winter.

water plentifully while active and sparingly in winter.

special needs liquid feed monthly in spring and summer. Prune in spring to keep it compact and remove dead flower heads. Propagate by stem cuttings in summer.

problems no real worries, but watch out for whitefly. Flowering deteriorates with age.

SCENTED

MINIATURE WAX PLANT (left)
Hoya lanceolata bella
These trailing plants are best in hanging baskets. They have pointy leaves and clusters of scented star-shaped flowers. The big brother, *Hoya carnosa*, is a fast-growing climber with bigger, glossy green leaves and similar waxy flowers. They thrive if left undisturbed apart from water and fertilizer.
light bright. A few hours of direct sun helps flowering of *H. carnosa*.
temperature average. *H. lanceolata bella* likes higher humidity.
water moderately from spring to autumn and then sparingly.
special needs only repot when it is unavoidable. Feed with tomato fertilizer every other week from spring to autumn.
problems sometimes mealy bug.

WAX FLOWER (below)
Stephanotis floribunda
This climber from Madagascar has clusters of pure white star-shaped tubular flowers that you get in bridal headdresses. It's tricky, but not impossible, to encourage back into flower in spring and early summer.
light bright light. Direct sunlight will damage the foliage.
temperature average warmth but hates sudden fluctuations. Keep the humidity up. In winter keep fairly cool.
water plentifully in summer and sparingly in winter.
special needs grow around a hoop of wire where space is limited. Liquid feed every two weeks in the active period. Repot in early spring.
problems scale insects under leaves and sometimes mealy bug.

PERSIAN VIOLET
Exacum affine
From midsummer to late autumn this little plant is covered in small, fragrant, violet-coloured flowers with a gold centre. Make sure you buy them mainly in bud rather than in bloom so you get the most out of them and then chuck them away when finished. They usually start off about 10cm tall and grow to about 25cm. There are also dwarf and white varieties available.
light bright light.
temperature cool or average warmth with high humidity.
water plentifully.
special needs liquid feed every two weeks. They can be grown from seed in late summer.
problems pick off blooms as they fade to prolong flowering.

Other scented plants *yesterday, today, tomorrow plant (p15), cereus (p142/143), peace lily (p18/21), hyacinth (p155/156), lily (p91)*

FENG SHUI

Feng shui is about living in perfect balance with your environment, so every aspect of your life benefits. It's about channelling the flow of energy, and apparently growing the right plants in the right place makes a big difference. Succulents are the most auspicious, their plump, round leaves being symbolic of money and goodness, but thorny plants send out poisoned arrows of bad energy. Bonsai should be chucked out because they are intentionally stunted and are very bad for wealth and luck. But good feng shui can only be achieved if your plants thrive so look after them or the bad energy overwhelms the good chi. Oh and don't forget to put the toilet seat down or all your wealth will disappear into the sewer.

SILVER CROWN (left)
Cotyledon undulata
This succulent brings good fortune to your house and is quite easy to look after. It can be placed anywhere. The flowers are orange.
light full sunlight to avoid spindly growth and poor-coloured leaves.
temperature average warmth. Dry air is happily tolerated.
water moderately but reduce in winter, so compost almost dries out.
special needs liquid feed every two weeks during active growth.
problems none really.

TI TREE (page 88)
Dracaena or cordyline
Plants are appreciated for their shape and silhouette and, like bamboo, these plants are disciplined and upright. A number of species are sold like this. The canes are cut into sections and shipped overseas. Buds burst out the side at the top of the stem when stood in water or planted.
light medium light close to an east- or west-facing window.
temperature average warmth.
water moderately, keeping compost moist. Reduce in winter but don't let it dry out.
special needs liquid feed fortnightly in active growth.
problems leaves go soft and curly if temperatures are too low.

LILY
Lilium
Lilies represent good feng shui all year round. The big trumpet flowers are often scented and come in a range of colours including white, yellow and orange.
light bright light but not direct sun.
temperature cool rooms, especially at night while the bulb is getting ready to flower.
water plentifully while the bulb is growing.
special needs reduce watering after flowering. Put outside or in a cool room and repot in autumn.
problems rarely flower well again.

POT CHRYSANTHEMUM (page 89)
Chrysanthemum morifolium
Pure and honest, chrysanthemums are held in high esteem but yellow ones in particular are associated with a life of ease and they create great happiness and joy. Buy when the buds are showing colour because tight green ones may fail to open. Discard or plant in the garden after flowering.
light bright light is essential, but shade from midday sun.
temperature cool rooms are ideal. They'll survive average warmth if you increase humidity but won't flower for so long.
water plentifully before and during flowering. Don't let them dry out.
special needs feeding isn't necessary.
problems letting them stand in water has dire consequences.

GOLDEN-GROOVE BAMBOO
Phyllostachys aureosulcata
'Aureocaulis' (right)
Bamboo wards off malign spirits and symbolizes longevity and endurance. Have it on the left-hand side of your home to signify the dragon, at the front to attract good chi and at the back to be lucky in business. Old or dead growth must be removed immediately. Many bamboos suitable for indoors are quite tall and you may need a lot of space.
light needs permanently bright filtered light throughout the year.
temperature cool rooms are best for most species.
water plenty during the active period and during the winter only sparingly.
special needs feed every other week in active growth.
problems underwatering and excessive heat makes the leaves curl.

JADE PLANT
Crassula ovata
You've probably seen these tree-like plants in Chinese restaurants by the door to attract prosperity, but you can also put them in the kitchen for abundance. Don't let them get more than a metre high and if they get sick replace immediately. Fortunately these succulents are easy to look after.
light bright with some direct sun.
temperature cool or average.
water moderately while active, in winter enough so it doesn't dry out.
special needs liquid feed every two weeks, except in winter. Repot every two years. Propagate by leaf cuttings.
problems overwatering is a killer.

Other Feng shui plants orchids (p137–139), philodendron (p19/21), bulbs, especially daffodil, (p155–157), orange trees (p128–131), lady's eardrops (p32), many succulents (p144–149).

KEEPING

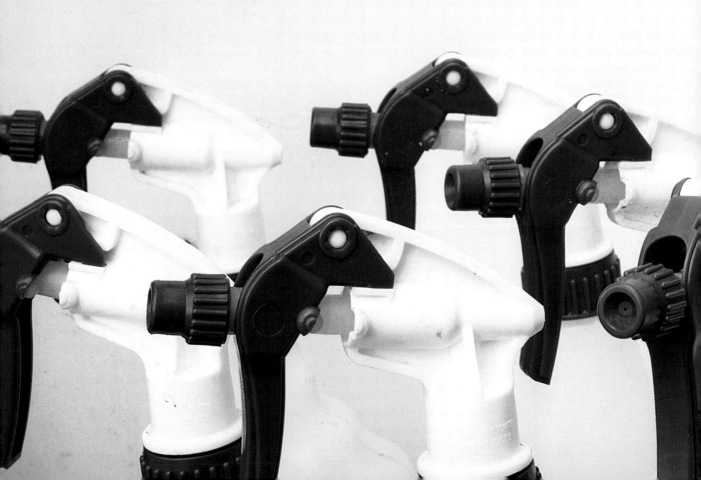

THEM HAPPY

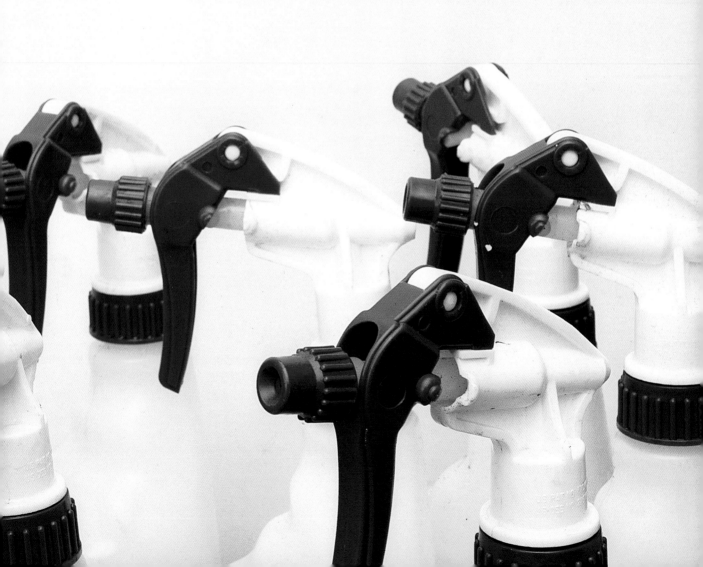

LIGHT + ARTIFICIAL LIGHT

THE CHINESE ROSE, *Hibiscus rosa-sinensis*, needs to be by a window, but the extra sunshine makes plants more thirsty, so keep an eye on the watering.

Light is probably the most important factor that governs where you can keep a plant. As a general rule, flowering plants need to be near windows with lots of sunlight and foliage plants are happy in dimmer conditions. Always check each plant's individual requirements before deciding where to put it and, if in doubt, remember that too much light is far more damaging than too little.

Your eye is a surprisingly hopeless judge of light intensity, and as you move away from a window, the intensity drops dramatically. You can buy a simple light meter from a garden centre to measure whether one spot is significantly lighter or darker than another.

HOW MUCH LIGHT?

Always check a plant's light requirements first.

Full sun Close to a south-facing window where 100 per cent direct sunlight pours in for most of the day. Few plants can stomach this unless they're more than 60cm away from the window. Most cacti, succulents and pelargoniums are common exceptions.

Filtered sunlight Full sun as above, but the intensity is reduced by a tree outside the window or a translucent blind or sheer curtain. Or it may be an east- or west-facing window that gets plenty of sun, except at midday, when the sun is strongest.

Bright This suits the greatest number of plants. It's the area beyond full sunlight, at least 60cm back from a sunny window and extending about 1.5m into the room.

Medium A bit further still into a sunny room or close to a north-facing window. This type of light is the most common. Foliage plants will do fine but flowering plants won't do the business.

Dim Not many plants will thrive here. This is well into the room, perhaps 2.5m from windows where the light is poor, but you could just about read a newspaper during the day without artificial light. Plants in the medium light group can also live here for a few weeks or so before being moved back into more light.

TOO MUCH LIGHT

- Leaves scorched by the sun, brown or grey patches form.
- Whole leaves shrivel and die.
- Leaves are bleached by the sun and become washed out.
- Potting compost is baked dry.

NOT ENOUGH LIGHT

- New leaves are much smaller and pale.
- Plant doesn't appear to grow at all – if it does, growth is leggy.
- Lower leaves go yellow and drop.
- Variegated leaves turn green.
- Flowers are hopeless or don't even form.

HOW TO INCREASE LIGHT

- Paint your walls and ceilings white and hang lots of mirrors.
- Wipe dust from leaves so they can absorb more light.
- Hire a window cleaner.
- Move plants closer to the window in winter.
- Use artificial lighting.

ARTIFICIAL LIGHT

Longer days encourage stubborn plants like orchids and bromeliads to flower and others to flower for longer periods. Artificial lighting can supplement daylight and it's also pretty handy if you want to grow some sort of crop in a windowless room.

Spotlights/floodlights Ordinary indoor light fittings can only boost low light levels and can't be used as a substitute for daylight.

Fluorescent strip lights These can be used as a substitute for daylight. Especially good for seedlings, salads, herbs and small plants that need to be close to the light – between 30–60cm for foliage plants and even closer for flowering ones. The lights don't give off as much heat as ordinary bulbs, so won't scorch the leaves.

High Intensity Discharge lamps (HID) These hang-up and plug-in appliances are perfect for vegetables, flowers and other light-loving plants. The most efficient bulb is a 600W sodium bulb with a reflector. A 400W lamp uses less than 5 units per 12-hour day to run.

Reflection Surrounding plants with reflective material massively increases the available light. For crops it's worth fitting white lino or painting walls with white emulsion. Lining your loft with aluminium foil is not the answer, because it only reflects 55–70 per cent of light. Flat white paint or polystyrene sheets reflect 75–80 per cent and Mylar sheeting reflects 90 per cent.

Duration Most foliage plants will need between 12–14 hours of light a day and summer flowering plants between 16–18 hours.

WATER

Overwatering is the biggest killer of indoor plants. As soon as they show symptoms of distress the loving owner gives them even more water and they are literally killed with kindness. So if you're in any doubt – underwater.

WHEN?

Shove a finger into the potting compost as far as it will go. It should feel damp but not soggy. This is by far the best test – those clever electronic testers are just a waste of money. Most plants need frequent watering between mid spring and late autumn when they do most of their growing. It's after this that people cock it up – in most cases, you have to cut down on watering in winter because the plant won't use it. The compost gets waterlogged and the plants either die or produce ugly misshapen leaves.

HOW MUCH?

Flowering plants usually need more careful and regular watering than foliage plants, but check each plant in the relevant sections. They mostly fall into the following four categories.

Water sparingly Pour a splash of water onto the surface of the compost and let it seep in, but not so much that it comes out of the holes in the bottom of the pot. The aim is to just moisten the compost throughout, then let it nearly dry out between waterings.

Water moderately Most foliage plants fall into this one. Let the top centimetre or two of compost dry out between waterings. Then add a little water at a time, letting it soak in, and continue adding until a few drops appear at the bottom of the pot. The compost will then be moist throughout. You soon get the hang of the amounts with each individual plant. For plants that are watered from underneath, pour water into the saucer until it is no longer absorbed and the top layer of compost is moist. Pour away any water not soaked up.

Water plentifully This applies to most flowering plants. The compost wants to be moist (but not soggy) at all times, so must never dry out. Pour water onto the compost until it comes out the bottom of the pot, but don't actually leave it standing in water or the roots will rot. Any excess that remains by the time you've put your watering can away should be tipped out.

Standing in water No clues here. There are only a few plants in this category.

HOW?

A watering can is better than a jug or a glass because it pours the water right onto the compost and some hairy leaves can be damaged if you get water on them. So you don't slosh water all over the carpet, stick your finger over the end of the spout on your way back from the tap.

WHAT KIND OF WATER?

Tap water is usually fine, but best served at room temperature because cold water can shock the plant, slow down its growth and mark the leaves. Add a little water from the hot tap if in doubt.

But if you have hard water that makes your kettle fur up with lime, it can cause a few problems to certain plants. The best solution is to use rainwater or a simple water filter which will take out harmful chlorine and fluoride as well. Even easier still is to use the water out of a kettle that has previously boiled and cooled.

YOUR PLANT WILL NEED WATERING MORE FREQUENTLY THAN MOST IF . . .

- You've got the heating cranked up.
- Humidity in the room is low.
- It's in direct sunshine – especially in hot weather.
- It's a large plant in a small pot filled with roots.
- It has large, thin leaves.
- It's in active growth – usually summer but depends on the plant.
- It's flowering or fruiting.
- It's in a clay pot rather than a plastic one.

IF IN DOUBT, UNDERWATER. Although they don't like it, some foliage plants can cling onto life for weeks or even months without a drop.

PESTS, DISEASES + PROBLEMS

FINDING THE PROBLEM

Most indoor plants can be ravaged by different pests and diseases which can wreak havoc if untreated. Give plants a quick once over each time you water and treat anything suspicious immediately. Tell-tale signs are discoloured leaves and blotches. Bugs tend to hang out under the leaves or at the junction of leaves and stems so always check there first. If you can't see anything, the likely cause is incorrect watering, the wrong amount of light, heat or even draughts. If that still doesn't solve the problem you're probably better off chucking the plant away and getting a new one.

TREATMENTS

Organic cure Organic cures include picking bugs off by hand and squashing them between your fingers, but sometimes you have to resort to chemicals. As luck would have it there are some organic ones such as pyrethrum, but if you don't have anything to hand, you can dilute a bit of washing-up liquid and spray that on.

Biological controls Predators and parasites that you introduce to a plant to seek out and destroy a particular pest. They don't really like the environment of our homes, but work well in the controlled environment of conservatories and greenhouses where certain organic chemicals can be used simultaneously. Never use synthetic chemicals at the same time. The downside is that they usually need constant reintroducing and can't cope with bad infestations.

Chemicals If you're using synthetic chemicals, be aware that they're potentially dangerous, so you don't want to go spraying them about in the kitchen or all over your goldfish. In warm weather, you can take the plant outside, otherwise open all the windows. Better still, stick to one of the other solutions.

PREVENTION

Keeping plants healthy, well fed and watered is the best precaution, but pest and disease can still mysteriously appear as they are easily spread from one plant to another on air currents or by clothes as you brush past. Problems can hit at any time of year so being vigilant and taking immediate action are your best weapons. Inspect new plants and remove dead or damaged leaves.

APHIDS

This is an umbrella term for a bunch of roughly 2mm long, sap-sucking flies that come in black, pink, yellow or the popular green. They congregate on soft shoot tips and leaves, distort growth and you get the tell-tale honeydew and sooty mould, but they also spread plant viruses. They spread rapidly and moult regularly leaving behind empty 'skeletons'.

Organic cure Spray with pyrethrum, derris or insecticidal soap. Or rub off with fingers, but be careful on young shoots. You'll end up doing more damage than the aphids.

Biological control Parasitic wasp, *Encarsia formosa*.

Chemical Pirimicarb.

MEALY BUGS

Ugly squidgy ribbed insects, about 4mm long, that come in an unpleasant beige or pale pink. You can't miss them under leaves and on the leaf and stem junctions where they cover themselves in a sticky white cottony fluff. They also excrete honeydew.

Organic cure Wipe them off the plant with a damp cloth or a cotton bud or tiny paintbrush soaked in methylated spirit or spray the leaves with insecticidal soap.

Biological control A small, but unfortunately very ugly ladybird called *Cryptolaemus montrouzieri* is particularly useful when temperatures are higher in summer.

Chemical Remove by hand and spray with malathion.

WHITEFLY

Sap-feeding insects, about 2mm long, these live underneath the leaves and look like tiny white moths. When you tap the plant, the adults, which have white wings, all go totally ballistic. Whitefly can spread rapidly, excrete honeydew and also cause leaves to turn yellow and drop.

Organic cure Spray with insecticidal soap which doesn't harm the biological control, *Encarsia formosa*.

Biological Control Introduce *Encarsia formosa* between mid spring and mid autumn.

Chemical Spray with Permethrin a couple of times a week.

MILDEW looks like dusty grey patches on the leaf, which soon becomes yellow and blotchy.

PESTS, DISEASES + PROBLEMS

APHIDS (top left) MEALY BUG (top centre) WHITEFLY (top right)
RED SPIDER MITE (bottom left) SCALE INSECTS (bottom centre) BROWN LEAF TIPS (bottom right)

RED SPIDER MITE

One of the hardest pests to wipe out, these tiny sap-sucking insects which lurk beneath the leaves look like minute yellowish green spiders with two dark blotches. In the autumn they're a bit bigger and easier to spot and they also turn more orange. They can infest most indoor plants, especially those stressed out by hot, dry air. The first obvious sign is when the leaf develops a fine pale yellow or silvery mottling, so investigate the underside of the leaf. You've got to look really closely for the adults and the specks of whitish eggs. Another giveaway in extreme cases is a fine white webbing between stems and leaves. Raising humidity is the best deterrent and part of the cure.

Organic cure Spray with insecticidal soap, remove badly infected leaves and repeat treatments. Sacrifice a badly infected plant in order to save others.

Biological control *Phytoseiulus persimilis*.

Chemical Spray with malathion as soon as you find them. Repeat several times.

SCALE INSECTS

Like tiny limpets, these insects hide under a brown, waxy shell that they secrete over themselves. The young ones crawl about until they find a nice juicy stem or perhaps the main vein on a leaf and then they set up home. Scale insects are about 3–4mm in length and also excrete honeydew.

Organic cure Pick off by hand and wipe with insecticidal soap.

Biological control Parasitic wasp, *Metaphycus helvolus*.

Chemical Spray malathion on undersides of leaves every two weeks. Repeat three times.

BROWN LEAF TIPS

Brown leaf tips or edges, especially on long, narrow-leaved plants like dracaena, are usually caused by dry air or soil and sometimes by cold draughts. Another likely cause of this is too much fluoride in the tap water, so use filtered water, boiled water from the kettle that has cooled down or rainwater instead. The dead bits won't grow back. Either remove whole leaves, put up with the damage or buy a new plant.

MILDEW AND BOTRYTIS

Mildew (pictured on page 98) is a white, powdery fungal growth that appears initially on the surface of the leaf and then on other parts of the plant. Affected leaves go yellow, distorted and blotchy, look sick and usually drop off. Caused by dry soil and humid air around top growth, botrytis or grey mould is similar, but more furry and spreads all over the plant including the compost. Infected bits may go brown and soggy.

Organic cure Remove badly infected leaves and dust remaining leaves with sulphur. Improve ventilation.

Biological control None.

Chemical Spray with systemic fungicide or carbendazim. Cut out all botrytis-infected parts.

HONEYDEW

Sap-sucking insects latch onto the plant with their mouths and a sticky gunk pours out of their back ends. This splatters onto the leaf below (see bottom centre photograph) and under damp conditions, black patches of fungus called sooty mould grow on it. Unsightly rather than harmful, you can wipe it off with a damp cloth, but you need to sort out the pest that caused the problem in the first place.

OTHER COMMON AILMENTS

- **Wilting** Underwatering or overwatering, too much heat or pot-bound plants. Sudden collapse could be vine weevil that munch the edges of leaves at night. Wash off all compost and repot.
- **Leaf curl** Too cold, draughts or overwatering.
- **Sudden leaf drop** Shock caused by relocation of a plant (very common for weeping fig) or sudden change in temperature, light intensity, cold draughts or really dry roots.
- **Flower buds drop off or flowers fade fast** Underwatering, dry air, too dark.
- **Never flowers** Too dark or overfeeding.
- **Leaves pale and sad** Too much light.
- **Leaves go yellow and drop off** Overwatering or cold draughts or severe changes in conditions.
- **Brown patches on leaves** Scorchmarks caused by too much sunlight or physical damage.

TEMPERATURE + HUMIDITY

TEMPERATURE

The best plants as far as us humans are concerned are those which like a temperature range of about 18–24°C, because this is how warm we like to keep our houses. In The Plants you'll see this referred to as average warmth.

Many plants remain happy at lower temperatures, but anything higher than 24°C and you'll need to do something drastic to raise the humidity or the plants will snuff it.

At night time the temperature should ideally drop by about 3–6°C but if you get massive differences between day and night the plants won't like that either. Check the range with a max-min thermometer if you're worried.

THE RULES ARE

- Always pick the right plant for the right place or it'll suffer.
- Avoid danger spots like radiators, cookers and boilers.
- Bakingly hot window-sills with strong, direct sunlight pouring through a single pane of glass during the day will heat plants up too much.
- Avoid great fluctuations in temperature especially between day and night. Occasionally cranking the heating right up is bad news for plants.
- The space between a curtain and a window traps harmful cold air at night and excludes the benefits of the heated room.
- Leaves touching external window glass can get too cold, go black and die.
- Plants near external doors are subjected to draughts.
- Heat rising from a radiator can be good for some plants, but needs deflecting with a shelf and you'll probably have to raise the humidity as well.

DANGER SIGNS

- **Too cold** Leaves curl, go brown and drop off.
- **Too warm** Flowers die quickly and plants grow small leaves or weak leggy growth in good light. Lower leaves wilt and get brown crispy edges.
- **Sudden change in temperature and draughts** Rapid yellowing and leaf drop.

HUMIDITY

Humidity is the amount of water vapour held in the air, but it has nothing to do with how wet the compost is. A plant breathes through its leaves and as it does this it loses moisture by transpiration. If the humidity is very low, the plant will lose too much water and the leaves will dry up and shrivel. Thick leaves, like those of rubber plants, don't really suffer, but thin papery leaves like Angel's wings and some ferns will quickly die.

At low temperatures there isn't a problem, but as a room heats up the amount of water vapour in the air can't keep pace and it becomes dry. The main causes are central heating and rooms and conservatories with windows that get lots of direct sunshine.

HUMIDITY TOO LOW

- Leaf tips brown and shrivelled (especially spider plants, palms and dracaenas).
- Leaf edges turn yellow and may wilt.
- Buds fall and flowers wither.
- Leaves may drop off.

HUMIDITY TOO HIGH

- Patches of grey mould appear on leaves and flowers.
- Patches of rot on leaves and stem tips of cacti and succulents.

RAISING THE HUMIDITY

A pebble tray is the best solution. Fill a plant saucer with pebbles or gravel and top it up with water so the plant stands on the pebbles, but doesn't actually touch the water. As the water evaporates, it raises the humidity around the plant. The width of tray should be the same as spread of plant, but anything is better than nothing.

You can always put your plants in the bathroom as the humidity is normally higher in there. Just grouping plants together also helps and if you're really fussed you could buy a humidifier.

Misting your plants with one of those hand sprayer things is more or less a waste of time for a lot of plants because the effect is so short-lived. (However, it is essential for air plants – see Bromeliads, page 132). To lower humidity, improve ventilation.

KEEPING PLANTS NEXT TO A RADIATOR IS USUALLY A BAD IDEA. Leaves get scorched and they suck moisture out of the air.

POTTING + REPOTTING

WHY BOTHER?

A plant can stay in the same pot for years if you give it enough food and water, but eventually the roots will fill the pot and the compost will have disappeared. This is called 'pot-bound'. The plant will continually dry out, leaves will yellow and drop, so basically it means repot or die.

WHEN?

Younger plants may need repotting each year. The beginning of the active growing period (usually spring) is the best time because they'll recover from the shock more quickly. But don't repot sick or recovering plants – they're suffering already and it could all be a bit too much for them.

If roots are poking out the bottom of the pot, take it off and have a look. If you can hardly see any compost and all you're looking at is a dense mat of roots which are growing in a circle at the bottom of the pot, then you know it's time.

WHERE?

Give yourself a bit of space, the bath is good and the kitchen is always a safe bet, although neither tends to please other members of the household, especially if you start using the cutlery to prise things out of pots. If you venture outside to do it, make sure it's not a cold day or the plants will catch a chill. Equally if it's a sunny day, pick a place in the shade or the roots will get frazzled.

HOW?

- Water plants before you start.
- Clean previously used pots with soapy water and rinse.
- Move up one pot size at a time – an increase in diameter of about 2cm. Soak terracotta pots for about 15 minutes first.
- Put a layer of compost into the new pot and tap it sharply down on a hard surface to settle it. Stand the old pot in it to check the level isn't too high.

- Gently take off the old pot (if it's plastic you can cut it off with secateurs if necessary), snip off any damaged roots and pull off any old crocks. Check for bugs and grubs (see pages 98–101).
- Place the plant in the centre of the new pot and pour compost down the sides. Settle it gently with your fingertips but don't squash it in.
- Tap the plant down again a few times, top up the compost and water. The top of the root ball should be about 2cm below the rim of the pot to allow space for watering.

COMPOST

Ready-mixed indoor plant composts are the easiest. They usually contain nutrients that will feed the plants for about three months before you have to provide additional fertilizer. Peat-free potting composts are the alternative for the environmentally minded. Soil from the garden contains too many nasties and shouldn't be used.

TOPDRESSING

Eventually, plants sort of become adults and they reach an ultimate pot size. Instead of repotting, scrape off the top few centimetres of compost with a spoon or trowel, but be careful not to damage any major roots. Replace it with fresh compost mixed with a little slow-release fertilizer (see Feeding, page 108). Do this once a year and your plants will look far more perky.

CONTAINERS AND DRAINAGE

Any kind of container be used, but drainage is extremely important. If there aren't any drainage holes, either drill some or put a 5cm layer of gravel in the bottom. Excess water will sit here rather than rotting the roots and a crushed lump of barbecue charcoal in with the gravel will keep the water sweet.

Terracotta pots need crocks – fragments of broken pots or lumps of polystyrene – in their base to stop drainage holes getting bunged up. Plastic pots already have plenty of drainage holes.

If things are getting a bit crowded in the root department and you can barely see any compost, it's time to repot. This **GRAPE HYACINTH** isn't ready yet.

106

HYDROPONICS

Virtually any pot plants, whether ornamental or crop, can be grown by this soil-less culture which replaces the compost with an inert growing medium and a solution of nutrients dissolved in water.

ADVANTAGES OVER COMPOST

- Produces a more vigorous plant or crop in a shorter time.
- Watering and feeding are very simple and give exactly the required amount of nutrient to a plant.
- Saves time and space and is less messy.
- Soil-borne pests and fungi are avoided.
- For passive systems repotting is not done annually but only when a plant looks awkwardly too big for its container.
- Holidays aren't a problem with passive systems as feeding need only be done once every few months.

PASSIVE CULTURE

You can buy special double pots for this simplest form of hydroponics. The inner pot with holes in contains the plant and growing medium, which acts as an anchor for the roots, and the whole lot is suspended inside a watertight pot. The bottom of the inner pot is immersed in a nutrient solution which is sucked up by capillary action to reach the plant's roots. It's this combination of constant moisture, constantly available nutrients and high levels of air supply that make up the perfect root zone which the plants love. A special gauge with a float ensures that the solution doesn't drop too low and cut off the capillary supply. Roots will eventually grow down into the solution and then you may only need to water once every few weeks but every plant is different.

TRANSFERRING COMPOST-GROWN PLANTS

There is an element of risk when transferring a plant from compost culture – nearly all plants can be grown hydroponically, but success is greater when started from seeds or cuttings. Carefully wash off the soil from established plants without damaging roots. Pour the chosen growing medium around the roots and tap the pot on a table to settle it and support the plant. Initially water from above with half-strength nutrient solution.

GROWING MEDIA

Perlite These tiny bits of expanded rock look like polystyrene. They're cheap, lightweight and reusable as long as you flush them through with a mild bleach solution and then rinse thoroughly. Always water from the top and dampen before use to avoid potentially harmful dust. Good for seeds and cuttings.

Expanded clay lumps (leca pictured) Attractive, lightweight and sterile, these are perfect for indoor plants. Being larger in diameter the capillary action is reduced, so they're not so good for big plants and pots. Water from below if possible.

Rockwool Spun fibres of molten rock made into preformed modules that you soak in water before use. Don't allow them to remain waterlogged and wear gloves as they can irritate the skin.

Greenmix The growing medium of the future; part rockwool, it holds far more moisture around the roots whilst still retaining air. It's more expensive, but well worth it for pricey plants like orchids.

NUTRIENT SOLUTION

This is specially formulated and should be purchased from hydroponic dealers or garden centres. It is normally sold in twin packs that must be made up and applied following the instructions. Ordinary fertilizers for soil culture aren't recommended.

ACTIVE SYSTEMS FOR SERIOUS CROPS

Active systems are scaled-down versions of the ones used by commercial growers. They may seem a bit complicated, but are well worth it if you're serious about growing a decent crop at home (see Buyer's Guide, page 170).

Any plant can be grown hydroponically, but it's a particularly good method for **GROWING INDOOR CROPS**.

FEEDING

WHY FEED?

Plants, like people, need to eat and if you don't feed them they start to look a bit rough and then they get sick. Different plants have different needs, but if you follow these basic rules and check individual plant requirements, you should be alright. If you don't feed, there's no way you can keep plants in good condition.

WHEN TO FEED?

Feed a plant when it's in active growth. For most plants that means between mid spring and mid autumn – when the days are longer and there's more sunshine. Feed much less or not at all in winter.

Potting compost normally contains fertilizers so when you first buy a plant it'll be okay for two or three months and then it'll start getting hungry. That's when you've got to begin feeding, unless it's winter, of course.

Don't feed sick plants, it's a fertilizer, not a medicine and if a plant is under stress already, it won't be able to cope with the additional pressure.

HOW MUCH?

A lot of plants like to be fed once a fortnight, but you won't go far wrong if you feed a plant at half the recommended strength once a week or even every time you water during the growing season. That way you won't forget to do it. In winter, cut it out altogether.

Feeding helps plants to grow vigorously, however, if you don't want your dracaena to outgrow your living room too fast, be a bit tight with the fertilizer.

SIGNS OF UNDERFEEDING

- Growth is slow, the plant barely changes size and pests and diseases take up residence.
- The plant doesn't flower or if it does they're small and pale and you wish it hadn't bothered.
- Stems are weak and lower leaves drop off prematurely.
- Leaves are pale, maybe yellow spotted and generally look sick.

SIGNS OF OVERFEEDING

- Useless, lanky growth particularly in winter.
- Stunted growth in summer.
- A white crust appears on the surface of the compost and the side of terracotta pots.
- Leaves wilt or have crispy brown edges and spotted leaves.

WHAT TO FEED?

Most indoor plant fertilizers are balanced. They include nitrogen for leaves, phosphorus for roots, potassium for flowers and fruit and then there are usually a few trace elements added for all the twiddly bits. Other fertilizers may be top-heavy in one of the main ingredients like tomato fertilizer, which is loaded with potassium but, if in doubt, go for a standard or balanced one.

Liquid feed This is the best and easiest way to give a plant the right amount of fertilizer. Keep it next to your watering can and add a couple of drops to each can of water. Don't pour it onto really dry compost or it can harm the roots by being too concentrated in one area. Water dry compost first. The organic options are seaweed extract, or if you have a wormery in the garden, dilute the liquid that you drain off with ten parts water.

Slow-release feed This comes as special granules which provide a good, steady dose for a whole growing season. Add them to the compost in spring when topdressing or repotting. Bone meal and seaweed meal are organic alternatives. Fish, blood and bone and pelleted chicken poo are also organic, but faster acting.

Tablets and sticks These are glued-together slow-release granules. They do work, but they're a bit gimmicky. The idea that it is a measured dose is a bit daft because they mostly feed the bit of compost that they're stuck into. You can push the tablets down near the roots with the blunt end of a pencil.

Foliar feed This is like a major caffeine injection. It provides instant zap and is perfect if the foliage is looking unhealthy. Mix with water and spray onto the leaves with a hand mister. Good for plants like bromeliads that don't have a lot going on in the root department.

PLANT FOOD The range of fertilizers in garden centres is mind-boggling. To keep things simple, just buy a single bottle of liquid feed.

047182

MEASURE CAPACITY

Small Bowl
Level fill measure =
1.25ml

Large Bowl
Level fill measure =
10ml

CONCENTRATED
WATER SOLUBLE

Miracid

SOIL ACIDIFIER
PLANT FOOD
with
SEQUESTERED IRON

FOR ALL ERICACEOUS
AND ACID-LOVING PLANTS

**AZALEA, CAMELLIA,
CONIFERS, DOGWOOD,
GARDENIA,
HYDRANGEA, LAURELS,
RHODODENDRONS,**

MIRACLE
GARDEN CARE   Net Weight 500g

250 g e

PHOSTROGEN

487

015

Plant

rich in nutrients
for healthy
& luxurious
flowering &
foliage
house plants

...ter on and see the difference in days

...all bedding plants • fruit and vegetables • salad crops and tomatoes
shrubs and trees • lawns • containers and baskets
seedlings and young plants • houseplants

Osmocote

CONTROLLED RELEASE

Plant Food Tablets

...ds Hanging Baskets, Containers
...t Pot plants when they need it

...TION FEEDS

Scotts

PROPAGATION

Some people will only ever treat indoor plants as pieces of furniture or part of the decor and will never get very attached to them. But for others it's a different story, and propagating their own indoor plants is likely to be one of their first encounters with gardening proper. In a lot of cases, propagation is a simple and deeply satisfying way to get new plants and, of course, it's virtually free. For others though, propagation is a complete pain in the backside, it takes ages and doesn't really work, so buying a new plant is probably the answer.

WHEN?

The best time of year to do most types of propagation is in spring and early summer. The days are getting longer, there's lots more sunshine and the plants have the whole of the growing season ahead of them in which to make new roots and shoots.

CUTTINGS

This can be the easiest way to get more plants. For some, like tradescantia and ivy, you literally just have to stick a bit in a glass of water on the window-sill and wait for it to root. For others, it's a bit more complicated, but not much.

Fill a pot with seed and cuttings compost (this is important because it must be low in nutrients or else you will get all sorts of problems) and insert the cuttings around the edge. Always use fresh compost because old stuff can contain pests and diseases. To cut down on water loss, poke four sticks into the compost, put a clear polythene bag over the top and fasten it onto the pot with an elastic band. You could use the bottom half of a plastic mineral water bottle instead, but don't cover cacti, succulents or pelargoniums as they don't like the close, humid atmosphere. Put the pot out of the reach of direct sun and remove yellowing leaves. Check them regularly and when new growth appears, water the compost first and pot up the new plants into individual pots, but be really careful not to damage the fragile roots and new shoots.

STEM CUTTINGS

This works for most plants, especially those with soft stems like philodendron. Cut a healthy, sturdy, non-flowering shoot between 8–15cm long (depending on the size of the donor plant). Cut off the leaves on the lower half and trim the stem just below a leaf joint with a razor blade or really sharp knife to avoid crushing the stem. Make a hole in the compost with a dibber or pencil, dip the bottom centimetre in hormone rooting powder, tap off the excess and put the cutting into the hole. Firm it in with your fingertips. Small cuttings like those of *Hoya bella* can be dipped in rooting powder and inserted in cubes of florist's oasis or rockwool and stood on a tray of water but make sure it never runs dry. Once they've rooted, you just pot up the whole thing.

Pelargonium and fuchsia cuttings can be taken in late summer, but woody-stemmed plants like sparmannia should be done in spring. Take a side shoot and tug it downwards to pull it off the main stem with a 'heel' of bark and pot up as above.

LEAF CUTTINGS

Some plants don't have stems at all and the leaves shoot straight out of the crown, level with the compost. These can be propagated from a single leaf or even a piece of leaf and the leaf cuttings will produce lots of tiny new plantlets. When they're big enough to handle, trim off the old leaf and pot up the plants.

Whole leaf With succulents like sedum, crassula and echeveria, take off the leaf and let it dry out a bit for a few days. Cover the compost in sharp sand, push the leaf base into the compost and lean the back of it against the rim of the pot.

Leaf with stalk For leaves that have a stalk, like peperomia and saintpaulia, cut a mature leaf with a razor blade, dip the stalk in hormone rooting powder and insert immediately in the compost.

Parts of leaves Big leaves can be chopped up. Streptocarpus can be cut into 3 or 4 strips, each with a bit of midrib. Place the base of each leaf section into a tray of compost. Sansevieria also can be

LEAF CUTTING (top left) **AIR LAYERING** (top centre) **CANE CUTTING** (top right)
DIVISION (bottom left) **STEM CUTTING** (bottom centre) **OFFSET** (bottom right)

PROPAGATION

chopped into 5cm-wide strips, but the new plant will only be variegated if you leave two nibs of the outer yellow part sticking down below (see picture on page 110). As a general rule, variegated plants can't be propagated by leaf cuttings.

CANE CUTTINGS

As they get older, plants that make stiff, erect canes such as yucca, dieffenbachia, dracaena and cordyline lose their lower leaves and look a bit shabby. You've probably seen those ready-to-plant canes or 'Ti plants' in the shops and it's the same idea here. Cut off a section of cane and chop the leafless part into bits about 6–10cm long. Lay them flat, half submerged in the compost and they'll soon sprout. The leafy top section can be used as a stem cutting and the butchered parent plant will soon sprout from just below the wound. You can also put cane cuttings vertically in the compost, but make sure they are the right way up by cutting the bottom at an angle.

OFFSETS

Some parent plants, like bromeliads, cacti and succulents, produce baby plants or offsets at the base. When they're about a quarter the size of the parent plant and beginning to resemble them, trim them off close to the parent stem with a sharp knife and pot up like a cutting. If possible, ensure the offset has some root already.

PLANTLETS

Some plants, like spider plants and saxifrage, produce new plantlets on the end of stems. If they already have short, stubby roots, remove the plantlets and pot up. Otherwise, peg them down into an adjacent fresh pot of compost with a hairpin of stiff wire and separate them once rooted. This works pretty well for trailing plants like ivy, if you peg down the stems.

DIVISION

Clump-forming plants, such as maranta and ophiopogon, can be divided. Take off the pot and carefully tease the clump apart ensuring your new piece of plant has plenty of roots. If there is a main root connecting it to the parent, cut through it with a knife.

AIR LAYERING

This is a good approach when things like rubber plants and cheese plants get leggy or start bashing into the ceiling. About 70–80cm from the tip of the plant, find a bare piece of stem about 10cm below where a leaf joins. Strip a 1cm-wide band of bark off by cutting two shallow rings with a sharp knife. Paint the wound with hormone rooting powder and then get a big handful of really moist sphagnum moss and pack it round the cut. Secure the moss firmly in place with a piece of clear polythene that is then wired onto the stem at the top and bottom. In a couple of months or so you'll see new roots growing in the moss. Cut the stem below the wire, remove the polythene and pot up the new plant. Keep it away from bright sunlight for the first few weeks and be careful not to overwater. The old plant should shoot again, so don't chuck it out.

SEED SOWING

Unlike real gardening, this is definitely not what indoor plants are all about unless you're growing edible stuff. Propagating most indoor plants from seed is difficult and is like watching paint dry except it takes a lot longer. If you must do it follow the instructions on the packet. Different seeds need different techniques, but as a general rule . . .

Fill trays or pots with seed compost to within 1cm of the rim. Firm it gently with the base of another tray or pot and sprinkle water onto it. Sow seed as directed on the packet and unless very fine, cover with a 1cm layer of sieved compost or vermiculite. Place a sheet of glass on top or seal in a clear polythene bag to make a mini greenhouse. Then put on a window-sill in a centrally heated room at a minimum 20°C. As soon as they sprout, remove the glass or bag and keep out of direct sun. Regularly spray with water and never let them dry out. Turn the pots or trays every couple of days so the seedlings don't bend towards the light. As soon as the seedlings are large enough to handle, hold a leaf and gently tease out the roots with a pencil. Plant them into trays of individual cells or pots and grow on in a bright spot at average room temperature for a few weeks before treating as adults and moving to a more permanent home.

PRUNING (right) actually encourages growth, so don't be afraid to do it, but most indoor plants never need to go under the knife.

PRUNING

Indoor plants don't need a lot of pruning because they just get on and do their thing, but they do sometimes become misshapen. There are two ways to prune: pinching out and cutting back.

PINCHING OUT

This is especially important for fast-growing, soft-stemmed species like tradescantia, coleus, pilea and beloperone to stop them getting lanky. You pinch out or 'stop' a plant by nipping the growing tip between finger and thumb just above a node where leaves join the stem. This tip might only be about 1cm long. Use nails scissors if this is fiddly. Keep pinching throughout the growing period.

CUTTING BACK

If plants are just too big or unbalanced, cut out thick woody stems just above a bud. If a plant like a yucca is already touching the ceiling don't just nip off the top or you'll be pruning it every five minutes. Be brave and chop off 70 or 80cm so it bushes out low down (see Air Layering, page 112). Make sure you cut back at the beginning of the growing season to give the dormant buds time to do their stuff. Use sharp secateurs or scissors so you don't crush the stems and encourage pests and diseases. Some plants, including ficus, bleed sap from cut wounds. You can stem the flow by rubbing bonfire ash, or for that matter cigarette ash, into the cut but wash your hands afterwards because the sap will cause havoc if you get it in your eyes.

DEADHEADING

Flowering goes on for a lot longer if you snip off faded blooms to channel the plant's energy into new buds. Badly timed pruning can stop plants flowering altogether so check in the relevant section before you do it. Remove dead, damaged and yellowing leaves as well, but be careful not to harm the main stem.

WHILE YOU'RE ON HOLIDAY

Most plants won't suffer at all if left for only a week, especially in winter when they aren't growing much anyway. Two weeks is pushing it a bit but three weeks, particularly in summer, is decidedly dodgy. So if you don't get on with the neighbours, you need a plan or your holiday will be like the Grim Reaper.

So after you cancel the milk and check the oven is turned off, give the plants a damn good soaking, move them away from sunny window-sills and group them together in a cool room out of direct sunlight. Keeping them all in the bath is a safe bet, but don't leave them sitting in water as that'll do more harm than good. Instead, stand the plants on pebbles in a water-filled tray. The pebbles raise the plant out of the water which, as it evaporates, raises the humidity around the plant and reduces its thirst. Some plants, like *Ficus benjamina*, hate being moved, so are best left to chance.

Alternatively, you can buy a piece of capillary matting from the garden centre and drape it over your draining board with one end trailing into the water-filled sink. Stand the plants on the matting and the water will be sucked out of the sink and up into the compost. Sadly, this only works for plastic pots because the thicker clay ones don't allow the essential contact between compost and matting. Do a trial run to check your sink is watertight or you could end up with a load of dead plants to welcome you home. You could always rig up the same thing with your toilet cistern because it tops itself up automatically.

You can also buy special wicks, one end of which you drape into a water-filled jar and the other into the compost or drainage hole. Or there are special porous clay bulbs that provide a constant, but limited supply to the compost. Don't fret about watering too much and remember that overwatering is far more likely to harm a plant than letting it go a bit dry for a week or two. In winter, make sure that the plants have got enough warmth while you're away. Don't be miserly and turn off the heating or you'll come back to a lot of very dejected plants.

If you do get back and find your plants have wilted, follow the advice in Bringing them back from the dead, page 117.

GIVE THE PLANTS A BREAK

Most indoor plants could do with a holiday too. Usually in winter they have a dormant period of R and R when they take some time out from all that growing. Some plants will let you know when they're ready by shedding their leaves or even dying down, but a lot of foliage plants aren't quite so communicative. You have to take your cue from the lower light levels and the shorter days of winter. The plant will stop growing and it's really important that you cut right down on feeding and watering and, if possible, lower the temperature by moving to a cooler room. Winter-blooming plants are the exception to this because they mostly need watering and feeding before and during flowering.

In summer, take your plants outside. The rain will wash layers of dust off the leaves, making the whole plant look happier and letting more light through to the leaf surface. Make sure they are in shade though, perhaps under a tree, or the massive increase in sunshine will scorch and bleach the leaves. Yuccas are a prime example, the leaves go a whitish brown in the sun.

GERBERAS are amongst the best air purifiers. They need watering plentifully during the growing season and shouldn't be allowed to dry out while you're on holiday.

BRINGING THEM BACK
FROM THE DEAD

Technically this plant has reached the Permanent Wilting Point and must suffer **THE ULTIMATE SOLUTION**.

DRIED-OUT PLANTS

If you've forgotten to water a plant it will usually wilt with the leaves drooping dejectedly. On top of that, the compost shrinks so when you add water it refuses to rehydrate and the water just pours down the sides without soaking in. Plunge the whole pot into a bucket of water and hold it under until all the air bubbles have escaped. Scrape out the top layer of compost and replace it with fresh, poking it loosely down the sides with your fingertips. The next few times you water it, add a couple of drops of washing-up liquid to act as a wetting agent and the old compost will eventually rehydrate. Then you can carry on watering as normal. If a wilted plant hasn't picked up noticeably in a couple of hours, you're probably looking at the ultimate solution.

Sometimes soil-based compost won't absorb water even though it hasn't dried out. Break up the hard surface with a screwdriver, being careful not to damage the roots, and immerse in water as above.

DUSTING AND SHINING

Dusty leaves look horrid, sunlight can't be absorbed for photosynthesis and their pores get clogged up so that the plants can't breathe properly. Support a leaf with your hand and wipe it with a wet sponge. Better still, put them in the shower and rinse it all off.

There is something of an obsession with leaf shine, which actually tends to make plants look plasticky and artificial. If you must do this, make sure you hold the nozzle of the aerosol at least 30cm from the leaf or the freezing propellant will damage the leaves. Leaf shine wipes are good because they clean the leaf at the same time. Some people use beer, milk and olive oil, but they should be stopped as these are all potentially harmful. Never shine ferns, palms, cacti, succulents and things with hairy leaves because it can kill them. You can remove dust from cacti and hairy leaves with a soft paintbrush.

DISPOSABLE PLANTS

Some plants must be treated as temporary. Like a bunch of flowers, they should just be chucked straight onto the compost heap once they're past their best. Certain flowering plants are prime candidates, as soon as they've bloomed – out they go. Otherwise you have to nurse them back into flower over the next 10 months during which time they'll just sit there looking back at you, begging to be put out of their misery and making your room look untidy (see the relevant plant section).

SOME PLANTS ARE FOR CHRISTMAS, NOT FOR LIFE

Some winter-flowering plants are traditionally sold at Christmas and Easter. They look good for a month or two and then you have to decide whether to keep them or not.

Poinsettia These are vile plants with large red modified leaves or bracts (the actual flowers are small, yellow things) that now come in white and a revolting pink. Well-heated rooms and draughts will make them wilt, so place them on a pebble tray to keep the humidity high and let them dry out a bit between waterings. Put them in a bright spot, give a weak feed occasionally and they'll last for three months.

To get them to produce their coloured bracts next year you'll need to give them about 14 hours of total darkness followed by 10 hours of daylight every day from early autumn for eight weeks. How very annoying. It's much easier to chuck it away and get another one next year.

Cyclamen Like African violets, these are old people's plants that remind you of granny. High temperatures and lack of water will make them wilt so ideally keep them in a cool room or on a cool window-sill at between 5–16°C. Lots of light and a weekly feed should keep them flowering for months. When they've finished, let the corm (the bulb thing) dry out completely until late summer, repot and start to water again. Watch out for vine weevils.

Azalea Draughts, erratic watering and droughts make the leaves fall off. Hot, dry rooms and radiators can also kill so 10–15°C is best. Water regularly by plunging the pot in a bucket until air bubbles stop escaping from the compost. You'll probably need to water three times a week, but avoid hard water (see Water, page 96). Remove flowers as they fade and they'll go on for a month or so.

Start to feed weekly after flowering and put outside in a bit of shade after the last frosts of spring. Sink the pot into the ground to stop it from drying out and bring back in before the first frosts of winter. It should flower again the following spring.

117

G30

DRACAEN

GROUPS OF

G90

1353

PLANTS

HERBS + EDIBLES

If you fancy yourself as a bit of whiz in the kitchen, there is nothing better than growing your own ingredients and being able to pick fresh herbs and vegetables straight from the window-sill. Most edibles are better off outside or in a greenhouse but if you don't have that choice these ones are worth a try indoors.

HERBS

Herbs should be treated as short-lived plants indoors. Some are annuals anyway and even the shrubby ones gradually peter out and the fact that you're obviously going to pull leaves off them doesn't help. But being easy to replace and grow, this isn't a problem. Some can be grown from seed (see Propagation, page 111) but all can be bought as plants from the garden centre to save time and fuss. Those pots of ready-growing herb seedlings from the supermarket are packed in so tightly and pumped so full of fertilizer that they have a very short life span so don't be disappointed when they meet their maker.

Grow on an east- or west-facing window-sill that gets lots of light. Full midday sun will be a bit hot and they'll suffer. Feed fortnightly in summer and always keep the soil moist, but do not overwater. Winter is a not a happy time for herbs because of the shorter days and lower light levels and you may be better off starting again in spring.

Basil is a must for Italian food lovers. You tend to get through quite a lot so you might need a few plants. If you grow it from seed, keep sowing every few weeks between spring and summer because plants don't last very long. Remove any flowers or the plants give up. Keep moist.

Coriander is for fish and curryholics and, like basil, you can make several sowings. Keep cutting and don't let it flower.

Parsley can also be grown from seed but unfortunately it's never wonderfully happy indoors.

Mint should be bought as a growing plant or a little clump can be lifted from the garden. Stand the pot in a saucer of water during summer but keep it drier in winter.

Chives, like mint, can be divided from a clump in the garden. Snip the leaves right down to the base when using it. Even the flowers can be eaten in salads.

HERBS (above) need a window-sill with lots of light but don't let them get frazzled by too much midday sun.
MINT TEA (right). Mint is really easy to grow if you stand it in a saucer of water.

Thyme likes a bit of grit or sand mixed into the compost and can stomach more sunshine and drought than most. It should never be stood in water and likes a scattering of garden lime added to the compost as a one-off fertilizer. Trim over with shears in spring.

Oregano, and **marjoram** which is a close relative, **tarragon** and **sage** can all be grown on a cool bright window-sill. The compost should be kept slightly moist and you can feed every fortnight with half-strength liquid feed. If you overfeed, the new growth is very leggy and weedy unless the light levels are very good.

Lemon grass is really easy to grow but you need to buy the stems as fresh and intact as possible. Unfortunately the base is always trimmed off the ones in the shops and if too much has been removed they won't root. Stand the thick end in a glass of water on a sunny window-sill. After a week or so, stubby roots should appear, so pot it up into compost. Keep moist and feed every other week once it's started sprouting leaves. A spring-grown stem should make a nice grassy clump by autumn and the following spring you can start harvesting stems for your Thai cooking.

SALAD AND VEG

Sow on a window-sill from early to mid spring or buy young plants. Give them lots of light, water and a fortnightly dose of tomato-like fertilizer once they're about a month old. Watch out for whitefly.

Tomatoes need to be kept moist and fed weekly with a tomato fertilizer. There are a few small varieties that do ok indoors such as Tumbler, Minibel, Santa Fi and Brasero.

Aubergines are quite small plants about 40cm tall. They may need staking and the leaves should be misted regularly.

Cucumbers aren't often grown indoors but the variety Fembaby is a small 90cm plant that can be grown up a cane and will produce several fruit. Stand in a saucer of water and mist daily.

Sweet peppers and **chilli peppers** are worth growing and, although they don't excel, you can still get a useful crop. Green peppers are just unripe red ones. Choose a small variety.

Okra, or lady's fingers, are used in Indian food and is surprisingly easy to grow. It reaches about 80cm and has pretty hollyhock-like flowers and interesting fruit.

SEEDS AND BEANS

Mustard and cress, like many sprouted seeds, are not only tasty but very nutritious. Sow cress evenly on soggy kitchen paper or loo roll in a shallow tray and place in a dimly lit spot. Three days later sow the quicker-growing mustard alongside. When they start to sprout, move to a window-sill and harvest a week later.

Bean sprouts, usually mung beans, are dead easy. Soak overnight in water and place in a single layer in a shallow tray and put somewhere warm and dark like the airing cupboard. Sprinkle with water every day and harvest in about a week when they're about 5cm long. If you leave them too long they lose their taste.

Wheat grass looks fantastic growing on the window-sill and its juice is a great natural medicine, which can be used for detoxing and for hangovers. It is also being researched as a possible complementary treatment for cancer. Buy seed from health food shops, or you can buy a wheat grass kit. Rinse and soak the seed in cold water for 12 hours. Sprinkle seeds on a 5cm layer of organic compost in a seed tray and pat down. Cover with a bin liner put in a warm cupboard and water sparingly. Once they sprout, bring them into the light and watch the grass shoot up. You will need a special juicer to extract the juice. (See Suppliers, page 173 for details).

FRUITS AND THINGS

These are familiar items worth diverting from your shopping trolley to a pot of compost on the window-sill. Most won't actually fruit unless you've got a warm conservatory but they do make excellent and unusual indoor plants, and it's nice to see where some of these things come from.

Avocado stones must be soaked for 48 hours in tepid water in a container on a radiator. Suspend the stone, pointy end up, over a jam jar of water by shoving four toothpicks or cocktail sticks into the sides. The base of the stone should just be submerged. Put in a warm dark cupboard. When a shoot appears, between 10 days and five weeks later, move the jar onto a window-sill and once the root almost fills it, transfer to a pot of compost. The pointy bit should just be visible. Once the main shoot reaches 15cm snip a third off. Repot after about two months, water regularly and feed every two weeks in summer. Keep pinching out the tips or it will get tall and leggy. A cane might be needed for support.

Papaya or paw paw turn into good-looking upright plants. Scoop out the black seeds, wash and dry them and plant a few in a pot. Once they've sprouted, thin them to one per pot and give average

COURGETTE FLOWERS (far left). Small varieties of squashes and cucumbers will live happily on a sunny window-sill.
SOME HERBS (left) like coriander and basil don't live for long, so keep growing new plants from seed.
MUSTARD AND CRESS (below) is a rite of passage for most gardeners.

warmth and lots of light. In a warm greenhouse they may fruit. Male and female on separate plants need to be cross-pollinated.

Dates grow on massive palm trees so you're clearly not going to get an adult plant with a crop but what the hell. Eat a date and spit out the stone, wash off any unpleasantness and rub the whole surface with sandpaper so that moisture can get in. Seal it in a bag of damp compost and put it in a warm dark place like an airing cupboard. It might take weeks but once a root appears at the end, plant 2cm deep in a pot of compost and put on a warm, light window-sill. As they grow repot into bigger pots of soil-based compost. Water regularly.

Coffee bushes are often grown as indoor plants in America. They have lovely shiny green leaves and in the third year beautiful fragrant white flowers followed by green berries that ripen to red and contain two seed beans. Eventually you should be able to get enough for at least one cup of coffee. You need to scrounge some unroasted beans from a grocer who roasts and grinds his own coffee. Sow 1cm deep in compost in July on a warm window-sill and cover with paper. Keep at about 16°C in winter and average room temperature in summer.

Sweet potatoes or yams are actually lovely climbing plants related to morning glory. Bury a couple of tubers on their sides in a pot of compost about 3cm below the surface. Put them somewhere as close to 18°C as you can. When the shoots appear, reduce them to two or three and chuck a few more centimetres of compost on top for good measure. They will grow quite quickly. Keep compost moist. They might flower but you're unlikely to get an edible crop of tubers.

Pineapple Buy a fresh pineapple with a really healthy looking crown of leaves on top. Slice off the crown with 1cm of flesh attached and leave it on its side to dry for a few days. Bury the fleshy bit into compost mixed with 25 per cent sharp sand, seal the whole lot in a clear polythene bag and place on a window-sill away from direct sun. When you see new growth sprouting from the centre of the rosette of leaves move to a really sunny spot. Pineapples will only fruit after two or three years in a warm conservatory. Water and feed regularly.

Mangos are huge tropical trees. Wash the seed of a very ripe fruit. Rub it all over with sandpaper and soak the stone in water for two

MOST HERBS AND EDIBLES (above right) can be grown from seed.
CUCUMBERS (left) and squashes prefer a greenhouse, but small varieties will grow on your window-sill.

HERBS + EDIBLES

weeks. Put the bowl in a warm place and change the water every day or it will go smelly. Plant about 3cm deep in a pot of compost, water really well, seal in a polythene bag and put it somewhere warm like the airing cupboard. As soon as it sprouts, take off the bag and put on a warm, sunny window-sill. Regularly repot and pinch out the tips to keep it bushy. Feed every two weeks.

Monkey nuts or peanuts. You need fresh ones still in their shells for this. Crack them slightly and plant three or four close together about 1cm deep in a pot. Seal in a polythene bag and put in the airing cupboard or a heated propagator. After about two weeks when they've sprouted, take the bag off and place on a sunny window-sill. Pot on as a clump into a 30cm-wide pot. Yellow flowers appear in summer followed by downward-facing pods which plunge themselves into the ground and turn into the familiar monkey nuts in autumn. They must never be fed.

Root ginger Buy a really fresh piece of root from a greengrocer. You don't need much – about 5cm. Treat it like a monkey nut but give it loads of water and feed fortnightly with a tomato fertilizer. It will grow about 1.5m and have a beautiful pink flower in summer. They prefer a warm conservatory and don't like direct sunlight.

You can also try growing **lychees**, **olives** and anything else you that takes your fancy.

A CARPET OF WHEAT GRASS (right) looks amazing and it'll cure your hangover. Allegedly.
OLIVE TREES (below) can be brought indoors for a few weeks but are more at home in the garden or conservatory.

CITRUS

You can easily grow your own lemon for a vodka and tonic as long as you have the right conditions in your home and follow some basic guidelines. Somehow, they'll never be quite as good as the imported fruit in the shops but if you grow your own tangerine you'll be so smug it won't matter.

The sweet-scented, usually white, star-shaped flowers are a couple of centimetres wide. They normally bloom in late spring and summer but occasional flowers appear at any time. In the right conditions, lemons and limes can flower almost continuously which makes them the best types to grow and you often get flowers and fruit on the bush at the same time. The fruits are green at first before spending as much as three months ripening to yellow, orange and, er, green. They can then last several months.

SHORTCUTS TO SUCCESS

• Water carefully, overdoing it is the biggest problem.
• Draught-free conditions in winter.
• Ventilate well or put outside in summer.
• Plenty of feeding.
• Cool but not cold in winter.

THE BASICS

Watering Get this wrong and you're stuffed, get it right and you're virtually home and dry. Use tap water, not softened water. Completely soak the thing so water pours out the bottom of the pot into the saucer and let the top 5cm of compost dry out between waterings until the leaves look slightly stressed. If in doubt leave it because overwatering is a killer. Never let it stand in water. In winter, when the plant is resting, water very, very occasionally to stop the compost from drying out totally.

Temperature In summer normal room temperature will do but they're much better off outside or by a permanently open window. In winter, they like to be cool but not cold. This means between 4–10°C, so if you've got an unheated room with a south-facing window you're in luck, otherwise a porch or a heated greenhouse or conservatory will do. Avoid draughts.

Humidity If too low, especially in warmer temperatures, red spider mite can be a problem. Stand in a water-filled tray and raise it up on a 5–8cm layer of gravel so the roots aren't in the water.

SOMEHOW THE FRUIT (above) is never quite as pristine as it is in the shops, but who cares.
CITRUS FRUIT (left) need regular feeding and a cool winter rest.

129

CITRUS

Feeding Citrus are greedy plants. Between spring and autumn, give a high-potash, tomato-type fertilizer every two weeks or when you water. In winter, a fortnightly foliar feed increases fruit set. Mottled yellow leaves is usually a magnesium deficiency cured by watering on sequestered iron, a readily available plant food.

Light In summer citrus yearn to be outdoors in bright light. After the late frosts, start in shade and creep into sunshine over a week. Bring them inside in autumn before the frosts start. They need at least four hours of direct sunlight each day and indoors the sunniest place is probably best for them especially in winter.

Repotting A soil- or loam-based compost is best. Each spring move up one size until you get to a convenient size for your space. *Citrus mitis* will flower and fruit in a little 13 or 15cm pot but most won't do the business until they've grown into a pot at least 25cm wide.

Pruning Very little is needed but branches can get a bit spindly. Shorten long branches by at least half in early spring. Nip out growing tips at any time during spring and summer to make the plant more bushy.

Propagation Cuttings can be taken in late spring and should root after 6 or 8 weeks. Start feeding when new shoots appear and move to brighter light.

VARIETIES

CITRUS MITIS (X *Citrofortunella microcarpa*) the Calomondin orange, makes a virtually spineless 1.2m bush and is one of the easiest citrus to get hold of and grow. It's popular because it flowers

NING
MPER WITH COIN BOXES
S AS THEY ARE WIRED
IC ALARM SYSTEM

sporadically and bears loads of small bright orange fruit throughout the year even when the plant is still tiny. The bitter fruit can be used for marmalade.

MEYER'S LEMON C. x meyeri 'Meyer' has thin-skinned pale yellow fruit 7.5cm in diameter but can be tricky. The 'QUATRE SAISONS' lemon variety, now known as 'GAREY'S EUREKA' is much easier.

'WEST INDIAN' is a spicy lime suitable for a rum punch and 'KAFFIR' leaves are essential in Thai cooking. 'TAHITI' is a good lime for beginners.

The OTAHEITE ORANGE, C. limonia, is a cross between a lemon and a mandarin and has purple-tinged flowers and yellow or orange fruit.

The SWEET or NAVEL ORANGE C.sinensis 'Washington' growing to about 1.2m is just about the only one you can have indoors which is actually sweet tasting. It flowers in spring and fruits in winter.

CLEMENTINES, MANDARIN, TANGERINE and SATSUMA are too big for a house and need a conservatory.

KUMQUAT is not really a citrus but it can be grown in the same way.

TROUBLESHOOTING

- No flowers and therefore no fruit is usually due to poor cultural conditions – lack of light and fertilizer and incorrect watering.
- Discoloration of leaves can be caused by either overwatering or underfeeding.
- Leaf drop is caused by warmth and too moist soil in winter.
- Red spider mite and scale insects are the biggest problems. Wash leaves with a mild solution of washing-up liquid and water to keep them at bay. Mealy bugs, aphids, whitefly can be kept in check the same way. Wipe off honeydew and sooty mould.

LEMONS AND LIMES (left and above) are the best because they can flower and fruit almost continuously. Apart from being pretty handy for your gin and tonic, they are actually good-looking plants.

BROMELIADS

Bromeliads are smart plants because they've figured out how to absorb food and moisture through their leaves as well as their roots. They mostly come from the jungles of North, Central and South America. Many are epiphytic and live up in the trees, taking nourishment from the atmosphere – hence 'air plants'. Most of the ones grown as indoor plants are stemless with strap-shaped, leathery arching leaves arranged in a rosette and often have a watertight vase at the centre which collects rainwater and dew. Some have both. Many varieties can flower at any time after two or three years when the plant is mature and then the parent produces offsets and slowly dies.

SHORTCUTS TO SUCCESS

- Average room temperature is perfect but over 23°C is more likely to induce flowering.
- Bright light but out of strong direct sunlight. (Ananas and cryptanthus like full sun).
- Keep the central vase topped up with water if there is one and keep compost on the dry side.

THE BASICS

Watering Keep the central vase filled if there is one. Use rainwater in hard-water areas. Empty and refill every two months so it doesn't get stale. Let the compost dry out between waterings but with non-vase types keep compost moist but never soggy.

Light A brightly lit spot is essential but generally those with thicker leathery leaves need more light (including a few hours of direct sun) than those with softer leaves. Give them an occasional shower with rainwater to wash dust off the leaves.

Temperature Normal warm room temperatures will do for most bromeliads and it shouldn't drop below 13°C. To get them to flower though, you may have to crank the heating up to about 23 or 24°C. Raise humidity, especially in centrally heated rooms, by placing on a pebble tray. Air plants need almost daily misting with water.

Feeding Every three or four weeks, spray a dilute liquid feed at half recommended strength, onto the leaves, compost and central vase.

Keep the central rosette of **GUZMANIA CONIFERA** (above) topped up with water, except when in flower.
VRIESIAS have flattened flower spikes and many **GUZMANIAS** have elongated rosettes (right).

Repotting Most don't need repotting due to their puny root systems. Largest pot size needed is often about 13cm.

Propagation Offsets appear at the base after the main plant has flowered which then starts to die off. When the offsets have stopped being elongated and start to resemble the parent, cut them off with a knife. They should have some roots attached so check before you do it. Plant shallowly in cuttings compost, enclose in a polythene bag and keep warm until established.

VARIETIES

AECHMEA The most common one, *A.fasciata*, with its alien pink flower-head and wide grey leaves has been consigned to the Kitsch section (pages 34–39).

AIR PLANTS – TILLANDSIA These mostly have grey-green furry scales that absorb water from humid air and nutrients from airborne dust. *Tillandsia usneoides* is the Spanish moss that hangs in great curtains from trees in the Florida everglades and would make a fantastic organic shower curtain. *T. ionantha* is only about 8cm tall and, like many of the other species, has a pretty flower spike. *T. cyanea*, with its big pink flowerhead, needs compost and a pot. Mist air plants almost daily with water or they won't survive, especially in heated rooms. Brightly lit bathrooms are the best environment.

NEOREGELIA The dramatic blushing bromeliad, *Neoregelia carolinae* 'Marechalii' stands nearly 20cm tall. It has glossy leaves about 20–25cm long and, just before the small lavender-coloured flowers appear in the central watertight vase, all the inner leaves turn a brilliant red colour for several months. The curiously popular cream and green striped *N. carolinae f. tricolor* is a real eighties' plant and looks like it's made of plastic. Neoregelias like brighter sun than many bromeliads and a liquid and foliar feed every two or three weeks.

NIDULARIUM These are really similar to neoregelia but often have small spines on the edges of the leaves. High humidity is needed.

GUZMANIA The scarlet star is probably vying for the title of world's most popular bromeliad. There are lots of species available including *G. lingulata minor* which has red and orange bracts which shoot up from the centre and produces small yellow flowers. Keep the compost moist and temperatures ideally above 18°C.

VRIESEA The flaming sword, *Vriesea splendens*, is something of a double whammy with exotic purple banded leaves and a sumptuous red flower spike up to 60cm tall. A little direct sunlight is needed to induce them to flower but avoid strong midday summer sun.

BILLBERGIA Definitely the easiest bromeliad to grow indoors, some of these will survive temperatures down to just above freezing and flower while still very young. *B. nutans* is the one you come across most. The 30cm-long green leaves are a bit wild and sometimes turn red in full sunlight and the yellowy green flowers are backed by 8cm-long pink bracts. They flower at any time of year and grow continuously if warm enough.

CRYPTANTHUS The earth stars are ground-hugging plants, often as little as 10cm across, and grown for their stripy or banded leaves rather than flowers. *C. bromelioides tricolor* is beautiful with cream and green striped leaves with a pink edge. Annoyingly, it is the hardest to grow because it can wither and die just for the hell of it.

They often have only five or six leaves and no central vase. They need loads of light but very little watering or feeding.

ANANAS You can only grow edible pineapples indoors if you've got a heated greenhouse. But there are a couple of varieties with green, cream or white striped leaves and inedible pink fruits on long flower spikes. *A. bracteatus striatus*, the red pineapple, is a compact 50cm in diameter. Sun improves leaf colour but it's hard to get them to flower and fruit indoors so buy them when they are.

TROUBLESHOOTING

- Pale brown patches can be caused by scorch from the sun.
- Brown leaf tips caused by lack of humidity in dry rooms or underwatering of central vase.
- Watch out for scale and mealy bug.
- Plants dry out and shrivel if underwatered or in poor light and cold rooms.

GUZMANIA (left) with its tall spike of coloured bracts must be the world's most popular bromeliad.
At flowering time, the central leaves of NEOREGELIA and NIDULARIUM (below left) turn deep pink or red.
TILLANDSIA CYANEA (below right) unlike most of the 'air plant' species needs to be grown in a pot.

ORCHIDS

Orchids have an erotic, exotic fascination. Collectors will pay fortunes for rare specimens and people have killed for them. Most of the 1,000s of different species and hybrids grow from egg-shaped pseudobulbs which give rise to the name orchid from the Greek meaning testicle. Each swollen water-storing stem that emerges from the pseudobulb flowers once, withers and dies. Most need the controlled environment of a greenhouse or conservatory to survive but there are at least five groups or genera that will be happy in your living room and some will even thrive.

SHORTCUTS TO SUCCESS

- Avoid overwatering, only water moderately.
- Humidity must be high.
- Bright filtered light is needed for most species.
- Keep a close eye on the temperature.

THE BASICS

Light Orchids need bright filtered light so grow near a window, but avoid direct summer sun. In winter move orchids to a really bright window and if possible give supplementary artificial lighting to stretch day length to 10 hours and improve flowering.

Temperature A steady temperature is needed to ensure flowering. As a general rule stick to 20°C in summer and 15°C in winter. At night they must have a slightly cooler temperature about 5°C less. Check with a thermometer. High humidity is essential, stand plants in pebble trays and hose down the floor of conservatories and green houses daily.

Water Overwatering is the most common problem. Moderate watering once a week is usually plenty, letting at least the top half of potting mixture dry out in between. In their brief winter rest period let them dry out almost totally. Use soft, tepid water; rainwater is good. Cold water can shock them.

Feed Give a weak foliar feed about once a month or every third or fourth watering but not during rest periods. Overfed plants produce lots of leaves but no flowers.

Potting Excellent drainage is essential. Grow in two parts rockwool or shredded bark to one part sphagnum moss and one of lime-free sand or

The **SLIPPER ORCHID** flower (above), *Paphiopedilum callosum*, lasts two or three months between autumn and spring.
ORCHID flowers (left) follow the same pattern with the same number of petals, but there are thousands of variations.

137

perlite with a little added charcoal to absorb toxins. Premixed bags are readily available. Put 5cm of broken terracotta pots in the bottom of a plastic pot for drainage. Repot every other year in spring, carefully removing any old potting mixture. Shake new potting mixture around the roots and poke it down carefully with a pencil. Newly potted plants should only be sprayed and not watered for the first month.

Propagation Divide into clumps of two or three pseudobulbs and repot as above. The stem types can be propagated from stem tip cuttings or side shoots taken with at least two aerial roots.

Resting period Most orchids need a rest period in order to flower well. This may only last for a few weeks and is indicated in some species by leaves dying back. The temperature should be lowered by about 5°C and watering decreased until the potting mixture dries out.

EASY VARIETIES

CYMBIDIUM are the easiest and best for virgin growers but they get more hungry and thirsty than most. Easily recognized by a clump of tall leaves about 40cm high, the plants need a short rest in autumn.

PHALAENOPSIS, the moth orchid, is also very easy to grow. A steady minimum temperature of 20°C is important. Shorten stems of dead flowers to just below the lowest bloom and new ones will grow on side shoots. They'll flower almost all year.

ODONTOGLOSSUM GRANDE, the tiger orchid, has bright yellow and rusty brown flowers about 17 or 18cm across from late summer to late autumn. They need a constant temperature of 15°C and a high humidity. Repot annually and divide large clumps.

COELOGYNE Mature plants produce lots of fragrant flowers in winter and early spring and the easiest is *C. cristata*. Water plentifully keeping potting mixture thoroughly moist and give a winter rest period. Rarely needs repotting.

PAPHIOPEDILUM The lone flowers of the slipper orchid, called so because the pouch-shaped lip looks like a moccasin, last between eight and twelve weeks and appear between autumn and spring. Give medium light, never direct sun and supplementary light in winter to promote flowering. They don't have a proper rest period but cut watering right down for six weeks after flowering.

Some **ODONTOGLOSSUM** (above) can flower almost continuously under the right conditions as long as the humidity is kept up.
PHALAENOPSIS (right), the flat-faced moth orchid – one of the easiest to grow in your living room and can flower nearly all year.

CACTI

Cacti are by far the easiest plants to grow indoors. They are tough, virtually indestructible, Schwarzeneggers of the plant world. They're specially adapted to cope with neglect and it is possible to keep certain cacti alive for over a year without even watering. Sure they won't grow at all, in fact they'll be hang gliding over the abyss of death but add water and they'll soak it up like a sponge and burst into life. This is good news for us as keepers of plants because they're guilt free. But in order to thrive, they must be watered and fed regularly during summer and this is where most people go wrong.

Plants usually lose water through their leaves so the cactus has cleverly got rid of them and the job of photosynthesis is done by the swollen stem. All cacti are succulents but not all succulents are cacti. Cacti have areoles from which sprout tufts of spines, bristles or hairs but if a succulent has spines they grow straight from the stem like the thorns on a rose. Most cacti come from the Americas and there are two kinds: those from the desert and those from the tropical jungle.

Coloured stems are sometimes grafted onto other cacti and **FAKE PAPER FLOWERS** are stuck in the top (above). Don't be fooled.
MAMMILLARIA MICROHELIA (left) Lots of sun, some food and water and you can't go wrong with cacti.

SHORTCUTS TO SUCCESS

- Full sunshine is essential all year.
- Feed and water regularly in summer and neglect them a bit in winter.
- Keep the plant slightly pot-bound.
- Give a slightly cooler temperature in winter.

DESERT CACTI

The flowering period may be over months, but individual flowers only last for a day. They may be red to pink, white, yellow or orange and trumpet or bell-shaped with petals. Some, including echinopsis and cereus, bloom at night and are scented but most cacti flowers don't smell. Most should start flowering after three or four years.

Light Give them the sunniest place in the house. In summer you can stick them on your balcony or patio, but remember the more sun they get, the more water they'll need. Rotate plants occasionally.

Temperature Normal room temperature is fine but in winter, most, apart from the hairy types, like to rest at 5°C, preferably in an unheated room, glazed porch or on a cool window-sill away from radiators. The hairy cacti *Cephalocereus senilis* and *Espostoa lanata* need a minimum winter temp of 15°C.

Watering In spring and summer soak the compost thoroughly every week or two letting the top bit dry out between waterings. Avoid splashing the stems. In winter, while they're resting, the compost should be dry or the roots will rot. But in heated rooms, water a little bit once a month to stop them from shrivelling.

Feeding Feed once a fortnight with a high-potassium, tomato-type fertilizer to encourage flowers. High-nitrogen fertilizers can make plants leggy and flabby and should be avoided. Never feed in winter.

Potting and repotting Cacti must have compost that doesn't hold too much water. Mix two parts loam, peat-based or peat-free compost mixed with one part perlite, sharp sand or fine grit for drainage. Most cacti don't mind being a little pot-bound. Repot every other year at any time except winter. Wrap a piece of folded newspaper around the plant to hold it or fashion a pair of tongs from a really stiff cardboard box. Remove the pot and shake as much compost off the roots as possible without causing damage and either replace in the same pot or move up one size.

Propagation Take cuttings in spring or summer. Some cacti produce offsets at the base and others, like opuntia, are segmented or branched. Dry the cutting for a couple of days so the cut surface doesn't rot, and stick it into some compost.

For non-branching columnar types, like cereus, cut at least 5cm off the tip of the stem and root as above. Shoots will appear around the cut of the parent plant and these can be removed and potted up once they've reached 5cm.

Pests, diseases and problems Watch out for mealy bug, scale and red spider mite and if you put them outside in summer, smear the side of the pot with grease to ward off slugs. Dust can be cleaned off with a paintbrush. Weedy, lanky stems are caused by too much heat in winter or too little light in summer. Localized corky patches are caused by physical damage, insects and sudden cold. Soft, brown patches are caused by stem rot disease. Cut out infected tissue and drench compost with a fungicide such as carbendazim. Lack of growth is usually due to underwatering and underfeeding in summer.

JUNGLE CACTI

These are a number of different species, including the ones you get at Christmas and Easter, with flattened trailing stems and showy pink or red flowers. Avoid strong sunlight at all times of year. Keep the humidity up and feed with high-potassium, tomato-like fertilizer from the moment the flower buds form until the last bloom fades. After flowering let them rest for a couple of months at a cooler temperature of 13–15°C, cut down watering and stop feeding. In the summer, put them outside in the shade.

ECHINOCACTUS GRUSONII (left) The bigger the better as far as the golden barrel cactus is concerned.
CEREUS JAMACARU (below) is a proper desert cactus that would make Sergio Leone proud.

SUCCULENTS

Succulents, as luck would have it, are specially adapted to cope with neglect. They've developed cunning ways to combat drought by storing water in plump fleshy leaves and thick juicy stems. But just because they take a long time to die of thirst doesn't mean they don't need water and food. Like cacti, which are a distinct group of succulents, they need regular watering right through the growing season and then to be kept drier and cooler in winter. They come in all sorts of shapes with attractive stems and leaves but they can also be coaxed into flowering if you treat them right.

SHORTCUTS TO SUCCESS
- Average room temperature from spring to autumn. Cooler in winter. • Full sunshine for most varieties.
- Feed during active growth. • Avoid very cold water or dramatic chills.

EUPHORBIA TRICHOMANIA 'RED' (above left). The leaflets fall off with age and this thorny plant becomes a impostor.
The ZEBRA HAWORTHIA (above right) is incredibly tough and never needs feeding.
ALOE VERA (right) grows well on a window-sill. Break off a leaf and squeeze the soothing gel onto scalds and burns.

Many **ECHEVERIAS**, like *E.* 'Perle von Nürnberg' (above) have a pale white bloom on the leaves that is damaged by touch.
The **GHOST PALM** (right), *Pachypodium lameri*, can easily grow to 2m tall.
ALOES (far right) will grow in cool or warm rooms and only need feeding a couple of times a year.

THE BASICS

Light Succulents need as much as possible so basically a really sunny window-sill. Give them a regular quarter turn so they don't develop a Pisa-like lean towards the light. In summer put them outside. Aloes, gasterias and haworthias don't like direct sunshine.

Temperature The warmth and low humidity of a living room is perfect for most succulents but a slightly cooler temperature in winter helps them to flower well.

Watering While they're growing between spring and autumn they actually need watering quite a lot. But the fleshy leaves are easily damaged by splashes so water from the bottom. Stand the pot in a tray of water about 5cm deep and let it suck it up by capillary action until the top of the compost is moist. Never let succulents remain standing in water. Allow the top 2cm of compost to dry out before you water again.

Feeding Give an ordinary liquid feed at slightly less than full strength once every two weeks. Don't overdo it or you'll get soft, weak growth and they won't flower.

Potting and repotting Drainage is paramount. Use any container as long as it has lots of holes in the bottom. Clay pots need a few crocks of broken terracotta at the base. Repot annually or every other year depending on how fast it grows. Use a potting mixture made up of at least one part sharp sand to two parts loam or peat-free compost.

Propagation Many produce offsets at the base that can be carefully pulled away and simply planted up. They'll soon develop roots. Branching types can be treated in the same way; cut off a small branch and, if necessary, support it with a small stick. Others are propagated easily by leaf cuttings. Dry cuttings for a couple of days and then lay them on the surface of the moist compost or bury the cut ends (see Propagation, page 110).

Pests and diseases Watch out for mealy bugs between leaves. They also live on the roots so keep an eye out when repotting. Plants put outside for the summer can be devastated by slugs and snails. Smear the edge of the pot with grease to stop them.

VARIETIES

AEONIUM ARBOREUM ATROPURPUREUM has rosettes of deep purple leaves and turns into a miniature tree. They need lots of light all year. Smaller varieties of AGAVE like the *A. Victoriae-reginae* and *A. filifera* are best indoors (see Outside In, p166–169). ALOE VARIEGATA, the partridge-breasted aloe has rosettes of thick dark green leaves with white bands. Spikes of tubular flowers appear in late winter. ALOE VERA is also easy to grow.

CRASSULA OVATA see Feng shui, page 91.

ECHEVERIA are mostly rosettes of bluey green leaves that send up spikes topped by bell-shaped flowers of orange, yellow and pink.

EUPHORBIAS come in all sorts of shapes and sizes, many of them masquerading as cacti with spines. *E. obesa* is a squat round thing that looks like it's eaten too much and *E. millii*, the crown of thorns, has spiny stems with red or yellow flowers.

GASTERIA VERRUCOSA has thick green leaves arranged in opposite pairs and covered in white warts and HAWORTHIAS are like aloes with banded and warty leaves. They don't need feeding.

KALANCHOE BLOSSFELDIANA, see Unkillable, page 71.

KALANCHOE DAIGREMONTIANA (*Bryophyllum daigremontianum*), the devil's backbone, can grow to about 90cm. The leaves are fringed with about 50 tiny plantlets that can be detached and potted up.

LITHOPS are called living stones because the pairs of squat leaves 3 or 4cm wide look exactly like pebbles. In late summer a daisy flower grows from the slit between the leaves. They don't need feeding and shouldn't be watered between October and March.

SEDUM MORGANIANUM, the donkey's tail, is a fragile plant good for a hanging basket with its trailing stems of overlapping leaves. Sedums don't need feeding either. SENECIO ARTICULATUS is known as the hot dog plant because the stems look like pale grey sausages with a few leaves sprouting out the top. SENECIO MACROGLOSSUS is a trailing ivy-like plant with glossy variegated leaves.

TROUBLESHOOTING

- Wilting, saggy discoloured leaves and rots at the base of the plant are due to overwatering. Prune off any soft or rotted roots and propagate some new plants.
- Soft brown spots are signs of disease. Water with carbendazim.
- Brown spots on the leaves are caused by underwatering in summer.
- Flabby growth is a result of lack of light or excess water in winter.

AGAVES (left and below) prefer a cool room and like most succulents can be put outside in summer.

FERNS

Ferns are very primitive plants, probably only a nose ahead of mosses and lichens on the evolutionary scale. They don't flower, but to make up for this, they do have wonderful leaves, or fronds, which come in all sorts of weird shapes and sizes and some, like the Boston fern, are extremely good at purifying air and raising humidity. They are pretty easy to grow and will thrive in less light than many other indoor plants, but if you neglect them even briefly, they will get their own back by dying. Their big enemy is central heating which sucks all the humidity out of the air in the room. Keep the humidity high and you won't have problems.

SHORTCUTS TO SUCCESS
- Never let the compost dry out completely; some species will suffer badly if it happens even once.
- Keep the humidity up and keep plants away from radiators. • Don't put them in full sunshine or in total shade. • Watch out for scale and mealy bug. • Never use leafshine.

The **BOSTON FERN** (above left), drops its frondlets if humidity is low and watering uneven.
The **STAG HORN FERN** (above right) has antlers up to 80cm long covered in a white bloom. *Platycerium grande* is chunkier.
ATHYRIUM NIPPONICUM PICTUM (right) The Japanese painted fern has silvery markings like many Pteris.

FERNS

THE BASICS

Light The idea that ferns love deep shade is actually a fallacy. Good indirect average light is needed. Strong summer sun is dangerous so put ferns further back into the room or in an east- or north-facing window.

Temperature and humidity Normal room temperature is fine but the warmer it is, the more humidity is needed. Stand plants on a pebble tray and, if you can be bothered, mist daily. Low humidity causes brown frond tips. Bathrooms are good places for ferns.

Watering Never let the compost dry out ever. Water plentifully and keep it moist but not soggy. Ferns get through loads of water especially in higher temperatures.

Feeding Feed every two to three weeks during the active growth period with a liquid feed high in nitrogen. Always use it at half strength to avoid burning the delicate roots.

Potting and repotting Repot in spring when roots fill the pot. Most are shallow rooting so only use a half-depth pot and don't bury the crown. Use an equal mixture of peat substitute, leaf mould and perlite. Crunch up a piece of barbecue charcoal to keep the compost sweet. Plastic pots are better than porous terracotta.

Propagation Some ferns, like adiantum and cyrtomium, have underground rhizomes. Tease the plant apart and cut them into sections each with a frond or two. For plants with overground rhizomes, like phlebodium/polypodium and davallia, cut off the end 5cm of rhizome with or without leaves. Place in pots, peg down with a loop of wire and cover with a clear plastic bag for four weeks. Growing from spores is difficult, takes ages, so don't bother.

EASY-TO-GROW TYPES

BUTTON FERN, *Pellaea rotundifolia*, has pairs of dark green leathery leaflets on wiry stems and like the holly fern, *Cyrtomium falcatum*, doesn't suffer too much from lack of water and humidity.

RABBIT'S FOOT FERN, *Davallia canariensis*, has furry brown rhizomes that grow on the compost surface. If you underwater or it gets too cold, the triangular fronds drop off but will soon grow back.

THE BIRD'S NEST FERN, *Asplenium nidus*, makes a shuttlecock of upright, soft green shiny leaves that could happily reach 60cm tall indoors. Don't touch the young fronds as they unfurl or they'll get damaged. Excess heat makes leaf edges go black. Cut watering right down in winter. The appropriately named mother fern, *Asplenium bulbiferum*, has feathery fronds with tiny plantlets growing on the fringes. Pull them off and pot them up.

DICKSONIA SQUARROSA (above) need cool, bright rooms. Water the trunk as well as the pot.
HART'S TONGUE FERN (left) is very similar to a bird's nest fern, but less shiny.

BOSTON FERN, *Nephrolepis exaltata* 'Bostoniensis', makes a large mound of herringbone fronds as much as 60cm long and is probably one of the best ferns. *N. obliterata* is a bit tougher.

A BIT HARDER BUT STILL NOT VERY HARD

PTERIS suffer badly from lack of humidity and water especially if left in small pots in which they quickly dry out and die.

DICKSONIA SQUARROSA and other tree ferns can be kept in cool, bright rooms. Water the trunk so that it is constantly damp.

BLECHNUM FERN, *Blechnum gibbum*, needs the same treatment and makes a neat rosette of elegant fronds which eventually reach 90cm long.

HARE'S FOOT FERN, *Phlebodium/Polypodium aureum* 'Mandaianum', has really thick hairy rhizomes creeping on the compost surface and wonderful silvery blue fronds eventually reaching over 60cm tall. Grow in a wide shallow pot.

STAG'S HORN FERN, *Platycerium bifurcatum*, is one of the most prehistoric looking of the ferns and looks best fixed to a wall or in a hanging basket.

HART'S TONGUE FERN, *Phyllitis scolopendrium*, is like a smaller, more open bird's nest fern but with less shiny, wavy edged fronds. It's lovely anyway.

MAIDENHAIR FERN, the delicate Adiantum, has rightfully earned a place in the Challenging section (pages 73/75).

BULBS

An onion is a bulb. It's a fleshy food and water store that produces flowers and leaves for part of the year and then dies down and becomes a bulb again. There are some bulbs that remain evergreen all year but they're treated as indoor plants elsewhere in this book. Some of the plants here are technically corms or tubers but it all amounts to the same thing. For this book bulbs are divided into two groups – those that are really outdoor garden plants temporarily brought inside in pots and those which are a bit more tropical and need to be indoors all year.

OUTDOOR BULBS MOVED IN

Most of these garden bulbs are sold in autumn and generally flower the following spring. They're a good way to cheer up your room in winter and spring, and some are scented and make brilliant air fresheners. There are snowdrops, tulips, daffodils, crocus and dwarf iris in yellow, purple and blue. Hyacinths have a really strong sweet smell and come in white, pink, mauve and a blue one which looks like Marge Simpson's hairdo. There are also delicate little blue flowers such as scilla and muscari, the grape hyacinths.

The autumn crocus, colchicum, is pink or white and their brown corms will produce leafless flowers in autumn even if you don't plant them.

SHORTCUTS TO SUCCESS
• When buying make sure bulbs are firm and mould free.
• Always pick the shorter varieties of tulips and daffs or they'll flop over.
• Plant as soon as possible and keep moist.
• Once indoors keep as cool as possible and away from radiators.
• Put in a bright spot. Rotate pots every other day to stop bulb shoots bending towards the light.

THE BASICS
Plant bulbs in quite shallow compost, close together. Some bulbs, like the grape hyacinths, look fantastic in in a row of individual shot glasses. Put pots outside for the winter and bring them in just before the buds open. Larger bulbs like daffodils and hyacinths can be 'forced' or duped into flowering much earlier than normal. After planting they must be denied light and warmth. Bury the pots in a flower bed and cover them up with

Bring **BULBS** (above) into a cool room once the shoots are 4–5cm tall.
LILIES (left) have a beautiful perfume, but never flower as well in the second year (see Feng Shui).

about 15cm of moist peat substitute. Or put them in a black bag in a shed or garage. After eight or ten weeks, once the shoots are 4–5cm tall, bring them into a cool room at about 10°C. When they're ready to flower move to a bright window. The warmer the room, the quicker the flowers fade and die. Hyacinths can be bought 'prepared' so they flower particularly early.

If you haven't got anywhere outdoors to put your bulbs I'm afraid you're stuffed and will just have to buy potted, already shooting bulbs in the spring.

After they've flowered Cut off dead flower-heads and either plant bulbs outside immediately or just bung outside and leave in pots. The foliage will die down, the bulbs will dry out and they can be planted in the ground the following autumn. They can't be used indoors again.

INDOOR BULBS

These are ones that can't tolerate frost and so can't be kept outside in cold areas. They flower at different times throughout the year and are left in the pot when the foliage dies down, moved somewhere out of sight and kept cool and almost dry until they shoot up again the following season.

Amaryllis, or hippeastrum has big, sometimes vulgar trumpet flowers in spring, but they look amazing in bud as one or two phallic shoots arise from the bulb. *Gladiolus callianthus* 'Murielae', the Acidanthera is leagues ahead of ordinary gladioli with white, purple-hearted scented blooms in late summer. Canna lilies have bold, banana-like leaves in green to bronzy purple and large flowers of red, yellow or orange. The spider lily is found in gardens in the tropics and veltheimia is a good one for indoors, though the winter temperature must stay below 15°C.

SHORTCUTS TO SUCCESS

- Water only a little after planting the bulb.
- Step up watering once in leaf.
- Keep in bright light by a window while in flower and leaf.
- Keep in cool rooms if possible.

After they've flowered Cut off the flower when it fades but leave the stalk. Feed with liquid fertilizer after flowering every two weeks then switch to a high-potash, tomato feed until leaves wither. Keep quite dry once leaves have died down. Repot every three to four years.

156

ALLIUM (left), the ornamental onions, are best kept outside until their globes of flowers are actually open.

AMARYLLIS or **HIPPEASTRUM** (below) has big, sometimes vulgar, pink, white, orange or red trumpet flowers in spring. They look amazing in bud as one or two phallic shoots rise from the bulb.

CARNIVOROUS

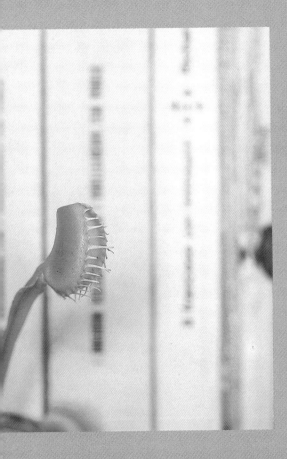

These easy-to-grow plants do actually eat insects. They live in places where nutrients are scarce so they've had to virtually give up on photosynthesis in favour of a more gruesome diet. Many are equipped with beautiful flowers, intricate patterns to lure their prey and cunning devices for trapping and killing. Victims are then dissolved in digestive juices leaving only the hard crunchy bits as evidence. Unfairly dismissed as novelty plants they are probably the most interesting indoor plants there are. Not only do they look good but they actually give you something back by keeping your house free of flies and mosquitoes and rid neighbouring indoor plants of aphids and whitefly. They are the height of organic pest control.

SHORTCUTS TO SUCCESS

- Always water with rainwater or defrosted freezer ice.
- Keep compost soggy in summer and moist in winter.
- Remove dead foliage as it dies down in winter.

THE BASICS

Water Hard or alkaline water is a killer so you must use rainwater, distilled water or defrosted freezer water. Just about all carnivorous plants need to have their feet wet during the spring to autumn growing season so stand them in a tray of 5cm of water. In winter all except the tropical species have a dormant period when plants form winter leaves. At this time let the saucer dry out before topping it up. This keeps the compost moist but not soggy.

Potting Generally they like an acidic peaty compost. Ironically their native habitats are being destroyed and drained for peat. To stop this gardeners should use peat substitutes (see Potting + Repotting, page 104). Individual requirements are listed for each plant. Premixed potting media are available from carnivorous plant specialists. When buying sphagnum moss check it is from a sustainable source. Plants won't need repotting for a year or two but when they do, put them into clay pots.

Light Give plenty of light. A south-facing window-sill is ideal, not least because they attract more flies than others. Conservatories and greenhouses are also good. Nepenthes and butterworts need a little shade but most hardy varieties can grow outside in sun.

VENUS FLY TRAPS (above) don't need any help from us as they catch enough flies on their own.
The SUNDEWS (right) have an incredibly sticky glob of glue on each of the tiny hairs. For small flies there's no escape.

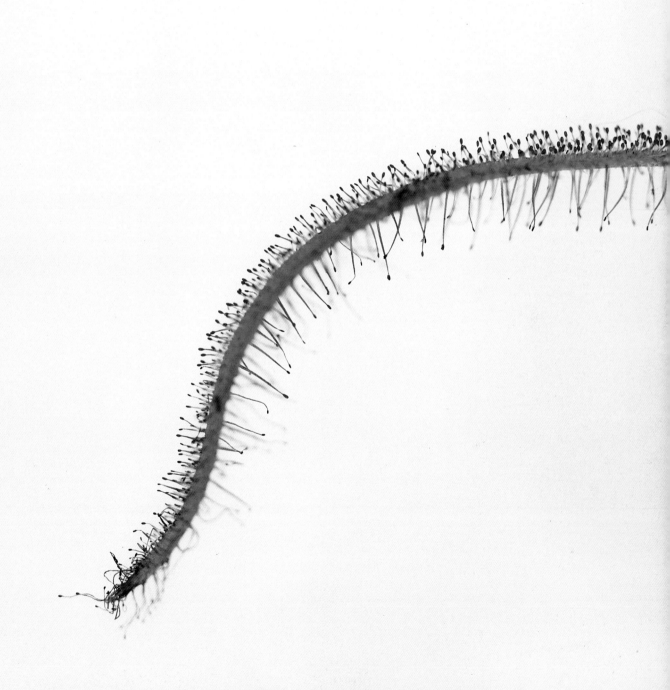

Feeding Of those listed here, only nepenthes ever need a fertilizer. All the others catch plenty of insects and don't need any help.

Temperature Normal room temperatures are fine for most from spring to autumn with a cooler winter temperature of about 4°C. This normally means a cold window-sill away from radiators or a cool, frost-free greenhouse or conservatory. In early spring move to a warmer spot and the plant will start growing new leaves. Plants can be put outside in summer, but they must be brought back inside in early autumn. Nepenthes favours warm rooms or greenhouses all year.

Pests and diseases Aphids can be a menace for some species and must be sprayed with a gentle organic insecticide like pyrethrum although butterworts and sundews catch small flying pests for themselves. Mealy bugs and scale should also be looked out for. Botrytis, the grey mould, can be a nuisance in autumn and winter particularly if you overwater. Remove any dead leaves as a matter

of course, provide ventilation and spray with a systemic fungicide. Copper-based fungicides will kill your plants, so read labels carefully. If you put plants outside, smear the side of the saucer with grease to stop slugs and woodlice getting in.

VARIETIES

VENUS FLY TRAP, *Dionaea muscipula* from the USA is really easy to grow. An unsuspecting fly lands on the open trap, touches several of the trigger hairs in quick succession, and bang – the trap closes and the fly is caught behind bars. They don't need many flies to survive so don't try and feed them or artificially trigger the traps. Grow on a sunny window-sill, in temperatures up to 30°C in summer and down to 5°C in winter when they must have a rest. Cut off the flower stalks which weaken the plants and remove dead traps as they naturally die back. Grow in 70 per cent peat substitute, 30 per cent lime-free sand or perlite.

SUNDEWS, *Drosera*, have rosettes of flattened leaves covered in tiny, often red hairs tipped with an incredibly sticky glob of natural glue. Flies get stuck to the leaves which then actually fold over the victim and dissolve it. *Drosera capensis* is easy and the giant Australian fork-leaved sundews are brilliant mosquito catchers perfect for a hanging basket. Pot in 70 per cent peat substitute, 30 per cent lime-free sand.

PITCHER PLANTS, *Sarracenia*, are the most efficient traps there are, capturing hundreds of house flies, bluebottles and wasps. A slender trumpet draws insects with its beautifully patterned hood and the lure of nectar. The insect loses its footing and tumbles into the tube to be digested. The tubes may be richly variegated or coloured red or yellow and the usually solitary flowers are equally beautiful. *S. flava* has yellow hooded pitchers 50cm tall. Use 60 per cent peat substitute, 30 per cent lime-free sand, 10 per cent perlite.

TROPICAL PITCHER PLANTS, *Nepenthes*, are good for hanging baskets because the short, dumpy pitchers hang over the edge on tendrils. Bristles and a slippery wax around the mouth prevent escape and a fly is gone within a few hours. Nepenthes have no dormant period and need warm temperatures night and day, regular high nitrogen feeds and a high humidity. Pot in 50 per cent live sphagnum moss, 30 per cent perlite, 20 per cent small grade bark.

BUTTERWORT, *Pinguicula*, have a beautiful flower and form rosettes of pale leaves and look a little like starfish. The leaves feel like melted butter and this surface traps tiny flies and eats them. *P. vulgaris* is hardy and can be grown outside in a bog garden. Pot in 70 per cent peat substitute, 30 per cent lime-free horticultural sand.

BLADDERWORT, *Utricularia*. The aquatic species native to Britain floats in water so grow in a glass bowl. They have very cunning underwater traps which when triggered open a door and suck in their prey. Feed with live daphnia (water fleas) bought from a pet store. In winter they form resting buds and sink to the bottom.

Slit one of the beautiful **SARRACENIA** pitchers (left) lengthways and you'll find it stuffed full of flies. The tropical pitcher plants, **NEPENTHES**, (below) need much warmer temperatures than most of the others.

CONSERVATORY

Whether you've got some sort of ramshackle glass lean-to or a state-of-the-art conservatory, you can use it to grow all kinds of fantastic plants. Things that just won't survive in the darker rooms of your home will thrive in the extra light levels and if you can heat it as well, the possibilities are endless. You can control the environment so it is actually more suited to plants than people and give them exactly what they want. Conservatories and greenhouses are usually either cool, warm or hot and it's mainly the temperature that dictates what plants you can grow.

THE TECHNICAL STUFF

Heating Unheated or cold greenhouses can be used to grow summer crops like tomatoes, overwinter tender plants and for propagation. But if you provide some form of heating your choice of plants is greater. Electric heaters with thermostats are the most reliable, efficient and convenient. Tubular heaters should be fixed to the wall just above the ground. Fan heaters can be moved around and create good air circulation providing an even temperature throughout and minimizing the spread of disease. Gas and paraffin heaters need good ventilation and aren't as good at regulating temperature. A maximum/minimum thermometer is essential for keeping an eye on things and a frost alarm which sounds indoors is useful to protect plants if there is a power cut or the fuel runs out.

Shading The high light levels make plants grow much faster than indoors so you'll probably have to do a lot more pruning. However, in summer, shading is particularly important on south-facing conservatories which can heat up very quickly and cause a lot of damage to plants. Sun-tolerant climbers grown under the roof provide natural shading to plants beneath and spraying a shading paint onto the glass is a practical but messy option for greenhouses. Otherwise blinds are the best solution. A cheap alternative is to buy rolls of hessian from a builders' merchant or upholsterers and staple gun it to the wooden glazing bars of the roof. In winter, on the other hand, some plants, particularly those from the southern hemisphere need as much light as possible and can even benefit from extra artificial light (see Light and Artificial Light, page 95).

Humidity The air can get far too hot and dry in summer so you'll need to raise the humidity to keep the plants happy. Each day, close all the doors

GLORIOSA SUPERBA (above) The glory lily grows to about 1.2m and must be kept dry in winter.
TIBOUCHINA GRANDIFOLIA (left) The purple glory bush needs lots of winter sunlight.

and windows for an hour or so and water the floor. As it evaporates the humidity dramatically increases which also keeps the dreaded red spider mite at bay. If you haven't got a wettable tiled floor place trays of water amongst the plants or purchase an electric humidifier. In winter, excess humidity is the problem.

Ventilation This is really important, even in cold greenhouses, to avoid a build-up of damp, stale air and to regulate temperature. In summer, doors and windows should be opened to cool the place down. Automatic openers can be fitted to vents, and kitchen and bathroom extractor fans controlled by thermostat are ideal.

Pests and diseases In an enclosed environment pests and diseases multiply and spread with the alarming rate of a biblical plague. Once established, infestations are hard to control so you have to be ever vigilant and stamp out problems as soon as you spot them. When bringing in new plants you should examine them minutely and, if possible, quarantine them for a month.

Introducing biological controls of insect predators, parasites and pathogens to conservatories can keep pests to a manageable level. But they are most successful in warmer temperatures and don't work so well in winter months (see page 99). Sometimes prevention is better than cure. Vine-weevil attacking nematodes can be introduced in August and September, and leaf pests can be kept at bay by routinely spraying with insecticidal soap every few weeks.

HOW WARM?

Cool Heated to about 2°C, just enough to keep it above freezing, you can overwinter tender garden plants and grow all sorts of exotic things. Many will even put up with an occasional frost, particularly if kept fairly dry at the roots and fed with a high-potassium fertilizer in late summer. The minimum daytime temperature should be between 5–10°C. Suitable climbers include *Plumbago capensis* with its powder-blue flowers, *Lapageria*, the Chilean bellflower, various passion flowers, jasmines and edible grapes. Flowering plants like pelargoniums, fuchsias, abutilon and salvias will thrive, and tender exotics like bottlebrush, ginger, palms and oleander will all be happy.

Warm Daytime temperature should be around 14°C dropping to a minimum 8°C at night. In summer you need to keep the humidity up. You can grow lots of the ordinary indoor plants listed elsewhere in this book but check the temperature requirements first.

Allamanda cathartica is a great climber for creating shade and produces lots of large yellow flowers for most of the year. It needs cutting back by a third each spring. The bizarre flowered heliconia will grow here, but needs a cooler winter rest. The deliciously scented frangipani, *Plumeria*, will make a large bush and the bird of paradise, *Strelitzia reginae*, with its orange and blue bird-like flowers will thrive. Citrus will also do well as will lots

The **LOBSTER CLAW** (right), heliconia, is a banana-like plant, reaching several metres high.
CUPHEA IGNEA (below left) The cigar plant and its purple-flowered relative are covered in flowers for most of the year.
ALLAMANDA (below right) The golden trumpet grows quickly and needs cutting back annually by a third.

of palms, certain orchids and that familiar plant of the Mediterranean, bougainvillea with its masses of papery, pinky purple flowers. *Tibouchina urvilleana*, with its big saucer-shaped purple flowers in summer and autumn, will grow into a large bush, but is prone to red spider mite, as are most conservatory plants – check under the velvety leaves. Feed monthly and keep fairly dry in winter. *Cuphea ignea*, the cigar plant and its purple-flowered relative, are covered in flowers most of the year. Leaf edges turn red in plenty of sun.

Hot These are truly tropical conditions with a minimum of about 20°C that let you grow some of the familiar indoor plants and plenty of things that would never succeed in your living room. The humidity must be kept high with the raised temperatures and it can get a bit sweaty for people. Indoor swimming pools usually fall into this range. Plants keep growing all year so you must continue watering and feeding.

Banana plants will fruit at this temperature, plenty of bromeliads, ferns and orchids will thrive along with tropical cycads and palms. The glory lily, *Gloriosa superba* carries red and yellow flowers in summer and autumn and grows to about 1.2m high. It needs full light and plenty of watering and feeding once growth begins, but dies down in winter, when watering should be stopped. All parts of the plant are highly poisonous and handling the tubers can irritate the skin, so wear gloves. *Heliconia rostrata*, the lobster claw, needs to be fed monthly, watered freely, and should be grown in sandy or gritty soil in plenty of light, but not direct sun.

OUTSIDE IN

Take a look in your local garden centre and it won't take long to realize that there are far more garden plants for sale than there are indoor plants. It seems a shame not to exploit this and there's no reason why you can't bring all sorts of garden plants into your home for a few days or even weeks. But instead of being binned afterwards, they can be put outside where they'll live to fight another day. Horticultural purists will probably want to have you flogged, but it's healthy to break a few rules now and again.

WHAT PLANTS ARE GOOD?

Scented and flowering plants are particularly worthwhile and containerized trees straight from the garden centre can be quite dramatic. In theory you can use anything but plants with thick glossy leaves, like laurel, tend to put up with indoor conditions for a bit longer than plants with soft, thin leaves.

Other things like agapanthus, which you couldn't possibly grow inside, can be kept in pots and brought in when they're in flower and put back out to recover when they've finished. But you can't just dig up plants to bring them in, they must live in pots all year-round.

The STAR JASMINE, *Trachelospermum jasminoides*, (above) can be brought inside for two or three weeks in a cool room.
The fragrant flowers of **SKIMMIA** (right) will last for about two weeks indoors.

OUTSIDE IN

SHORTCUTS TO SUCCESS
- Check for bugs beforehand.
- Avoid really warm rooms.
- Place near windows in lots of light.
- Always keep the compost moist.
- Watch the plants for signs of distress.
- Rotate plants almost daily so all sides get some light.
- Only keep indoors for a short time, don't torture them.
- Don't bring the same plant in two years in a row.
- Put plants back outside into some shade at first.

WHEN CAN YOU BRING THEM IN?
If it's only for a really short time, perhaps a matter of days, then you can bring a plant indoors virtually whenever you fancy it as long as you follow the shortcuts. For longer stays, the time of year that you bring plants in is really important. If you take in a deciduous tree or shrub in winter, for example, the warmth of your home will force it into leaf prematurely and then when you put it outside, the cold weather could kill all the buds and maybe the whole plant. The extremes of temperature are what are most likely to make the plants suffer. In summer it's not so bad because the temperature of your home isn't going to be a great deal warmer than outside and may even be cooler. Remember this is only a temporary exercise and that even if they look fine, garden plants will start to get stressed out as soon as they enter your home.

Ideally you need a garden or some sort of outdoor space so you can move things in and out as you please and then let them recover outside for a year or two. It's best to give plants a bit of time off before bringing them in again.

Always check plants thoroughly for pests and diseases. You don't want slugs and woodlice running around your carpet and things like aphids and vine weevil will happily set up home on your ordinary indoor plants. The cosy environment of your living room could even cause a population explosion. If possible, slip the pot off and cast your eye over the compost.

Spring In early spring deciduous trees and bushes with interesting bark make really different indoor plants. Silver birch, willows and the red-stemmed dogwoods are particularly good. All are likely to come into leaf and should be protected from frosts once they're put outside or they may suffer as a result. Clipped topiary of box and lonicera will also do well in cool rooms. There are scented shrubs like the Mexican orange blossom with its white flowers and

CORDYLINE AUSTRALIS (above) will last for several months in a cool room in winter, but needs high light levels in summer.
AGAVE AMERICANA (left) can be brought into a cool, bright room in winter, but watch out for the spines.

aromatic green leaves, and *Skimmia japonica* will fill a whole room with its sweet smell which is wasted outdoors in late spring. Exochorda and *Spiraea* 'Arguta' are absolutely clothed in white blossom and will really bring the excitement of spring indoors.

Summer All through summer there are heaps of perennial plants that can be brought in for a few days: aconite, columbine, cosmos, day lilies, osteospermum, cone flowers, chrysanthemum and crocosmia. Experiment with anything you like. Bamboos can mostly be brought in, but the low light levels will eventually be a problem. Keep watered well and if the leaves show any sign of curling rush them back outside. Other candidates are buddleia, ornamental grasses, liriope, mock orange, lavender, laburnum, and climbers like the star jasmine, *Trachelospermum jasminoides* and wisteria.

Autumn Apart from flowering shrubs like hydrangea there are plants with autumn colour as well. The hardy plumbago, ceratostigma, goes bright red and then there are trees like *Sorbus aucuparia* with red berries. As autumn progresses, frost-tender palms can be brought into cool, bright rooms.

Winter There are a number of shrubs which often have scented flowers on bare stems in winter like chimonanthus, corylus, corylopsis, hamamelis and *viburnum fragrans*. The conifers with needles like pines and spruces will survive a few weeks indoors in winter but those with flat leaves like chamaecyparis and thuja will probably die but it won't be obvious for months.

BUYER'S GUIDE

An unhealthy indoor plant is a sad, depressing creature and should be avoided at all costs. Most of the time, plants offered for sale by shops and nurseries are perfectly healthy. But there are a few caveats to observe to make sure you're not buying one which has already had its death warrant signed and that isn't going to infect and kill any plants you already have. If you get something that's been suffering since before you parted with any cash, that plant is going to struggle from day one, no matter how green-fingered you are and, if it's diseased or infected, it will spread to everything else.

WHERE TO BUY?

Markets can be very cheap places to buy plants, but in winter the plants may suffer from being outside in the cold. Shops are okay but they are often darker than they should be and if indoor plants are put out on the pavement in all weathers they can get bashed around in the process and scorched by the chilling winds. They may look fine when you hand over the money but when you get them home the damage starts to show up. It's pot luck when it comes to supermarkets and DIY warehouses, so garden centres and nurseries are usually your best bet.

CHOOSING A HEALTHY PLANT

Check out the nursery or shop. It should be clean and tidy because hygiene is really important to plant health. If there are fallen leaves and flowers around this is very bad news as bugs and diseases will probably be lurking amongst them. I'm not suggesting an official tour around with a clip board, a casual glance should be enough, but if the place is a mess then the plants are less likely to be in fine fettle. You should probably leave immediately.

If your chosen vendor passes the first test you need to look at the plants themselves. Stick your finger into the compost; well looked after plants should generally be moist. If it's very soggy or very dry this may be bad news, unless of course the plants specifically need those conditions. A crusty whiteness on the surface of the compost or the side of clay pots is a tell-tale sign of incorrect feeding. That certainly isn't the end of the world but it helps to build up an overall picture.

If you find something you like, look to see if there are other plants the same. Retailers normally buy in batches and it's nice to have a few to compare it with. If it's on its lonesome there's every chance it's the worst of the bunch and may have been kicking around for some time.

A plant should generally look healthy without damaged or discoloured leaves or broken branches. If you're buying a flowering plant, try and get one with buds that are about to open but if it's in flower already check that there are still more to come.

Once you've chosen a plant, inspect it meticulously for pests and diseases – this is the single most important thing you must do. Look very closely under the leaves, on the shoot tips and where the leaves join the stems. Search for tiny whiteflies, brown scales, little bits of white fluff, tiny cobwebs and fine grey furry mould. Any suspicions and you should walk away. White blotches on the surface of the leaves is usually a harmless residue from watering, just check that it easily rubs off with your thumb. Next, when the shopkeeper isn't looking, give the plant a gentle shake to see if any leaves fall off – this is a bad sign.

THE JOURNEY BACK

Finally, you need to get your immaculate plant home safely. Make sure fragile specimens are really carefully wrapped and, if you're putting one in a car, get someone to hold it or wedge it in really well. It only has to fall over once to be spoiled. The most important thing is not to expose it to wind so you should keep the windows shut and if you're going on public transport make sure all the leaves are covered up. If you've bought a big plant you'll be tempted to stick it out through the sunroof but this is very dangerous. As you drive home the plant will be subjected to the equivalent of gale force winds, all the leaves will get damaged and the plant will probably die.

A NEW HOME

Some plants get a real shock when you take them out of their cosy home and put them into your own. Some, like the familiar weeping fig, start to drop their leaves but they normally grow back. Try to acclimatize plants slowly and don't subject them to a massive change in temperature. Avoid draughts and if a plant has been grown in lots of light, start it off near the window before inching it back into the room over the course of several weeks.

SUPPLIERS

PLANTS

BONSAI
Bushukan Bonsai
Ricbra, Lower Road,
Hockley, Essex SS5 5NL
Tel 01702 201029
Fax 01702 200657

BROMELIADS + INDOOR FERNS
Newington Nurseries
Newington, near
Stadhampton,
Oxon OX10 7AW
Tel 01865 400533
Fax 01865 891766
www.newington-nurseries.co.uk

British Pteridological Society
www.nhm.ac.uk/hosted_sites/bps/index.htm

BULBS
The International Bulb Society
www.bulbsociety.com

P. De Jager & Sons
The Nurseries, Marden
Kent TN12 9BP
tel 01622 831235
fax 01622 832416
PdeJag@aol.com

CACTI + SUCCULENTS
British Cactus and Succulent Society
http://cactus-mall.com/bcss

Brookside Nursery
Elderberry Farm
Bognor Rd, Rowhook,
Horsham,
West Sussex RH12 3PS
Tel 01403 790996
Fax 01403 790195

Southfield Nurseries
Bourne Rd, Morton, Bourne,
Lincs PE10 0RH
Tel 01778 570168

CARNIVOROUS
Carnivorous Plant Society
66 Pine Crescent,
Hutton, Brentwood,
Essex CM13 1JB

Hampshire Carnivorous Plants
Ya-Mayla, Allington Lane,
West End, Southampton,
Hants SO30 3HQ
Tel 023 8047 3314
Fax 023 8047 3314

CITRUS
The Citrus Centre
West Mare Lane,
Pulborough,
West Sussex RH20 2EA
Tel 01798 872786
www.citruscentre.co.uk

CONSERVATORY
The Palm Centre Ltd
Ham Central Nursery,
Ham Street,
Ham, Richmond,
Surrey TW10 7HA
Tel 020 8255 6191
Fax 020 8255 6192

The Conservatory
Station Road,
Gomshall,
Surrey GU5 9LB
Tel/Fax 01483 203019
www.conservatoryplants.com

Fleur de Lys
Restharrow Cottage,
Lower Street,
Fittleworth,
West Sussex RH20 1EL
Tel 01798 865475
Fax 01798 865475

HERBS + VEGETABLES
The Herb Society
Deddington Hill Farm,
Warmington, Banbury,
Oxon OX17 1XB
www.herbsociety.co.uk

ORCHIDS
The Orchid Society of Great Britain
Athelney,
145 Binscombe Village,
Godalming,
Surrey GU7 3QL
Tel/Fax 01483 421423

Burnham Nurseries
Forches Cross,
Newton Abbot,
Devon TQ12 6PZ
Tel 01626 352233
Fax 01626 362167

ORGANIC HERBS + VEGETABLES
Jekka's Herb Farm
Rose Cottage,
Shellards Lane,
Allveston,
Bristol BS35 3SY
Tel 01454 418878
Fax 01454 411988
farm@jekkasherbfarm.com
www.jekkasherb.com.demon.co.uk

WHEATGRASS
Wheatgrass juicer
www.discountjuicers.com/wheatgrass.html

Wheatgrass Seed
www.wheatgrasskits.com

BUYING PLANTS FROM ABROAD
Ministry of Agriculture, Fisheries and Food
Plant Health Division,
Foss House,
King's Pool,
1–2 Peasholme Green,
York YO1 7PX
Tel 44(0) 1904 45 5191/5192/5195
Fax 44(0) 1904 45 5199
q.info@ph.maff.gsi.gov.uk

SEEDS
Chiltern Seeds
Bortree Stile, Ulverston,
Cumbria LA12 7PB
Tel 01229 581137 (24hr)
Fax 01229 584549
info@chilternseeds.co.uk
www.chilternseeds.co.uk

Thompson & Morgan
Poplar lane, Ipswich,
Suffolk 1P8 3BU
Tel 01473 688821
Fax 01473 680199
Tmuk@thompson-morgan.com
www.thompson-morgan.com

Mr. Fothergill's Seeds Ltd
Newmarket,
Suffolk CB8 7QB
Tel 01638 552512
Mailorder@mr-forthergills.co.uk

FENG SHUI
Feng Shui Association
31 Woburn Place,
Brighton BN1 9GA
Tel/fax 01273 693844
www.fengshuiassociation.co.uk

ARTIFICIAL LIGHT
Philips Lighting Ltd
The Philips Centre,
420–430 London Rd,
Croydon CR9 3QR
Tel 020 8665 6655
www.philips.com

FERTILISER, INSECTICIDES + COMPOSTS
The Scotts Co (UK) Ltd
Salisbury House,
Weyside Park,
Catteshall Lane,
Godalming,
Surrey GU7 1XE
Tel 01483 410210
Fax 01483 410220
www.scotts.co.uk

Scotts (Levingtons) Advice Line
0500 888558

Chase Organics
River Dene Business Park,
Molesey Rd, Hersham
Surrey KT12 4RG

BIOLOGICAL CONTROL
Hendry Doubleday Research Association
Ryton Organics Gardens,
Coventry CV8 3LG
Tel 024 7630 3517
Fax 024 7663 9229
enquiry@hdra.org.uk

Defenders Ltd
Occupation Rd,
Wye, Ashford,
Kent TN25 5EN
Tel 01233 813121

CERAMIC POTS
Pret-a-Pot
6a Cow Lane,
Sidlesham, Chichester,
West Sussex PO20 7LN
Tel 01243 641928
Fax 01243 641945
enquiries@pret-a-pot.com
www.pret-a-pot.com

HYDROPONICS
Greenfinger Hydroponics
182 Hook Rd,
Tolworth, Surbiton,
Surrey KT6 5BZ
tel 020 8255 8999
or 2 Jowett Street
Peckham, London
SE15 6JN
Tel 020 7708 4999
puddle@vanoord.u-net.com

INDEX

Abutilon 30, 164
Acalypha hispida 37
Acidanthera 156
Acorus gramineus
 'Variegatus' 80
Adiantum 73, 75, 153
Aechmea 34, 35, 37, 134
Aeonium arboreum
 atropurpureum 147
Aeschynanthus lobbianus
 16, 17
African hemp 75
African violet 41, 43
Agapanthus 166
Agaves 147, 148–9, 168
Aglaonema crispum 20
Air layering 110, 112
Air plants 134, 135
Air purifiers 9, 36, 44, 59,
 65, 114
Allamanda 27, 164
Allium 156
Alocasia x amazonica
 (Kris plant) 78
Aloe 146, 147
Amaryllis 156, 157
Ampelopsis
 brevipedunculata
 'Elegans' 30
Ananas 132, 135
Angels trumpet 83, 84
Angel's wings 26
Anthurium scherzerianum
 38, 39
Aphelandra squarrosa
 (zebra plant) 38, 44
Aphids 99, 101
Araucaria heterophylla 60
Aristolochia gigantea 72, 74
Asparagus fern 65
Aspidistra elatior 'Milky
 Way' 71
Asplenium 152
Athyrium nipponicum
 pictum 151
Aubergines 122
Avocado 123
Azalea 117
Azolla filiculoides 78

Bamboo 91, 169
Banana plant 58, 165
Basella rubra 49
Basil 120
Bead plant 46, 48
Bean sprouts 122
Beaucarnea recurvata 60
Begonia 16, 31, 38, 42
Beloperone 16, 113

Bertelonia marmorata
 (jewel plant) 75, 78
Big plants 8, 56–62
Billbergia 135
Bird of paradise 75, 164
Bird's nest fern 152
Bladderwort 161
Blechnum gibbum 80, 153
Bonsai 49, 90, 173
Boston fern 9, 150, 153
Botrytis 100
Bottlebrush 164
Bougainvillea 55, 165
Bright conditions 14–17, 95
Bromeliads 27, 112, 132–5,
 165, 173
Brugmansia 83, 84
Brunfelsia (calycina)
 pauciflora 14, 15
Bryophyllum
 daigremontianum 147
Buddhist pine 32, 59
Bulbs 91, 154–7, 173
Bulrush 76, 79
Burle-marxii 27
Busy lizzie 44
Butterwort 161
Button fern 152

Cacti 111, 112, 140–3, 173
Caladium hortulanum 26
Calathea 37
Cane cutting 110, 112
Cape cowslip 31
Cape leadwort 32, 53
Cape primrose 38
Capillary matting 114, 115
Cardomom 21
Carnivorous plants 158–61,
 173
Caryota mitis 57, 58
Cast iron plant 21, 71
Catharanthus rosea 12, 14
Celosia 36
Cereus 87, 142, 143
Ceropegia linearis woodii 52
Chamaedorea elegans 21
Cheese plants 19, 21, 36,
 63, 65, 112
Chemicals 9, 99
Chenille plant 37
Cherry pie 85
Chilean bellflower 164
Chives 120
Chlorophytum comosum
 'Vittatum' 69
Christmas cactus 143
Chrysalidocarpus lutescens 64
Chrysanthemum 9, 89, 91

Cigar plant 164, 165
Cissus rhombifolia 54
Citrus 128–31, 164, 173
Clay lumps 106, 107
Clementines 131
Clerodendrum thomsoniae
 53
Climbers 50–5, 74
Clivia miniata 32
Club moss 77, 79
Cock on a plate 38, 39, 49,
 80
Cockscomb 36
Cocos nucifera 56, 58
Codiaeum variegatum.
 pictum 38, 44,45
Coelogyne 138
Coffee 125
Coleus 38, 44, 113
Columnea x banksii 14, 15
Compost 104, 108, 111,
 117, 173
Conservatory 74–5, 162–5,
 173
Containers 8, 104, 173
Cool conditions 28–33
Cordyline 24, 88, 91, 112,
 169
Coriander 120
Cotyledon undulata 90, 91
Crassula 91, 111, 147
Creeping fig 52
Crocus 155
Crossandra
 infundibuliformis 75
Croton 38, 44, 45
Cryptanthus 132, 135
Ctenanthe 27
Cucumbers 122
Cuphea ignea 164, 165
Cutting back 113
Cuttings 111–12
Cycads 165
Cycas revoluta 48
Cyclamen 117
Cymbidium 138
Cyperus alternifolius
 (umbrella plant) 16, 69,
 80, 81
Cyrtomium falcatum 152

Daffodils 91, 155
Damp conditions 76–81
Dark conditions 18–21
Dates 9, 59, 125
Datura 83, 84
Davallia canariensis 152
Deadheading 113
Devil's backbone 49, 147

Devil's ivy 38, 44, 54
Devil's root 48
Dicksonia squarrosa 153
Dieffenbachia 36, 37, 112
Dim conditions 18–21, 95
Dipladenia 22, 24
Diseases 100, 170
Division 110, 112
Dizygotheca elegantissima 27
Donkey's tail 147
Dormant period 8, 114
Dracaena
 conditions 24, 108
 cuttings 112
 D. deremensis
 'Warneckii' 59
 D. fragrans
 'Massangeana' 65
 D. marginata 67, 69
 feng shui 88, 91
Drainage 104
Drosera 161
Dumb-cane 16, 36, 37
Dutchman's pipe 72, 74
Dypsis lutescens 64

Easter cactus 143
Echeveria 111, 146, 147
Echinocactus grusonii 143
Elephant's ear 78
Elettaria cardomomum 21
Emerald tree 25
Epipremnum aureum
 (Devil's ivy) 38, 44, 54
Episcia cupreata 80
Eucalyptus 28, 29, 30
Euphorbia 144, 147
Exacum affine 87
Exochorda 169

Fairy moss 78
False aralia 27
x Fatshedera lizei 20
Fatsia japonica 65
Feeding 107, 108–9, 114
Feng shui 88–91, 173
Ferns 65, 75, 80, 150–3, 173
Fertilizer 107, 108–9, 114,
 173
Ficus (fig)
 F. 'Audrey' 60, 61
 F. barteri 'Variegata' 64, 65
 F. benjamina (weeping fig)
 60, 64, 70, 71, 114, 170
 F. elastica 'Decora' 42
 F. pumila 52
 pruning 113
Firecracker flower 75

Fittonia verschaffeltii
 argyroneura 24, 25
Flame nettle 38, 44, 113
Flame violet 80
Flaming katy 69, 147
Flowering maple 30
Flowering plants 14–17, 95,
 100, 113
Foliage plants 18–21, 95
Frangipani 164
Fuchsia 32, 33, 111, 164

Gardenia 75, 82, 84
Gasteria 146, 147
Genista 31
Geranium, scented 84
Gerbera 9, 114
Ginger 126, 164
Gladiolus callianthus
 'Murielae' 156
Gloriosa superba 163, 165
Golden trumpet 164
Goldfish plant 14, 15
Goodluck plant 24
Goosefoot 16, 21
Grape hyacinths 105, 155
Grape ivy 54, 65
Grass 48
Greenhouse 162–5
Grevillea robusta 16
Guatemalan rhubarb 16,
 47, 48
Gum tree 28, 29, 30
Guzmania 132, 133, 134
Gynura sarmentosa 23, 24

Hare's foot fern 153
Hart's tongue fern 153
Haworthias 144, 146, 147
Heaters 103, 163
Hedera helix 53
Heliconia 164, 165
Heliotropium arborescens 85
Heptapleurum arboricola 69
Herbs 120–2, 173
Herringbone plant 36
Hibiscus rosa-sinensis 13,
 15, 87, 94
Hippeastrum 156, 157
Holidays 77, 114–15
Holly fern 152
Honeydew 100
Hormone rooting powder
 111
Howea forsteriana (kentia)
 60, 65, 68
Hoya lanceolata bella 86,
 87, 111
Humidity 22, 78–80, 103

Hyacinths 87, 155, 156
Hydroponics 106–7, 173
Hypoestes phyllostachya 40, 43

Impatiens walleriana 44
Insecticides 173
Iris, dwarf 155
Ivy 21, 53, 71, 111, 112
Ivy tree 20, 71
Ixora coccinea 74

Jade plant 91
Japanese aralia 65
Japanese painted fern 151
Jasmine 55, 84, 164, 166, 169
Jatropha podagrica (Guatemalan rhubarb) 16, 47, 48
Jewel plant 75, 78
Jungle flame 74
Justicia brandegeeana 16

Kaffir leaves 131
Kalanchoe 69, 147
Kris plant 27, 78
Kumquat 131

Lachenalia aloides 31
Lady's eardrops 32, 33, 91
Lantana camara 16
Lapageria 32, 164
Leaves
  buying plants 170
  cleaning 114, 117
  common ailments 100
  cuttings 110, 111–12
  foliage plants 18–21
Lemon 131
Lemon grass 122
Light 8, 94–5, 173
Lilies
  arum/calla 80
  canna 156
  feng shui 91
  glory 27, 163, 165
  kaffir 32
  peace 18, 21, 65, 71
  scented 87, 154, 169
  spider 156
Lime 131
Lithops 147
Lobster claw 165
Lollipop plant 15
Lychees 126

Madagascar dragon tree 67, 69
Madagascar periwinkle 12, 14
Maidenhair fern 73, 75, 153
Majoram 122
Malabar nightshade 49
Mammilaria microhelia 140

Mandarin 131
Mandevilla sanderi 22, 24
Mangos 125–6
Maranta 21, 32, 36, 112
Mealy bugs 99, 101
Medinilla magnifica 74
Medium conditions 18–21, 95
Mildew 98, 100
Mind Your Own Business 79
Mint 120
Monkey nuts 126
Monkey plant 27
Monstera deliciosa 36
Moss 78, 79
Moth orchid 138, 139
Mother-in-law's tongue 69
Musa acuminata 'Dwarf Cavendish' 58
Mustard and cress 122

Narcissus 91
Neoregelia 134, 135
Nepenthes 161
Nephrolepsis exaltata 'Bostoniensis' 150, 153
Nertera granadensis 46, 48
Nidularium 134, 135
Norfolk Island pine 60

Odontoglossum grande 138
Offices 62–5
Offsets 110, 112
Okra 122
Oleander 32, 164
Olives 126
Ophiopogon 112
Orange 91, 130–1
Orchids 75, 91, 136–9, 165, 173
Oregano 122
Organic treatments 9, 99
Outdoor plants 155–6, 166–9

Pachypodium lameri 147
Pachystachys lutea 15
Painted drop-tongue 20, 65
Palm
  adonidia 65
  Alexander 65
  areca 76
  coconut 56, 58
  conditions 164, 165
  corn 62, 65
  date 9, 59, 125
  ghost 147
  kentia 60, 65, 68
  parlour 21, 71
  pony tail 60
  sago 48
  tufted-fishtail 57, 58, 80
Papaya (paw paw) 123, 125
Paper flower 55
Paphiopedilum 137, 138

Parsley 120
Passion flower (Passiflora) 55, 164
Peanuts 126
Pelargonium 84, 111, 164
Pellaea rotundifolia 152
Peperomia 43, 111
Pepper elder 42
Perennials, indoors 169
Persian violet 87
Pest control
  buying plants 170
  carnivorous plants 158
  greenhouses 164
  outdoor plants 168
  treatment 8, 99–100, 173
Phalaenopsis 138, 139
Philodendron
  conditions 19, 21, 71
  feng shui 91
  habit 55, 60
  offices 63, 65
  P. scandens 52
Phyllitis scolopendrium 153
Phyllostachys aureosulcata 'Aureocaulis' 91
Pilea 113
Pineapple 125, 132, 135
Pines 59, 60
Pinguicula 161
Pitcher plants 160, 161
Plantlets 112
Plants
  benefits 8, 9
  buying 170, 173
  care 8, 170
  challenging 72–5
  conditions 12–32, 76–81
  disposable 117
  sick 99–100, 104, 108, 117
  unkillable 66–71
Platycerium bifurcatum 150, 153
Plectranthus (flame nettle) 38, 44, 113
Plumbago 32, 53, 164
Plume flower 36
Plumeria 164
Podocarpus macrophyllus 59
Poinsettia 117
Polka-dot plant 40, 43
Polypodium aureum 'Mandaianum' 153
Porcelain berry 30
Prayer plant 21, 32
Propagation 110–12
Pruning 113
Pteris 153
Ptychosperma elegans 65
Purple glory bush 163, 165

Rabbit's foot fern 152
Radermachera sinica 25
Red spider mite 100, 101

Repotting 104
Rheum rhaponticum 20
Rhubarb 20
Rosa chinensis 32
Rose of China 13, 15, 87, 94
Rose grape 74
Rubber plant 42, 60, 112
Ruellia makoyana 27

Sage 122
Saintpaulia 41, 43, 111
Salvia 164
Sansevieria 69, 111–12
Sarracenia 160, 161
Satsuma 131
Saxifrage 112
Scale insects 100, 101
Scented plants 82–7
Schefflera 27, 60, 69
Scindapsus aureus (Devil's ivy) 38, 44, 54
Scirpus cernuus 76, 79
Sedum 111, 147
Seeds 112, 173
Selaginella 77, 79
Senecio 147
Shrimp plant 16
Shrubs, indoors 168–9
Sick plants 99–100, 104, 108, 117
Silk oak 16
Silver crown 90, 91
Silver net leaf 24, 25
Skimmia 167, 169
Slipper orchid 137, 138
Smithiantha 26
Snowdrops 155
Soleirolia soleirolii 79
Sparmannia 75, 111
Spathiphyllum 'Mauna Loa' 18, 21
Spider plant 41, 69, 112
Spiraea 'Arguta' 169
Stag horn fern 49, 150, 153
Star jasmine 84, 166, 169
Stem cuttings 110, 111
Stephanotis floribunda (wax flower) 55, 75, 87
Strelitzia reginae 75, 164
Streptocarpus 38, 111
Succulents 90–1, 111, 112, 144–9, 173
Sundews 159, 161
Sunlight 14, 95
Suppliers 173
Sweet flag 80
Sweet peppers 122
Sweet potatoes 125
Sweetheart plant 50, 52
Syngonium podophyllum 16

Tangerine 131
Tarragon 122
Temperature 8, 103, 114
Temple bells 26

Tetrastigma voinierianum 54
Thyme 122
Ti tree 88, 91
Tibouchina 163, 165
Tiger orchid 138
Tillandsia 134, 135
Tomatoes 122
Topdressing 104
Trachelospermum jasminoides 84, 166, 169
Tradescantia 69, 111, 113
Trailing plants 50–5
Tree ferns 153
Trees
  bonsai 49, 90, 173
  eucalyptus 28, 29, 30
  indoors 168, 169
  palms 58, 59
  pines 59, 60
Tulips 155
Turf 48

Umbrella plant 16, 69, 80, 81
Umbrella tree 60
Urn plant 34, 35, 37
Utricularia 161

Vegetables 122, 173
Veitchia merrillii 65
Velvet plant 23, 24
Venus fly traps 158, 159
Vine
  bleeding heart 53, 80
  chestnut 54
  grape 164
  lipstick 16, 17, 80
  pepper 30
  rosary 51, 52
Vriesias 133, 135

Wandering jew 69
Warm conditions 22–7
Watering 77, 96, 100, 114, 117
Wax flower 55, 75, 87
Wax plant 86, 87
Weeping fig 60, 65, 70, 71, 170
Wheat grass 122–3, 173
Whitefly 99, 101
Wilted plants 100, 116–17
Windows, light 14, 95

Yams 125
Yellow sage 16
Yesterday, Today, Tomorrow Plant 14, 15, 87
Yucca 66, 69, 112, 113, 114

Zamioculcas zamiifolia 48
Zantedeschia 80
Zebra plant 38, 44
Zebrina pendula 69